# Reading Yeats and Striving to Be a College President

*John O. Hunter*

iUniverse, Inc.
Bloomington

iUniverse books may be ordered through booksellers or by contacting:

iUniverse
1663 Liberty Drive
Bloomington, IN 47403
www.iuniverse.com
1-800-Authors (1-800-288-4677)

ISBN: 978-1-4502-8542-1 (sc)
ISBN: 978-1-4502-8543-8 (hc)
ISBN: 978-1-4502-8544-5 (ebook)

Printed in the United States of America

iUniverse rev. date: 01/12/2011

*Dedication page*

These memoirs are dedicated with love and respect to

My family

My students

My colleagues and friends

William Butler Yeats thought that his best work was always ahead of him. He was still producing poetry when he died at seventy-four and published posthumously.

I am not satisfied with anything I produced before the age of seventy, but at the age of eighty I shall have improved, and at one hundred I shall finally have got to the bottom of things. I call on those who are still with me to see if I live up to my word.

And at the end, my hope is to join the merry Fiddler of Dooney:

When we come at the end of time
To Peter sitting in state,
He will smile on the three old spirits,
But call me first through the gate;

For the good are always the merry,
Save by an evil chance,
And the merry love the fiddle,
And the merry love to dance:

And when the folk there spy me,
They will all come up to me,
With 'Here is the fiddler of Dooney!'
And dance like a wave of the sea.

(W.B. Yeats)

# CONTENTS

# CHAPTER I

## Introduction to a Career in Higher Education

I served as president of four different colleges in the period of 1978 to 2005. Most of my research and writing focused on higher education topics and organization development, but my richest discovery was the power of poetry. Since my retirement I have developed a website, http://loveofpoetry. net , which includes poems by poets who have meant the most to me.

Some of these poems I memorized, forgot, and memorized again. I think I began my memorization catharsis with the poem, *Ulysses*, by Alfred Lord Tennyson. I have used these lines many times to inspire students and sometimes myself:

*Come my friends,*
*'t is not too late to seek a newer world...*
*Though much is taken, much abides, and though we are not now*
*that strength which in old days moved earth and heaven,*
*that which we are, we are...*
*One equal temper of heroic hearts, made weak by time and fate,*
*but strong in will, to strive-- to seek-- to find-- and not to yield!*

Now in the closing years of my life, I think of myself like Tennyson's Ulysses, wishing that I could still be on the plain of action and remembering events that marked my career, and especially the many good people who were my colleagues, students, and associates.

My story is bound with the institutions I served, the people I served and learned with, my family and my faith. In these memoirs, I engage in some tendentious naming of colleagues because a large part of my purpose here is to express my gratitude to many folks in my colleges and communities who made our lives -- Lyla Beth and me -- more event-filled and exhilarating than we anticipated when we began almost 50 years ago.

When we began, I thought that I would spend my entire career in the classroom because I loved teaching, but six years into history and government at Niagara County Community College (NCCC), the founding president, Dr. Ernest Notar, offered me the position of chief academic officer. I accepted, gave up tenured full professor status, and launched my career in higher education administration.

Afterwards, I sometimes thought, was I crazy? A tenured full professorship is the best job in the world! But then, why did so many of those I knew complain about it and the administration they had to endure, even when they/we accomplished so much?

That was my territory for nine years as dean and 28 years as president of five colleges, each different but each with the same pressures and dialectical struggles. Gradually, it became clear to me that I was where God wanted me to be.

He gave me a way to sustain myself in office -- through poets who began slipping into my life: first, Dylan Thomas -- how I loved "Over Sir John's Hill" -- then Tennyson and Frost and Rilke. Finally, I settled on two choices for the best of the English poets, neither of whom were English – Robert Burns, a Scotsman, and William Butler Yeats, an Irishman. They have inspired me not only by their beautiful poems but because of their life stories.

These poets and others have helped me to learn the profound difference between happiness and the "inescapable quality of great art—joy!" (Rilke) Most salvifically, they taught me a trick of memorization that clears the mind, and they became my pinions in a search for lyrical meaning when it seemed that my work was a dull, hardscrabble burden.

Because presidents are naturally multitask oriented and required to range broadly for information, sometimes it is difficult to penetrate deeply on one kernel of thought. Memorizing poetic lines is made easier by lyrics and wit, but complete concentration is necessary. In this state of mind everything else is abandoned. The thought may bring an element of tranquility or vision --or something serendipitous.

The founding president of NCCC, Dr. Ernest Notar, was the only administrative colleague I could call my mentor. Ernie Notar was not a strategist, but he was an honest, humble, and completely reliable man whose unassuming personal leadership set the tone and direction for the early development of this community college. Many of us hired by him continue to give him allegiance and respect; we have had to make our own way since, of course, but Ernie set us on our career paths.

Later in my career, I also became a founding president. I cannot compare my experience with Dr. Notar's, but I know the thrill and burden which he knew before me. We are among few educators who have shared this unique experience.

During my years as Dean of NCCC, I learned about organization development and settled on my administrative approach which I outlined in my 1977 book, "Values and the Future: Models of Community College Development." This was a transitional experience in my career which I look back on now as exquisitely ironic.

In 1978, I took my family-- except for oldest daughter, Elaine, who had just been married--to Illinois where I became the second president of the College of Lake County (CLC), Grayslake. This was an excellent opportunity, and I believe we made the best of it. With the support of a stellar board, I gave the College a new vision and direction for development, including the founding of the CLC Naval Training School under federal contract at Great Lakes Naval Base and the establishment of a second campus in downtown Waukegan. The concept of "open campus development" greatly enhanced the mission and reach of the college.

For family reasons, we moved back to New York in 1986 when I succeeded Dave Huntington as president of the State University of New York at Alfred (Alfred State College). Again, we looked beyond the immediate College and found a great opportunity to establish a twin college of technology in El Salvador. This proved to be an enriching experience for several faculty members who traveled to the *Instituto Technologico Centro Americano* (ITCA) as curriculum consultants. But there was also a rougher side to the Alfred story when the financial situation turned dire. We survived this crisis, however, and set the stage for a new mission involving development of baccalaureate engineering technology programs.

In 1994, after completing consultancy at ITCA, El Salvador, I actually thought that I had retired. Either I did not know myself very well, or God had more in store for me: the El Salvador experience was a bridge to becoming founding president of Cambria County Area Community College (CCACC), now renamed Penn Highlands Community College, in Pennsylvania. I never worked harder anywhere than in Pennsylvania building that college from scratch. My wife, Lyla Beth, worked right alongside, and when we left in 1999 the College was well-established.

There was a physical cost to me personally because I developed acute hypertension, I think not so much because of the long hours, which are normal in any presidency, but traveling every day up and down the length of Cambria County bent on trying to pull together the disparate elements of a college community. In any case again we thought we had retired.

A year later, I took the presidency of West Virginia Northern Community College (WVNCC). The college was undergoing a serious decline in enrollment and stature in its district and had a structural deficit of over a million dollars. The challenge to pull it out of a desperate downward spiral was enormous -- and I relished it. Lyla Beth again was eminently present and helpful. When we left in 2005, these problems had been resolved and the college had begun a major facilities transformation of the Wheeling campus.

Upon leaving West Virginia, retirement finally became real except for a brief visit in 2006 as a consultant to China where I delivered a keynote address at an international conference on technology education at Tianjin University.

In the following chapters I will focus more concretely on some of the projects, problems and accomplishments at each of these colleges. First, however, I need to acknowledge the generous and loving God who inspirited and sustained us in these efforts. It does not seem remarkable to me now that each of my appointments to office of president was as easy as walking through an open door. In each case, relationship with my governing board was quickly formed and held positive to the end. College governance is not easy, but I carried away no grievances or dissatisfaction with the support I received, and I gave each of these boards a significant boost in understanding of collegial governance.

This testimony also extends to the faculty and staff at each of these institutions despite the occasional episodes of alienation that darkened and twisted our paths. Sometimes the alienation ran so deep it was surprising, partially explained perhaps as defense of a sense of inadequacy or insecurity.

I am not suggesting that alienation was the general condition in my higher education environment, but there is something about the teaching profession -- perhaps the basic loneliness of it-- that inhibits social interaction. I remember a conversation with two professors well experienced in business/industry as well as the college classroom who expressed their wonder about the sensitivity and defensive attitude of fellow faculty members. Other faculty and staff members shared their presentiments of it as well.

I felt it too. I felt no hesitation interacting with Board members or community leaders or my presidential colleagues, but there were occasions when a wall of dislike or distrust daunted me in approaching faculty on congenial terms. Whose fault? They are not to blame. Desire for excellence and ability to break through resistance to a common ground are compatible traits of leadership which I did not always evoke in full measure.

It is a mistake for a president to want to be liked; nevertheless, reflecting on regret of disconnection, commingled with the satisfaction of major accomplishments, often against the odds, I consider what grade I should give myself in faculty leadership and conclude that it is a "B." Maybe there are some who would give me the "A" I would like to have, for my evaluation surveys were mostly positive -- but there are others who would balance it out. (And still others more professionally mature who would wonder about this gratuitous pre-occupation.)

It doesn't fit into a true picture of the many faculty and staff members I have known to try to grade or classify them, but as the years passed I noticed similarities in the best and the worst (admittedly judgmental on my part.) Even when they had to put up with bureaucratic ineptitude (and would frequently complain about it), the majority of faculty I knew in all of my institutions were committed to the teaching- learning process and were quite competent in their disciplines. This was especially so in the nursing/ allied health and engineering technology programs.*

It would be wrong and foolish to say that I admired every one of my administrative associates equally--indeed, there were some whose lack of commitment or resentment bothered and even angered me-- but others whom I remember fondly for their professional maturity and commitment to excellence. I was lucky to have them.

I never felt that I had an imperious attitude toward any of my faculty or administrative colleagues -- I think the best of those I worked with would agree -- but I know there was resentment by some who did not like to be challenged -- sometimes deviously expressed, because one way or another it has to be released.

There was a middle level of those who did not fail their tenure, yet their beginning commitment did not hold career long. I felt sorry for those few who began to hate their vocation and the institution by which they made their bread. It must have been a life of daily torment.

I am grateful to God that I did not react in the face of malice and animosity towards me personally or the college. I regard this as one of the most important victories of my career.

**\*Among the best , the Directors of Nursing were always outstanding: Elena Perone (NCCC), Dee Swan (CLC), Marilyn Lusk (Alfred), Regina Jeannette (WVNCC) were almost like clones in their disciplined systems approach, their loyalty to yet independence from the administration, their dedication to nursing excellence; and in each case, their programs, among the most rigorous, always had the best success rates.**

*I have believed the best of every man. And find that to believe is
enough to make a bad man show him at his best, or even a
good man swing his lantern higher.* (W.B. Yeats)

Did I miss opportunities to strengthen my relationships with my faculty
and staff? Yes, I am sorry to say that I did. My demeanor was too often
grim-faced: I remember one time passing a faculty member whom I liked
very much in the hall, and she called me later to ask if anything was wrong.
In my usual way, my mind had been too intensely occupied and I did not
flash warmth of greeting, which confused her. Fortunately, by this time
I had become acquainted with the dialectical thinking that Yeats so well
espoused, and so immediately began to think of a way to make an honest
correction that would take us to a higher plain (synthesis). In retrospect,
it may have been a better improvement just to learn to smile more often,
as Lyla Beth does, but it did not come to me as naturally as the art of the
dialectic.

Our personality is not the most important thing. Of course, we should
strive for cosmetic improvements that make personal connections easier,
but what is most important for someone who bears executive responsibility
is personal and professional integrity. This quality leads to respect for
another person's dignity and integrity, as well as institutional integrity—
and that I dare to say to all my friends and colleagues is at the very heart
of institutional development. These are universal values.

I do not subscribe to the military line that "familiarity breeds contempt,"
but it is the case that friendship is difficult to combine with rank, especially
on the way up. Even so cognizant, I regret very much a mistake I made
early in my administrative career that caused me to lose a good friend.

We had been close colleagues in the founding of NCCC, bonded by
excitement of the adventure. I was unduly concerned that my promotion
to chief academic officer would mislead him in our future relationship,
and so I told him that henceforth there would be a difference. I know this
wounded him—and me as well. "Three things come not back-- one is the
spoken word." To this day I grieve my error.

It was a mistake of false understanding of leadership. No one instructed
me in this way, and I had the example before me of a president who would

7

not have made this mistake. When we get into a position of leadership, it is of course imperative to call upon new skills of decisiveness and courage. But there is no formula. The neophyte may become enraptured by theories and exemplary personalities thrust upon him. These are not worthless, but learning to be an effective leader depends foremost on personal energy, integrity and vision.

Sitting in many councils over the years, and hearing the drumbeat of goals and crunched numbers carefully crafted by bureaucratic officers into a grand plan, impelled by the latest popular doctrine, and cast on executive officers eager to prove their worth (who may or may not have been consulted beforehand) -- I often heard myself thinking...

"What are they talking about? Is it really possible to expect results according to these demands without knowledge of changing field circumstances, the unknown, unquantifiable human potential? Why cannot they see that too many things may change in the course of one day's action that may bring entirely unforeseen opportunities -- or new risks not worth taking? Do they really think development is a straight line from authority?"

No, it is a crooked path; circumstances always color the reality of application, however principled and conscientious. A leader must be free, hopefully to see clearly, to innovate and adapt to the changing needs of the institution and community.

**The Assessment Game**

Here's a recent story: a professor of English with a PhD in literature notes that his primary role is to teach the basic skills of composition, and he correctly believes that this is his most significant contribution, but he also still enjoys his lifetime preoccupation with literature and would like the opportunity to teach some sections of that as well. Though he does not deny the need for competency outcomes he says, "I would like my students to enjoy literature." Well, that's fine, but it is not a measurable value.

.It isn't wrong to follow the Assessment curve. The average citizen/taxpayer without a Ph D is entitled to answers to simple questions:

"What are you doing with my money? How do I know the results are worth it?"

Education reform at all levels is critical and if assessment can give the cause a boost professional educators should welcome it rather than cry about it. But accountability/assessment in the offices of politicians and bureaucrats is a game often divorced from school and college realities.

There is a "missing link" between the legitimate aims of policy makers and those of educators on the front lines who in the end must carry the day. Some of these front line members are master teachers, some are enablers, some are new to the profession, some are still competent but no longer driven to stay current, and some are cynical or jaded by personal disappointment or because of having seen too many educationist fads come and go.

There are differences among them which can create a healthy dialectical struggle if it is fostered intelligently. The majority of college faculty still believes in the academic community and a professional lifestyle. Most of them resist the idea that they are only "facilitators."

In their academic communities there are serious issues which are dividing and polarizing the disciplines. (The sharp divide of the American Historical Association and the Historical Society is a case in point.) Marxism and other ideological persuasions and political correctness have taken a heavy toll. These wars notwithstanding, the classrooms and laboratories and studios of the institutions which are the targets of reform are still in the hands of the faculty.

The salient question of reform is not whether the teaching professoriate can adapt to the basic requirements of accountability and assessment. The question is whether academic renewal and scholarship shall continue to be a clarion call, or shall it be pushed aside by political expediency to make a different kind of progress, by the numbers.

The ancient Athenians defined happiness as "the pursuit of knowledge and the full exercise of creative powers, along lines of excellence, in a life affording scope." This ideal may be still relevant, hopefully, to education, but it has nothing to do with assessment.

There was a time when a college education was supposed to lead the student through an inquiry process about the most important life matters. Why am I here? Where am I going? What is more important than me? What do I owe to my community and my country and the world? What is justice? What is beauty? What is truth? Even in technical education there have always been core courses which address such questions.

These are not the concerns of assessment. There the questions are: what percentage of students graduated? Graduated on time? How many dropped out? How many high school students are enrolled in college courses? etc. Collecting such data may be useful, but not if it is the end-all of the process.

Disraeli said we have lies, damn lies and statistics. Carefully generated, statistical data may not be lies, but they can easily mislead. Data always require interpretation and analysis, and then comes judgment as to what changes should be made. How are the data being used? Who does the analysis? What knowledge do the analysts have on the issues framed? Are data being interpreted appropriately? Are comparisons that are being made appropriate, or are oranges being confused with apples? Does the analysis itself strive for critical objectivity, or give way to extremes of naïve acceptance or cynical rejection?

There may be something to learn in the assessment game by reflecting on Werner Heisenberg's "uncertainty principle" which is now commonly accepted in science. That principle is that "the more precisely you measure one variable, the less precise measurement of the related variable can be." I am not saying this can be directly applied to our thoughts and intentions about the meaning of our data; it's just that our intentions are often shifting and elusive. They cannot be precisely established and so this uncertainty in our thinking is also fundamental to the problem of change, especially in a culture which is experiencing countervailing demands for change. It's a simple fact of human behavior that people don't automatically fall into place because of statistics. (I think most educators would agree with Emerson that, "consistency is the hob-goblin of little minds.")

The mature professional does not deny that something must be done about student attrition, for example, or graduation rates, or field placements. Within that mature perspective there will be an awareness of the needs for data analysis and the demands of institutional integrity. A mature professional wants to know how the numbers are going to go up, especially if resources seem inadequate to the goal.

In the community college, for example, the idea that high school graduates can earn the associate degree at the same time they obtain their high school graduation diploma without degrading the degree is suspicious. Let me be stronger: I always thought it was an insane idea.

If such genuine concerns are dismissed as mere resistance to the need for reform, the leadership needed in the trenches to achieve the reform will not be forthcoming...

Over the past several years, teaching faculty have experienced a growing problem of students who are unprepared and, even more troubling, unmotivated to become active learners. The majority of the students are in the traditional college-age bracket and too advantaged to have picked up a work ethic. It's a problem of lack of shared commitment. Increasingly, faculty see that incoming students do not know how to make a commitment. The signs are obvious: lack of regular class attendance and lack of class preparation. Less obvious is the start of addiction. Alcohol and marijuana are big on all campuses. Nor, of course, does the problem begin in college. (Diane Ravitz reports that a 2003 Public Agenda survey found 43% of public school teachers spend more time trying to maintain order than teaching.)

While most faculty are aware of the changes occurring in the learning environment and the need to adapt, they are caught in crosscurrents of the student failure/attrition syndrome and rising expectations of greater student success.

In dealing with these issues, as well as the incursion of ideological themes, the case for professional and organization development resources has become urgent. If the assessment game is going to yield greater results, it needs to propel a steady, multifaceted, ongoing professional development program aimed at the needs of the front-line educators ultimately responsible for those results. It's also a matter of style: teachers at all levels need to be respected for their professionalism and encouraged in it.

I just want to report again from my experience that effective leadership is not born of management science --despite the brilliance of Peter Drucker-- and we shall not get effective governance and administration of our schools and colleges from those who continue to think that somehow we can marshal bureaucratic driving forces to that end. I never had any problem reporting good numbers, but there was never any magic in them. All the data that are constantly churning in political image making have an Orwellian impetus that should be recognized for what it is and distrusted.

It is highly questionable that increased governmental authority can achieve greater cost-effectiveness or even cost-efficiency in an educational institution, but even if we could get this outcome, Thoreau reminds us that, "you never gain something but that you lose something."

I knew very capable higher ed officers and politicians enamored by the compilation of productivity data and cost analysis, but the Holy Grail of cost-effectiveness remained elusive for the simple reason that it cannot be measured in an educational institution. Cost-effectiveness is primarily a qualitative matter in which value judgment is controlling.

Forget about it! Much better to focus on organization and staff development! Allocating resources for staff development is never a mistake provided there is a strategic framework for it.

Education can be an enervating profession. Sabbaticals, long recesses, tenure appointments – – though little understood by the public, these are essential factors in meeting the challenge of "staying alive" professionally. At the same time, I do not countenance the notion of "burnout." It is incumbent upon all of us in the profession to summon our own Angels of fortitude and resiliency.

*How can I, that girl standing there,*
*My attention fix on politics?*
*Yet here's a traveled man that knows*
*What he talks about,*
*And there's a politician*
*That has read and thought,*

*And maybe what they say is true*
*Of war and war's alarms.*
*But O that I were young again*
*And held her in my arms. (W.B. Yeats)*

Most people probably understand that any college campus, given the premium on individuality, may experience erratic behavior-- even dangerous and unhealthy -- as well as being an erogenous zone. There are lots of social, psychological and just plain odd ball problems that are difficult to compartmentalize. Increasingly, however, mission success depends upon effective organization development and strategic planning led by a strong president.

## The OD Approach

Assuming the office of president, my first move was to call for an assessment of the college's needs and financial situation -- what we used to call a SWOT analysis-- and I would try to enhance my understanding of what I faced as president by entering into small conversations with as many people as I could reasonably see. With some I could immediately detect underlying animosity toward administration in general, but mainly this interaction allowed me to identify leaders. Then I would request cooperation across the college for administrative reorganization and transition, beginning with a functional analysis and evaluation of the need for every position. In all cases we ended up with fewer positions, and by modest retrenchment found funds for salary increases in applying the reorganization, which reinforces my bias that all schools and colleges are administratively top heavy.

When the new table of organization was set, a Charter of Responsibility for each administrative officer was required, specifically delegating authority and major responsibilities. Job descriptions were required for all office and technical assistants. These documents were used in evaluations along with statements of goals and objectives. But we strove to avoid a top- down, impersonal cast to the process. Each associate was charged with taking the lead in his/her own evaluation.

In my view as an Organization Development (OD) administrator, the ability to evaluate and make changes based on that evaluation is the key to developing an effective organization.

I was always talking about an "OD approach." I don't know how much of it survived me. In retrospect I wonder how many listeners asked themselves, what's he talking about? OD? overdose? overdrive? I recall a humorous report back following presentation of the Blake and Mouton Managerial Grid, asking that we all strive to be "9/9 administrators": "does he mean that we should all work 9 to 9?" It reminded me again of my need to hone my communication skills—and the story of conversation between two women:

> "What did you do to your hair, it looks like a wig?
>
> It is a wig.
>
> Strange, it doesn't look like a wig."

The reorganization was instrumental in laying down some basic principles and concepts that were to be the values framework of the college organization. Following are some of the most important:

#A student is not an interruption of our work; he/she is the purpose of it.

#Don't complicate the teaching process; back it up! Simplify and streamline procedures as much as possible.

#Expect integrity in all relationships: when reporting a mistake tell the whole truth of it; above all don't tolerate dishonesty or lies.

#Tight/ loose principle: on a few essentials, such as budget control, stay tight, don't fold. Otherwise, be loose, flexible, and open to ideas. Set as a goal the claim to innovation within good management.

#Don't rely on memos to solve problems, and don't try to fix the blame, fix the problem.

#Responsibilities should be energized not by exhortation or propaganda but by clearly laid out duties and expectations.

\# The key to good staff performance is training: a well trained staff member will claim the job as his/her own.

"If we cannot express what we are trying to do, do we really know?"

In administrative council, I constantly reinforced the importance of mission vitality and the differences between strategic and operational (action) planning. The concept of mission (or purpose) did not apply only to the institution as a whole but to each unit of the organization.

At the time of the appointment or reappointment, I expected each administrator to make the following claims:

1.  I am competent to hold this position.

2.  I understand the relationships necessary for my office to be effective.

3.  I know the mission of the college and of my department.

4.  I recognize the importance of goal setting and evaluation and will take the lead in my own evaluation and professional development.

Each summer a retreat was held to create or confirm our goals for the coming year, measured in the context of our strategic plans as ratified by the governing board (and state authority if necessary.) At mid-year a conference to assess progress was always scheduled.

Other important organization development guidelines included such documents as "Building Partnerships," "Academic Integrity and Work Ethic," "Flexible Learning Methodology," and "Principles of Evaluation."

I pressed upon the Board the principle of *"governance by policy,"* which was accepted in every case. I also pledged that if ever there was a Board vote of lack of confidence in me as president, I would resign regardless of my contract. I did not warrant any presidential inaugurations (but we did have some good parties.)

These were all aspects of a "natural systems" approach to governance and administration which we called "Goals Setting and Evaluation."

The president needs a set of principles and rules that he/she tries to promulgate as a driving force for institutional excellence. Lest he forget, however, that they are not meant for his great credit, she should also respect *Murphy's Laws:*

> *If anything can go wrong, it will.*
>
> *If anything can't go wrong, it still will.*
>
> *Nothing is ever as simple as it seems.*
>
> *Everything takes longer than you expect.*
>
> *Whatever you set out to do, something else must be done first.*
>
> *You can't do just one thing – – there are always consequences.*
>
> *If everything seems to be going well, you have obviously overlooked something.*
>
> *Nature always sides with the hidden flaw.*
>
> *Mother Nature is a bitch.*

\*\*\*\*\*\*\*\*\*\*\*\*\*\*\*\*\*\*\*\*\*\*\*\*\*\*\*\*\*\*\*\*\*\*\*\*\*\*\*\*\*\*\*\*\*\*\*\*\*\*\*\*\*\*\*\*\*\*\*\*\*

> *The intellect of man is forced to choose*
> *perfection of the life, or of the work,*
> *and if it take the second must refuse*
> *a heavenly mansion, raging in the dark.* ( W.B. Yeats)

I chose work. I have never met a college president who did not choose work, although I have heard of some who lost because they could not do the work (or, regrettably, could not handle a distraction.) There is no way around it: the purpose of work is the work, and it must get done. We glory in it, but in the middle of it, we cannot see the day's vanity or where the energy might have better placed. So we drive on.

I was by nature an "academic president." I wanted to follow the old high way of those presidents who spoke with a strong sense of values—spiritual as well as intellectual---exemplified by Samuel P. Capen of my alma mater,

University of Buffalo, who stood so resolutely on academic freedom; or Harvard's Charles W. Eliot or Chicago's Robert M. Hutchins, both of whom had enormous influence on liberal education. As a young dean and president perusing their speeches and notes, I was impressed how fearlessly they carried their views into the public arena.

Although I worked and studied to become adept at financial planning and audits, it was too prosaic for me to enjoy. I depended upon my chief financial officers and gave them more latitude than academic officers. Fortunately, I had some good ones: Vern Manke at CLC, Bob Granger at Alfred, Jim Wagner at CCACC, and Larry Bandi at WVNCC. I also had a "bad one" at CCACC (before Wagner) and a "shaky one" at WV Northern (before Bandi) who got no latitude; they gave me a headache and I ended up firing them.

I was proud of all our achievements in the colleges I served, but I was always concerned about what I saw as a decline of the liberal arts tradition and the "objective scholarship" –- was it real?--that so impressed me as an undergraduate at the University of Buffalo. The concern did not emanate so much from our community colleges as it did from the universities which influenced higher education more. As president, I saw for the first time the effects of a steady rise in the "isms" --Marxism (even in the English classroom), Freudianism, deconstructionism and feminism -- cascading and running over the historic values of the pursuit of knowledge -– *beauty, truth, the good*. It seemed that these now belonged in a category of hopeless naïveté. They were also being jammed by political correctness and cultural relativism.

I was not alone, of course. When I had just about come to the conclusion that my worldview was retarded beyond repair, I would come across marvelous new works, such as Allan Bloom's *The Closing of the American Mind and* Roger Kimball's *Tenured Radicals*. Bloom's book especially had a strong influence on me. I was also grateful for meetings of the *National Association of Scholars,* to which I did not contribute much, but they saved me from my dreary feelings. These folks are my chosen masters of cultural analysis.

I'm also grateful for a suggestion from a colleague at Alfred State College, Dick Kellogg, to add Theodore Dalrymple (pen name of Anthony Daniels) whose work on politics and culture of decline continues to impress me. I used to think that we needed another Eric Vogelin, the German political philosopher who brilliantly reviewed the Gnostic tendency in modern politics, but now I believe that Dalrymple, Kimball, Charles Krauthammer, Thomas Sowell, a few others can provide the critique stimulus we need.

The "alienation of the intellectuals" on university campuses may have been going on for decades earlier, but the assault on traditional values and standards began in the late 1960s just as I was beginning my administrative career-- at least that's the way I see it now.

On reflection, the slide is an integral part of my personal story because my views were staunchly liberal when I began teaching in the early 60s, but gradually evolved to conservative. (When did I first reflect on Disraeli's comment that "all great minds are conservative"?) Was my personal transformation because I shifted from teaching to administration (as some critics would say, went over to the "dark side"?)

Or did my administrative work require a more realistic and rigorous approach? Maybe. For one thing, I worked a lot harder as an administrator, and I think the work gave me a bit more humility than I otherwise would have had (probably still short on that stick.)

The switch is interesting for another reason: teaching history, I had an older, bright and conscientious student, emigrated from East Europe, who was as conservative as I was liberal. We had friendly disagreements, but I understood his perspective. We met again years later when he was a college instructor, and he admitted that my position had been the sounder one.

Lo and behold! Our views had completely interchanged. Why did I/he cross over? I wish I knew the answer to these questions, but my introspective memory is not strong enough.

I have known many college faculty, the majority of them excellent in the classroom. It is a curious thing that most of them were liberal or radical in their political and socio- economic views. In fact, it is usually anticipated.

I recognized that most of my fellow presidents were also in that lineup; some even accepted right-wing/left wing labeling. For example, some thought of the NAS as a "right-wing bunch" without knowing anything about the organization or the eminent scholars in its membership. This tendency among my colleagues may partly explain my hesitation to be bold in the "higher circles." I was contrarian, perhaps "maverick" is more apt, but did not share fully my critique of what was going on, probably because I did not want to be looked on that way. (If that is so, shame on me.)

I took some personal risks, some of which I will outline in following chapters, but now I argue with myself that I did not do enough to oppose the ideological fanaticism and the threats to academic freedom and integrity coming from within our institutions, nor did most of my presidential colleagues.

There were a few champions who stood up, and usually won their battle, whatever it was against radical takeover. I admired S.I. Hayakawa, president of San Francisco State, and John Silber, president of Boston University, and Bob Ketter, president of SUNY Buffalo. On the other side, I could not understand President Summers' self-lacerating response to his critics at Harvard University. He had an opportunity to stand up for important academic values, which would have heartened many who are tired of the PC nonsense, but he just yielded.

Most of us in office during the last 40 years of the 20th century were too complacent. When and why did we give up on the real liberal tradition of Capen/Eliot/Hutchins?

Or am I simply too "contrarian" on the change front?

---

From the beginning to the end, I wrote thousands of pages, perhaps hundreds of thousands, about the work we were doing in my tiny sphere. It was not until near the end that I saw what I had been skipping—or perhaps stating it more deliberately, the circumscription of the life I had chosen.

I took time for family celebrations (though not enough for my children when they were young), and time for the Rushford Lake cottage, and time for Stratford plays and movies and music with Lyla Beth. I traveled: twelve trips to the United Kingdom including one to Oxford for Round Table, one to Rome for John Paul II's funeral, one to China, several to Central America; and took personal retreats at Ft. Sill, OK and Genesee Abbey, one of the most serene places in the world. But in due course we surrendered again to the work, which was never really left behind. In the profession this is called "dedication." I do not think it is wrong to spend one's life this way if it is meant for something to outlast it, but reflection also tells us that between the ideal and the reality there falls a shadow. These activities are not a path to self-fulfillment.

I could have made more money, but it has never motivated me and I never used my office exploitatively (as some presidents have, sad to say). I could have placed myself more in the spotlight, but I was there often enough and, thank God, was able to see the foolishness of desiring more of it: In all of my presidencies I refused inauguration ceremonies and was resolved to maintain a tough and decisive but humble office; I tried to focus the attention on faculty and students.

I could have moved higher in the state systems, but I was not a good enough politician. I could have published more, but I did not see that published journal papers made as much difference as the documents I provided to explain and move my institution. (I did publish over 150 Letters to Young Friends and local op-ed columns.) I could have contended for more prominence in my professional associations, but I was too much of a contrarian and too busy at home (and maybe too arrogant.) I have some regrets along these lines but not very serious. No, these were not my losses. So where did I lose out?

I lost in not giving more attention to my children, a fount of regret in my reveries.

I lost when I did not sustain a closer walk with my God, and secondarily, did not spend enough time on poetry and theology. During my professional life, I was also on a journey to conversion. It has been a long and slow process. I should know better where I am now on that path, and so am sorry to say that I was negligent earlier when more dedication transferred could have brightened it. Encouraged by other devotees, I followed too many dry branches of the river.

I confess that my search for God through Christ is partly intellectual, but I cannot help it, I am an intellectual man. I have fallen short, but not without some salvific discoveries along the way. I found Immanuel Kant's definitive answer to the God question (God's existence can neither be proven nor disproven by "pure reason"; it is a postulate of "practical reason.") I found Rilke. I found process theology and seminal works by George Land ("Grow or Die: The Unifying Principle of Transformation") and George Kennan("Around the Cragged Hill"). I found Thomas Merton at Genesee Abbey, and wish that I had found Fr. Richard John Neuhaus and "First Things" much earlier. I found General Booth and the Salvation Army. I found Alexander Solzhenitsyn and John Paul II. All of these heroes helped to direct my quest for an enduring faith. They are all gone now, but I owe them a great debt.

Preceding them in my soul was an anchor seed from the first lines I ever memorized at the age of seventeen from John Milton's *Areopagitica* (how I ever came across it I cannot fathom but I have never forgotten it).

> *Though all the winds of doctrine were let loose to play upon the earth, we do injuriously by licensing and prohibiting to misdoubt Her strength; Let Truth and Falsehood grapple: whoever knew Truth put to worse in a free and open encounter?*

I am an eclectic scholar, so much so that I fear being a dilettante and pray for depth. I am grateful, however, for my three years of part time study at St. Bonaventure University while I was president at Alfred State College. I took graduate theology courses from professors there who were excellent theologians and teachers. (They are not responsible for any errors of mine.) I almost completed a Master of Theology degree (six hours short) but had to give it up for CCACC.

On a lovely campus with an abiding Franciscan spirit, those evenings were a nice respite from the travails of Alfred. What did they contribute to my search for the triune personal God? I'm not entirely sure of that either, but faith is an important part of my story so I will try to write myself clear on my ongoing conversion.

## WHAT I BELIEVE

"No one believes anything unless one first thought it believable... Everything that is believed, is believed after being preceded by thought... Not everyone who thinks believes, since many think in order not to believe; but everyone who believes thinks, thinks in believing and believes in thinking." (Augustine)

I believe in evolution as I believe in God. Both physically and spiritually, God uses an evolutionary process in His creation. The primordial nature of God (or Divine Eros) is the urge to change—" the force that through the green fuse drives," as Dylan Thomas put it -- to realize new possibilities -- creative and not mechanical-- the immutable principle of "grow or die." He is a God of surprises and paradox. (Yet as Herman Melville said, "we may surprise Him as much as He surprises us.")

I also accept W. B. Yeats' poetic argument that the process is dialectical: In other words, God has two poles or opposites which may be in conflict but strive for synthesis. He has allowed evil to come into the world, but Jesus died on the Cross for love. Like many others with so little knowledge I just accept the mystery of it. God is Love; there is no other explanation. But I also believe that it was not so from the beginning. Love evolved with the human soul when God decided to become "three persons in one." The acceptance of the Trinity is the core of my belief.

> *"We rise today through a mighty strength,*
> *The invocation of the Trinity.*
> *Through belief in the Threeness and confession*
> *Of the Oneness toward our creator:*
> *Christ to protect us today,*
> *Christ to deliver us from all fears today."*
>
> (From St. Patrick's Lorica, Isle of Iona)

If my belief is true, it can be reconciled with any truth given through science. At the same time I am not willing to stay in a worldview that seeks to bend everything to natural interpretation and cannot see the paradox and mystery in the way God works His will.

I confess to a degree of mysticism, yet it is reconcilable in my mind with rational understanding. This is a lesson taught by Victor Frankl, founder of the school of logotherapy, whose mystical reference to his survival in a German concentration camp during World War II profoundly impressed me. The suffering he endured would have been unbearable except for his remembrance of his beloved wife, whom he could not know was alive or dead. One day, while working in unbearable cold, his soul dying, Frankl received confirmation that communion with his wife was real. In that moment he was restored to life for he knew that his wife was still alive and returned his love:

*"The guard passed by, insulting me, and once again I communed with my beloved. More and more I felt that she was present, that she was with me; I had the feeling that I was able to touch her, able to stretch out my hand and grasp hers. The feeling was very strong: she was there. Then, at that very moment, a bird flew down silently and perched just in front of me, on the heap of sod which I had dug up from the ditch, and looked steadily at me."*

The skeptic may see this story as mere coincidence or delusion or some such curiosity of little value because it cannot be replicated; but it was a moment of reality for Frankl, fragile as life itself but hard as stone. Here is miraculous love with the power of resurrection no science can match – at least so it seemed to me in that first reading and remains so.

Compelling as they are, I do not mean that these mystical examples are the foundation of my belief in the Trinity. In His primordial nature God was the First Cause, the Primary Mover. Through what scientists call the "Big Bang," God fired the universe into motion billions of years ago. Immediately, I must recognize that this statement is disputable too because of the work of Stephen Hawking and cosmologists who posit a "no boundary" universe.

A few years ago Hawking spoke of his work as finding "the mind of God."But more recently he has apparently concluded that there is no place for God in the creation of the physical universe. I shudder before the knowledge and courage of a Hawking, and it would be absurd for me to take him on in scientific matters. However, I am not willing to cede ground to him on the possibilities of a spiritual universe, about which he has dismal acquaintance, at least until there is definitive and not just theoretical proof that something can come out of nothing. I doubt we shall ever reach that point. Just as we cannot fathom infinity in time or space, we cannot know God's purpose in the origin of the universe. Ever to claim such knowledge is just arrogance.

At the same time, in the first instance of fashioning the universe and subjecting it to the physical laws by which its further development was governed, it just seems to me highly unlikely that God as Primary Cause would have concern for the later development of a tiny planet on the edge of a solar system, among billions of similar systems opening out, each with billions of stars, and earth's sun a minor one, on which billions of years later human beings evolved.

We risk making God in our image, a current tendency of many Christian evangelical believers, whom I think mock God in their arrogance. Does it not seem to fit the Logos better that this God was impersonal and naturally indifferent to the world He was creating? Yet He made it full of potentialities, including those of spiritual evolution as expansive as His physical universe. Without being dogmatic about it, I am comforted by this view because it answers the eternal mystery of the problem of evil: why does an omnipotent, omniscient and loving God allow it?

I think the problem is confused by those evangelicals who insist the substance of the Trinity could not have evolved; it had to be there at the Beginning. There was no reason why God as Primary Mover should have exhibited a benevolent character at a point of His creative process when there were no creatures to shine it upon. The natural order came first, and then what is referred to in the Nicene Creed as "the holy spirit, the Lord, the giver of life." This Spirit, as Jesus himself called it, is distinguished from the all powerful Creator and bears no responsibility for the natural order of things. The world was a given.

> *"In the Beginning was the Word…*
> *and the Word was made flesh…*
> *and dwelt among us…*
> *We have seen his glory,*
> *who came from the Father,*
> *full of grace and truth."* (Gospel of John)

Again we cannot know how or when exactly: the human creature became self aware—thus, the emergence of the human soul! For God the Creator it may have been an act similar to the emergence of the first flower: for millions of years vegetation rioted on earth without flowers; then one morning a flower appeared and soon thereafter this miracle covered the planet in a blaze of color. It would also be so for humans.

In any case, at that point another Deity, sprung from the First, and merciful and caring whereas the First, in a vaster recess of power and majesty, was not, became a part of human consciousness, imparting an awareness of the divine presence and making us forever capable of Faith and Hope and Love. Praise God!

If I am wrong in this, then I am indeed a wayward heretic, but I believe I am faithful to the truth as God leads me in this attempt to reconcile rational understanding and acceptance of divine mystery.

## Tempus Dei Gratia

So how does all this fit into my story as a college president? And where am I now on my path of conversion? With Merton, I believe that my desire to please God in my work does please Him. I believe that He works through us, in spite of our failures, if we are faithful.

Christian evangelicals have much to say about prayer. Does prayer work? For me that's the wrong question. I believe prayer works if God wills it, at least for the one who prays, and possibly for the one prayed for, because it is part of His creative force; but true prayer is about a relationship that is deeper than the mere words can express. Prayer is a search for God but also a revelation of God that may be best rendered through silence.

The evolutionary process has been steadily upward – – from vegetation to flowers to poems – – from material substance to spirit – – from brute existence to self-awareness to the power of love.

God is majestic beyond our poor power to grasp. His Majesty is revealed in evolutionary patterns which move inexorably to greater complexity, greater elegance, greater beauty, greater love. The dialectical nature of the process is evidenced by the still abounding presence of ancient evil.

I believe that despite the relentless pain and misery of our chaotic world, God is trying to unite us with Himself through Christ. We go to the Father through the Son in the Spirit. Thomas Merton expressed this faith in a prayer ending *The Seven Story Mountain:*

*Now my sorrow is over, and my joy is about to begin... I hear You saying to me: you shall taste the true solitude of my anguish and I shall lead you into the high places of my joy... That you may become the brother of God and learn to know the Christ of the burnt men.*

Whitehead speaks of an event as pervading its future. The Christ event pervades all future events in the history of civilization. I believe that to live heroically in this world we need to see beyond the appearance of things, get beyond literal interpretation of our sources and the narrowness of our minds, accept our responsibility to confront evil when it appears, yet above all stay centered on Christ.

What does it mean to stay centered on Christ? It means to live with mystery. It means to believe in His mercy, to believe that, having looked at the alternatives, there is nothing more essential than this faith, even when we suffer doubt. Christocentrism means putting Jesus in the very center of the Holy Trinity, understanding that Jesus had to die on the Cross to finish his mission of becoming the Christ, all in accordance with Scriptures: What happened in Christ is how God works to bring about communion with Him.

Given the seemingly endless strife and scorn among Christians, it is hard to reconcile the zealotry with the redemptive example of Jesus. Yet through all this I can see His splendor!

Genuine Christian love I think also means leaving room for the possibility that others may find their way to God by a different faith. Knowing how small and poor we are when we do measure ourselves by Christ, how can we pretend to have all the truth of God's purposes and ways?

When we look up at the night sky, it seems so peaceful and serene, yet we know it is anything but that. The universe is a terribly active place, full of creations even more majestic than those we see. Cosmologists estimate that there are 400 billion suns in our galaxy we call "the milky way" and billions of galaxies in the universe, moving in various directions at tremendous speeds. They speculate on parallel universes, an infinity of possibilities racing, bending and collapsing. We know and speculate on these things by our intelligence and reason. This is the physical universe evolving.

There is also a spiritual one. We know of it because of our faith and love, also active, growing and evolving.

There is an eternal process of creation and worship going on-- in which men and women throughout the world are engaged according to their faith and thought and action. This process is like a dance, a cosmic dance of touch and counter touch, current and countercurrent, a reverberation between us and God, an unending spiritual movement of grace and beauty and purpose flowing out of His immense depths.

John Paul II said, "Be not afraid"-- not afraid of what? -- the truth about ourselves – of God's love—of man's weakness—or his grandeur.

This remarkable poem by Alexander Solzhenitsyn, who endured the Soviet gulag concentration camps, is testimony to the connections of faith and courage and grace:

*"How easy it is to live with You, O Lord,*
*how easy it is to believe in You.*
*When my spirit is overwhelmed within me,*
*when even the clearest see no further than the night,*
*and know not what to do tomorrow,*
*You bestow on me this certitude*
*that You exist and are mindful of me,*
*that all the paths of righteousness are not barred.*
*As I ascend to the hill of earthly glory,*
*I turn back and gaze, astonished, on the road*
*that led me here beyond despair,*
*where I too may reflect your radiance upon mankind.*
*All that I may reflect, You shall accord me,*
*and appoint others where I shall fail."* (Solzhenitsyn)

How great is that freedom then to which we are called?

In my presidencies, my ambition, pride, insecurity, desire to be liked were part of my bondage, not freedom. Is not my spiritual quest conditioned by the circumstances of my life as well as by the myths and language and culture which shape me and to which I have adapted?

I think all men have great capacity for self-delusion. We have difficulty assessing our motivations, our knowledge and our guilt. As we move into God's wilderness we fall short of the prize of His calling to freedom again and again.

Yet if we try to be faithful, somehow a growth path is laid out for us. God may be hidden in the affairs of men, yet somehow He works in these realms. He does not leave us to face our trials alone.

Cursom Perficio

# CHAPTER II

## *Niagara County Community College 1963—1978*

"Should auld acquaintances be forgot,

and never brought to mind?

Should auld acquaintances be forgot,

and days o' auld lang syne?

We'll tak' a cup o' kindness yet

for auld lang syne." (Robert Burns)

I began my teaching career in 1959 at the high school in Newfane, New York, where I was born, but my career in higher education administration was launched, unexpectedly I must confess, when Niagara County decided to open a comprehensive community college in 1963. This was an era when community colleges were spreading across the country at a rate of one every two weeks and changing fundamentally the scope and purpose of American higher education. It was an exhilarating time. Those of us chosen to assist in this institution's birth were indeed blessed. Most of us knew it; some did not.

I look back now at this period of my life with gratitude I cannot fully express. NCCC was my training ground for everything that followed in my career. Perhaps for that reason, my connections with people there were vital to me in the ensuing years of development, there as well as at the institutions I led as president. My loyalty did not flag, even in the dry periods when I had no news and was caught up in new crises.

I was appointed Dean of the College by President Ernest Notar in 1969. Time blows away the details of many accomplishments and crises that Dr. Notar and I enjoyed or endured together. Here I can only deal with a few that stand out for me, and which of course represent the early formative years only.

I have almost mystical memories of my NCCC experiences with some folks who were personally dear to me and, I think, continued to respect me, even when the suspicion wafted that I may be going astray—God bless them. I'm sure it did not always appear that I would "go to the wall" for them, for the intensity of my desire for excellence was shaping my demeanor too strongly (yes, I was too intense), but that conviction entwined with loyalty was deep in me.

With Dr. Notar at the helm, we founded NCCC in facilities we shall not forget: the Shredded Wheat building in Niagara Falls, pictured on cereal boxes; an old motel renovated for classrooms; a couple of old mansions used for office space. The college became known as Nabisco Tech. The facilities were awful, but that did not really make any difference then (Bob Olans reflected the spirit of the enterprise when he said, "I could teach in a barn.") Today, NCCC is a beautiful, well equipped campus in the heart of the county—but with a lot more morale problems. Such is the case with all the colleges I have known.

There were 18 faculty/staff members in our first year, 1963-64. I still have personal contact with one of them, Meredith Kellogg, who taught physics, and his wife Marjorie. The following year we doubled.

This outline is incomplete, but these were some of my teaching colleagues whom I remember (for six years I taught history and government):

Ray Harvey, economics, my first office mate and good friend; Doug Farley, sociology, also an old friend from high school days; Dick Cavall, hired with me, we team taught history of western civilization; Clyde Tyson, history, replaced me as social science coordinator; Gern Jaeger (my first appointment to division chair) and Hal Polanski, biology, both life-long friends; Steve Stepus, biology and Stan Herowski, chemistry—both "original 18" members;

Elena Perone, the first of many nursing educators I have admired -- something special about them – Irene Costanzo,Sue Grobe, Roseanne Roberts, Olga Bopp, Catherine Farina;

Bob Kenyon, Business Division Coordinator (Dr. Notar's first promotion to full professor, I was jealous) ; Al Penzotti, Paul Power and Bob Cinelli, business; Judy Serbacki and Teresa McGlennon, secretarial; Brenda Webb, accounting;

Don Stellrecht and Jerry Repetski (I ran cross-country at UB with him),technology coordinators; Angelo Gillie, electrical (left after one year to become community college president in Hawaii); Pat Zanzano, Lloyd Jones and John Fulciniti, technology; Ken Raymond, Larry Law, Sam Richbart, Jeannette Lenczyk, Art Hadley, Ken Burg, Dave Brown—all math; Dr. Paul Kwitowski and Ted Georgian, a great boost to chemistry; Dick Panek, physics; Doc Ray and Dorothy Oldham, Dental assisting;

The health/physical education department--Ed Voetsch, chairman; Roy Sommer, basketball coach (took our team to national championships); Eric Knutilla, wrestling coach; Bob Heisner, martial arts, creator of Bushido Kai systems;

Min Jack, Claire Ives (we taught together at Newfane), Catherine Ainsworth, Ken Hennig ,Eleanor Robinson (excellent advisor to "Spirit" student newspaper edited by my daughter Elaine), Don Sleight, Jean Adjemian ( my student and proud appointment), Ed Thomas, Humanities division chair; Marg Laurie, Lee Buffan (also my student),Bob Baxter, John Marohn, Brandon Warden, Dave Tobin, Gene Miller, Norm Tederous, Don Ferrick, --all English;

Gerry Reinagel, music; Paul Seland, speech; Larry Plant, psychology; Sam Loliger, Ralph Race and Mike Ryan, sociology; George DelGrosso ,anthropology (left to become president of a Canadian community college); Don Harter, fine arts chairman; Kathy McWhorter, reading specialist;

and a few younger teaching colleagues who came later—Carl Heintz, culinary arts (I saved Carl in a crisis after Dr. Notar left); Jim Mezhir and Alex Greenburg, criminal justice; Rosemary Sweetman, Bob Flock and Peter Schwartzott, fine arts; Pat Willie, secretarial; Rog Wright and Kathy Dolce, phys ed; Nick LoCasio, Bryce McMichael, Gene Carella, Tom Mangan and Tom Martin--all biology (we were determined to build a strong department}; Sue Bland and Paul Kankolenski, psychology; Bart Nigro, computer tech (I had to come to Bart's defense too in a dispute over computer configuration);Dave Truesdale, business; Barb Falsetti, Ann Catalano and Marian Hannigan, speech/ communications.

In a special category of *"distinguished professorship"* I would place Tony Gullo, anthropology, long-term outstanding faculty leader as Chair, Social Science Division and president of Faculty Union; Bob Olans, psychology, well respected leader of Senate; Graham Millar, history, the "old prof" and a great Scot, an originator of the "Academy" and internal "Hibernian" chronicler, one of the few faculty with whom I still have contact; Bill Warthling, philosophy, an ordained priest who belonged only in a college setting, one of the most fertile minds I have known and perhaps the best lecturer; Jim Abbondanza, psychology,an innovator, creative in both technology and curriculum development; Paul Ferington, music, a distinguished conductor of the Buffalo Philharmonic, succeeded me as chief academic officer -- and lasted longer (Paul has great time management skill); Roger Lehman and Don Voisinet, independent but dedicated teachers and developers of technology programs; Carol Jamieson, chair of English and Humanities; Cathy Griebner, speech and creative student activity; Paul Dominick, anthropology and Tim Tomsen, history—retired, but young lions in my mind still;

and Jerry Miller, who started in English but became renowned for his theater productions, was appointed Dean of Students when Norm Shea left, and finished his career as NCCC president. I also had to defend Jerry in his first stage creation for some language. Jerry had a lot of guts! His transgression was mild by today's standards -- "Vagina Monologues"— you've come a long way baby (down!)

Early Counselors -- better than the current Rogerian or even worse Marxist types-- included Dan Rogala, Len Sabato, Len Longley, Joe Colosi, John Mooney, Carol Henschel, Larry Bolster, Judy Shippengrover, Gary Livent;

and Librarians Eleanor Seminara, Director, Sue Mirabelli, Katherine Thompson, Dan Nicoletti.

Backing up any good faculty are the enablers, those administrative staff members whose competence is indispensable to the college operations. Dr. Notar hired some good ones. There was Felicia "Fanny" Bongiorno, our indefatigable first Registrar, who confided to me one time that she would like to put the computer out in the parking lot (remember, this was the early sixties long before Bill Gates and Steve Jobs); replaced by Ted Meyers, who had some problems with the president; Ed Trask, our first Business Manager, whom I think I annoyed with too many purchase requisitions ( low cost but voluminous) for his small office; followed by Mike Kisiel with his wife, Jeanie—an ardent young couple I liked very much; Jim Pletcher, first Dean; Ron Mirabelli, Director of Admissions (Ron and Sue came together in '67); Joe Linza, maintenance, actually the college's first employee; and Jerry Wenger, public relations officer, whose leaving of the college was a sad affair (see below)—fortunately, he was succeeded by an equally competent and enthusiastic professional, Jane Haenle, generously and efficiently helped as Jerry was by Janet Schultz.

When I became Dean, there was Marianne Corrieri. my superb secretary— we got off wrong footed because I messed up her files, but she forgave me and we had a splendid partnership for nine years; and one of the most loyal colleagues I have known, my Associate Dean, Ed O'Keefe; and a young lady whom I did not work with, but she apparently became a vital member of the president's office for many years—her name was Louise Volpe.

My memory has a special place for my fellow dean, Norm Shea, Dean of Students, whose career path was similar to mine (see below for our adventures together at NCCC.)

" Think where man's glory most begins and ends,

And say that my glory was, I had such friends." (W. B. Yeats)

It is somewhat surprising to me how easy it is to remember these folks— many of them I hired-- but perhaps it shouldn't be: We have a bond, even if it is forgotten, for we were *present at the creation*.

The college would do its history a favor if all of these names (and others mistakenly not mentioned) were commemorated – an honor roll! I regret that I did not take this action when I had the opportunity.

\*\*\*\*\*\*\*\*\*\*\*\*\*\*\*\*\*\*\*\*\*\*\*\*\*\*\*\*\*\*\*\*

Fully forty five years ago, when I was teaching, there was a Professor of English at NCCC who taught for one year only; he had a drinking problem and his appointment was not renewed. I believe he committed suicide. I did not know him well and did not include him in my list above for that reason. But he was the sort of person in whom one recognizes depth. His name was Ross Hogue. As a professional, he seemed highly competent, especially in Shakespeare. Perhaps not unlike the Bard whose words he loved to recite, he was the "unaccommodated man."

Ross Hogue represents for me now the loneliness of the teaching profession that wears heavily on some who cannot quite balance the life style. There is no compensation in extravagant language for this kind of loss, but I was proud that the college wanted to remember and honor him—he was, after all, "one of us," or at least wanted to be -- and so I suggested to the memorial committee an inscription for his plaque, in the Shakespearian words he knew:

To the Memory of Ross A. Hogue

Professor of English

"I know a bank whereon the wild thyme blows,

Where oxslips and the nodding violet grows

Quite oe'r-canopied with luscious woodbine,

With sweet musk-roses' and with eglantine."

There sleeps our teacher and our friend.

The plaque was made and hung in the library at the old Nabisco Tech building for awhile. I don't know what happened to it thereafter.

\*\*\*\*\*\*\*\*\*\*\*\*\*\*\*\*\*\*\*\*\*\*\*\*\*\*\*\*\*\*\*\*

There are sorrows given and taken on any college campus that sometimes do not light a candle of understanding. One that was particularly upsetting, to me at least, was the firing with prejudice of Jerry Wenger. This event occurred during the administration of the college's second president, Jack Watson.

Jack's misfortune was in following a founding president who was destined to become an icon. It was a difficult situation for him because he got caught up in forces beyond his understanding and control. He came from Illinois where the politics were much different than in New York, as I learned later when I became President of the College of Lake County. He was quirky but had some good ideas and challenged us, as a president should. His dismissal of Wenger was understandable from a traditional governance viewpoint.

Yet I saw it as the cruelest action I knew of in the early history of the college.

Founding members of the faculty and staff knew that Jerry had a ghost in the closet. He could not verify the degree he had claimed. This is, of course, a serious offence in higher education and indeed cause for dismissal. False degree claims are not unlike false medal claims in the military, where I remember a top general with many decorations for valor committing suicide because one of them was unearned. Very critical stuff.

When President Notar appointed me Dean of the College in 1969, I was also assigned as Director and Editor of the Self Study for Accreditation. In this capacity, I checked our personnel records for completeness and removed Jerry's file from the Personnel office. I gave it to Dr. Notar and suggested that it would be better if he kept it in his confidential files. I am certain he understood why. We were involved in a silent conspiracy to conceal Jerry's tragic mistake. Why? Because we both knew and respected Jerry. We knew of his commitment and personal loyalty, his enthusiasm and willingness to put in long hours to do whatever was asked of him. He was a fine colleague who had simply made a mistake. His wife, Bea, was also fully committed to the college, serving as our archivist. (I wonder what happened to her work?)

President Watson must have discovered Wenger's file. I don't know what inquiries he made but with the Board's acknowledgment he took the immediate action he believed to be justified and necessary.

Jerry of course was devastated, and he came to me for advice or sympathy, I'm not sure which. I could see that he was a shattered man and I was not much help to him. I understood the President's ground. Nevertheless, I regret with all my heart that I did not stand up for Jerry before the Board even if to no avail.

Years later I exchanged notes on the case with the "Old Prof", Graham Millar. He did not agree with me. He told me that the faculty did not respect Wenger's work and felt that President Watson's action was correct.

There are arguments to be sincerely voiced that objective truth is all that matters and Wenger got what he deserved. But I saw it then and now as a doctrine of truth without mercy and without appreciation of our own human frailties. It does not lead to justice. Jerry was a good and decent man who loved the college and served her to the best of his ability.

Wenger's dismissal was an unalterable decision. Yet, later, I believe the Board too had regrets. Ernie Curto, Board Chair, called me to see if there was a way to put Wenger on part-time.

Jerry just disappeared. I heard shortly after that he was still living in the area, but we never saw him again.

******************************

President Notar and I had an extraordinary relationship from the beginning. I did not realize it until later, but his willingness to delegate to me responsibility and authority for all academic affairs and his reliance upon me in policy matters gave me an excellent opportunity to grow and develop as an administrator. I did not have this same relationship with Jack Watson and, spoiled as I was, that is one of the reasons I decided to pursue a presidency elsewhere.

In internal affairs I always felt that I had to keep my hand upon the throttle and my eye upon the rail. Dr. Notar handled all external affairs, and it was not until collective bargaining came along that I had any association with outside political authority. Interesting enough, that is also the area where I encountered the most severe crises.

Before that however, I was ushered into a job for which I had no experience or knowledge or expectations. I was a neophyte in all aspects of my new administrative position. This first job was to write the self study report and organize documentation for the college's first Middle States accreditation. While I had done some administrative report writing as Social Sciences department coordinator, the extensive nature of the self study summary work quite overwhelmed me. Lyla Beth saw very little of me during the weeks when I stayed overnight at the college writing the report and cataloging our accreditation files. I remember at one point going to President Notar to plead that I could not finish the job on time without some writing assistance, which he graciously granted through an assistant, but it was more hindrance than help. It was then that I remembered a line from Napoleon that had struck me as uncommon when I first came upon it:

"The first quality of a soldier is constancy in fatigue and hardship."

I realized that it must apply to executive management as well, and so I pressed on -- and took that big dog with me for the rest of my career – – though there were times when I faulted myself for not measuring up.

By the time the self-study report was finished I felt that I "owned" the college right down to her founding bowels. The report drew accolades from the Middle States visiting team. Singularity was achieved as the College -- a collaboration of Board/administration/faculty/ students gloriously stood up with its President to earn its initial status as an accredited institution. I don't remember it being that strong again.

Accreditation came at a time of fever. For students of today it seems like ancient history, yet the 60's were a revolutionary period on college campuses, even including Nabisco Tech. The most blistering issue was the war in Vietnam which I vehemently, publicly opposed. I began to feel keenly the strictures of my administrative office when our students joined in the protests going on all over the country. What made these protests interesting, more than the excitement, was that students were divided. I admired those who spoke out in defense of our troops even though I felt contempt for our policymakers. I was young too.

One day, in order to maintain campus control, we held a college wide convocation on the war. I delivered a history lecture which put me smack in the middle because the Asian reporter who covered the event liked my presentation and made it headline news. Fine, in one way, but I was beginning to worry more about the disruption of our teaching mission and the need for some academic leverage. I felt that some of the faculty, including some visiting professors from the University of Buffalo, were too radical and were basing their arguments about the university's role on superficial grounds. So it was a soul-searching time for us all.

That evening there was a march through the city of Niagara Falls— much energy expended! -- an event that allows me to introduce the third member of our top-level administrative team, an engaging and confident young administrator who served as our Dean of Students, Dr. Norman Shea. Norm had responsibility, of course, for dealing with our students and keeping them out of trouble if he could. Norm was physically fit, mentally awake, and morally straight, so we came through this mini-crisis all right.

The next day, students gathered around the flagpole to raise or lower the flag, as they would, because of the Kent State massacre and the continuing blaze of protest against the Johnson administration. The flag came down to half-mast. The flag went up. The flag came down. Last time I looked, it was at half-mast,, and students had apparently exhausted their incentive. We escaped any injuries.

Presumably, our political recess was over, but a week later there was violence at Jackson State similar to Kent State and some black students were killed there. I noticed that there was no commotion on our campus about it and wondered why there was no flag action to honor the black students. It seemed to me that it was a matter of equality and fairness, so I ordered the flag reset at half-mast. No one said anything.

I felt concerned for Dr. Notar, who was suffering from a bad back and this was not the sort of thing that his generation was used to anyway. I was not the least concerned for Norm Shea who I think relished the action. We went on to share other episodes of the college development, including one that made the year of 1975 the most dangerous to the college stability and autonomy in its brief history to that point.

Unwanted by both sides, a crisis never-the-less developed during negotiations over a new contract between the College Board, the County and the Faculty Association that began in February 1975 and continued throughout the year.

Harkening first to seven years earlier, a major decision was made by the faculty in 1968 that permanently changed the ground rules for the college governance. A faculty meeting to debate the options available through New York State's new collective bargaining law(Taylor Law) held in the Parkway Inn, across the street from the Shredded Wheat building -- I recall the meeting as clearly as this morning because it was so significant-- resulted in a solid majority decision to form a union for contract negotiations under the law, but to remain independent from the larger unions, such as United Federation of Teachers. With this option, we hoped to preserve a collegial concept of governance alongside contractual (dual governance.) The parties to the contract negotiation were the College Board, the County government (College sponsor), and our newly formed union, the Faculty Association, officially recognized as bargaining agent.

I was elected the FA president and led our team to the first contract. Other team members included Gern Jaeger, vice-president, Jeannette Lenczyk, secretary, Roger Lehman, John Marohn, Ken Hennig, Al Penzotti, Ed Voetsch, Sam Loliger, Steve Wilson. The circumstances were stressful (and sometimes humorously difficult) because of our lack of experience, but we had a good, innovative result which established direct faculty participation in determining salary and classroom conditions. Equally important, a mutually respectful, supportive relationship was established with the governing board.

In 1968 we felt that we had won a great victory: there was a grand celebration. A few months later, Dr. Notar offered me the Dean position. I received from John Marohn on behalf of the faculty a comic photograph of a chimpanzee dressed up like a doctor with the inscription, "whatever it was you had you've got it again." I still have the picture.

For the next few years the college made outstanding progress in curriculum development and student services, and dual track governance seemed to be working. We had met and accommodated change.

Then in 1975 change of a more radical and indecipherable nature occurred. It was a lesson for all of us that governance is a game of billiards where the balls bounce a little rather than pool where the balls are racked up and then pocketed.

> "These events draw me back to the
> streets of the speech I learned early
> in life. I also was engaged in the
> battle of thought and language. " ( W.B. Yeats)

I saw the difference early on when the board heard that the faculty union had hired an attorney: this caused them to back off their first plan to proceed as in the past with an informal approach conducted by Ernie Curto, Board chair. They countered the faculty's move by hiring their own professional negotiator who came into the process with a different value perspective. His name was Bob Gray.

From the first meeting, the faculty did not like dealing with Gray; they wanted direct contact with the County. Their focus on Gray as a personal enemy tended to hamper a better understanding of the process and Gray's role in that process. He was a tough but thoroughly professional negotiator, and in the end, the best and fairest advocate for the faculty on the County side.

The union presented extensive proposals, a much bigger package than I had earlier been led to believe would be submitted. For the most part, however, the items seemed negotiable to me. The faculty focused primarily on salary. At this early stage the County was not ready with a salary counter- proposal, another factor which, though not abnormal, increased the faculty's anxiety. I understood it and was not concerned at this point. My participation was understood by all parties to be limited to academic governance items, and on this we made fairly rapid progress.

Then the negotiations turned sour. In May, the County finally made a salary counter- proposal which included elimination of increments, ultimately the issue that blew up the prospect of orderly settlement. Earlier on, I had written to Gray as chief negotiator and our new president, Jack Watson, expressing concern about total elimination of increments. I knew that the faculty would not understand the County's desire to eliminate them.

It was sad and ironic that the Faculty Association team on this contract negotiation was probably better prepared than any previous team and achieved the most gains, yet somehow they could not claim victories. Without doubt, the increment problem preyed heavily on everyone's mind.. Yet the faculty had done well in obtaining the County's agreement of a $1600/1500 two-year across-the-board raise.

In September, the mountain had been climbed and we were at the peak. Yet closure did not happen. The faculty put their faith in the fact-finding step; in its fact-finding submission the union referred to the County proposal as " The Assault on the Increment System," a label which symbolized the depth of feeling engendered by an issue on which the union leadership had sought and obtained complete unity. Outside observers, both the mediator and fact finder, were honestly puzzled that this issue could cause a breakdown. "It's not a strike issue," they said. But for the faculty leadership, it was.

I have not seen worse communication in any negotiation. The essential facts were that with a two-year across-the-board application, a regular step schedule is eliminated and any incremental language is of psychological value only upon expiration of the contract. A state Court of Appeals decision made it clear that there was no guaranteed bridge from one contract to the next. Any inclusion of an incremental concept would be subject to new negotiation . Given knowledge of this fact, the board and administration argued for its inclusion. From his experience, Gray felt in his bones that a settlement was near and fought for an accommodation on both sides. He was so strong pressing his point as to arouse the ire of his employers at County level.

The County's adamant opposition seemed to be based on a view that the fact finder's salary recommendation was so large that it could only be justified to their constituencies and other unions with the argument that at least the automatic increment had been bought out. Gray and the County personnel director, Don Ehringer, even developed some language in order to mask it, referring to " economic progression through the ranks."

The original ground on which the college governance and sense of collegial community was built was being thoroughly shaken. The College board and administration had adopted a philosophy which emphasized congenial and close relations with the faculty while retaining necessary autonomy in policy matters. The overall college record in its programs and services was also outstanding. Prior to the contract crisis, the college readiness for reaccreditation was excellent .

It seemed to me, and some others as well, that an alarm was sounding that the faculty's first allegiance was not to the college but to the faculty union. If so, it would be necessary in the future for the administration to adjust to this likely continuing reality. How it would do so, and how the faculty leadership would respond, was the new challenge for the future.

It was a lesson for me that collective bargaining had brought the faculty new power, yet they stood to lose greatly on another dimension of values if balance could not be achieved. In retrospect, some of the speculation-- such as whether or not a liberal arts faculty plunging deep into a corporate style of behavior in pursuit of monetary interest could say anything meaningful about the needs of society at large -- seems hopelessly idealistic. The battle for the liberal arts had already been lost at the university level.

In a letter on the crisis at the time, I said, "It is the sheerest romanticism to believe that collective negotiations will not set the tone and pattern of college governance in the future, but surely an educational institution with such potential as exists at NCCC ought not to stultify on such a singular plane of vested interests and power interplay." This thought was even more germinal in the next stage of the crisis.

Looking back so long ago, I am still puzzled, but I don't believe that the faculty as a whole understood what was happening. The union leaders had no sense of the dialectical nature of the process. They were inflexibly sure of their position on the increments issue, yet on the other hand, expected their demands to appear reasonable and their allegiance to the college to be acknowledged. I felt the need to intervene, but powerless, lacking credibility to do so.

Like stepping off a dock into water without knowing how deep it was, the Faculty Association decided to call a "strike day," an illegal move under the Taylor Law. It was not only a bad tactical move but ultimately very unproductive.

By law, the Board and President Watson had to respond to it, and they knew there was no way the faculty could win. When the strike action happened, lines became drawn much harder. That was a defining moment. One of the costs was a reinforced rigidity in regard to the salary increments so dear to the union. The Board was not entirely unsympathetic to the increment concept; it was the County Legislature that wanted to abolish it, but eventually a compromise resolution could have been achieved with Board support.

On November 3, 1975, President Watson sent a memorandum to all members of the professional staff which I drafted for him. The memo made it clear that "job actions will not be tolerated... Appropriate disciplinary action shall be taken in each and every case of neglect of duty, intentional failure to carry out assignments, or disruptive activity."

The crisis finally ended when the faculty capitulated, but there was no joy in Mudville that day-- no celebration or victory claims. Actually, the Faculty Association could have, and should have, claimed victory for the substantial gains made, but there was just a feeling of relief that the ordeal was finally over. There was also lingering dissatisfaction on both sides, altogether a sad outcome.

This history is not what I foresaw when we began the Faculty Association, but neither would I contend against the view that it was a natural evolution. Thereafter the union leadership matured and apparently provided a responsible part of dual track governance for the college for many years.

I cannot testify to it, of course, for I was gone to Illinois, but I suspect that the election of Tony Gullo as union president in 1978 was an important factor in achieving stability-- thus illustrating again how essential it is to have leading professors who know how to balance the conflict in pursuit of legitimate aspirations.

There is little difference between this kind of professor and the college dean. When these leaders understand each other the dialectic works. If one accuses the other of going to the "dark side," good things don't happen.

> "So we come back to the place from which we started-- seeing that place in a wider perspective. The place is a college and we are the faculty. The wider perspective is about perspectives, and the question posed is this: do we, as the faculty, foster whatever will promote in students, in faculty, and around the table those wider perspectives which will bring our system back into an appropriate harmony between rigor and imagination?"
>
> *"As teachers, are we wise?"* (Gregory Bateson)

\*\*\*\*\*\*\*\*\*\*\*\*\*\*\*\*\*\*\*\*\*\*\*\*\*\*\*\*\*\*

Pulled out of context, the above description of our biggest crisis in the early history of the college may make it appear that 1975 was a wasted year for development and student service. On the contrary, disregarding the problematic undermining of the reaccreditation effort-- ultimately we were successful in that effort too-- the record of development and student success was very good.

It was the year of approval of the Culinary Arts program (Carl Heintz) following contentious debate over the appropriateness of an OAS degree (limited general ed courses), the Service Technician program, enhancement of the Learning Skills program under the leadership of Ed Thomas and Dr. Kathleen McWhorter, Medical Office Assistant program, and several feasibility studies for more programs to come. Nor was teaching innovation ignored: a fine example was team teaching, involving the classes of Cathy Griebner ( speech) and Eleanor Robinson (English).

The final enrollment report for the year exceeded the anticipated FTE by over 300 students. Significant progress was made in the goal of transition from the former traditional library set up to an integrated Library Learning

Center project -- the idea was to make the library a "vital center" on campus, to include computer technology. There was a major breakthrough in co- curricular organization in Student Affairs and a significant increase in the activities of student clubs and organizations, such as the Veterans Club (Dan Rogala). Community education programs were also expanded, such as the Tuscarora project to strengthen relations with the Tuscarora people; chief Kenneth Patterson was appointed project coordinator with Tony Gullo.

Yet, undeniably, it was also a year of discontent, kicked up a notch probably by the faculty contract dispute. But it was more than that: we were beginning to experience the cognitive dissonance natural to rapid growth. For a decade, the college had been moving aggressively on several fronts with many new faculty and staff members coming on board. In retrospect, I don't believe we were prepared to receive them, taking nothing away from their commitment. We did not see how the communications problem is exacerbated when the number of personal relationships rises exponentially. (Doubling the number of department members, for example, increases the number of interaction routes by the square.)

Still, the drift of cynical responses was by no means justified in my view. In one particular case which annoyed me more than usual was a strident bit of satire submitted anonymously by an administrative staff member (for God's sake!) to the student newspaper, "The Spirit," providing a litany of what he perceived as the college's failures and stupid mistakes with a cute, concluding conceit. I knew who it was but could not remonstrate, of course. So after pondering it for a day or two, I responded in the same format. I believe it serves here as a fair, positive summary of this paradoxical year:

"Spirit Chitter Chatter"

Are you aware...

That no other community college in the area has a Library Learning Center like ours... that Dr. McWhorter's College Prep program for incoming freshmen is unique... that Dr. Polanski is the only community college faculty member attending the medical ethics series at the Hastings Center... that Mr. Abbondanza's biofeedback training course is the only one in the state's community colleges... that the planetarium has many potential uses beyond the study of astronomy... that the math department has a tutoring program... that the recent high school articulation conference for English teachers sponsored by the Humanities Division was the first in this area since 10 years ago...that the opportunity for our students to study with professional artists at Art Park is unmatched anywhere else in the country... that the nursing faculty has developed a totally integrated teaching approach... that the technology faculty annually conducts technology orientation days on campus... that Mrs. Griebner's students in "These Days" have already given nine performances... that the ORT program is one of only two in the state... that the wrestling team earned Academic All-American honors... that the college's recent Energy conference was carried by three American and three Canadian television stations... that the Organization Development Project for Older Adults is unique among two-year colleges in the state... that the college has applied to become the first Bicentennial campus in the state... that the secretarial science faculty was responsible for a luncheon honoring the college's secretaries and secretarial students during National Secretaries week... that a Service Technician program was begun this year... that Ms. Jamieson is an officer on the State Community College Faculty Council... that the Niagara Chorale, college band and orchestra are an outstanding tribute to the college's desire for excellence... that the college trustees spend an enormous amount of time on college business without salary -- ?

In the immortal words of the mountain lion," it all depends on your landing devices." Balance! Balance! Balance!

At this point of my personal history, I was six years into being an academic Dean, still low on the learning curve, but I began to see that the old cliché," you can't see the forest for the trees," was apropos for many faculty and staff in our college organizations. But then I also had my own blind spots.

\*\*\*\*\*\*\*\*\*\*\*\*\*\*\*\*\*\*\*\*\*\*\*\*\*\*\*\*\*\*\*\*

"Though you are in your shining days,

voices among the crowd,

and new friends busy with your praise,

be not unkind or proud,

but think about old friends the most:

Time's bitter flood will rise." (W. B. Yeats)

I was at this community college for 15 years, the longest I have served at any institution. NCCC has been special to me because it was first in my career and the last institution I served where I enjoyed genuine camaraderie with colleagues whom I knew first as personal friends. " We knew each other." At those colleges where I served as president I also enjoyed personal relationships as well as very productive alliances, but it was not possible to develop the same kind of familiarity, nor did I expect it. Even at NCCC in my Dean years I could sense the gradual loss of it and estrangement.

Yet there are fond memories of good times at faculty events where I was welcome, such as the "academy" -- an informal group for philosophical exchange but mostly beer- blasting, bragging and bullshit. Great times!-- as were lawn parties, ping-pong and basketball games, a canoe trip down the Niagara River with Stan Herowski, Roy Sommer and Gern Jaeger, spirited but gentle discussions with Clyde Tyson, an arm wrestling contest with Jim Abbondanza (I think he won), the distribution of initiation Tiger cups (I remember presenting one to Ray Harvey) and tiger prints on the walls, scraggy sarcasm (sharp but never cruel) from Roger "if you can't plug it in to hell with it" Lehman, and standard complaints about high-handed administration. (I don't even recall the issues but have some regret now that I went after Dr. Bodkin so hard.)

These are as vital in their own way as faculty meetings to discuss academic standards, but when I became president they were replaced by wine and cheese parties with formal invitations.

I respect all of my colleges and have extensive, sterling memories of their people and development, but feelings of nostalgia only for Niagara County Community College. The core of it was the social science department where I began. I always accepted invitations for their retirement parties, but Thomas Wolfe was correct, *"you can't go home again!"*

\*\*\*\*\*\*\*\*\*\*\*\*\*\*\*\*\*\*\*\*\*\*\*\*\*\*\*\*\*\*\*\*

I took six months sabbatical leave in 1976 at Harvard University where I wrote my first book, "Values and the Future." So leave was productive, but when I returned it had not given me the morale boost I needed. By this time I had been drained of my imagination for the college and wanted desperately to move on, so I began to apply for presidencies. There was never a prospect that I would become president of NCCC, although I briefly considered it when a later president resigned during my time in West Virginia.

My last consultation on the college governance occurred in my last month when I was invited to a conversation with three members of the Board-- Ernie Curto, Ed Pawenski and Al Certo. I respected them highly along with other Board members for their selfless dedication to the college. They wanted to know my evaluation of Jack Watson. This was a difficult topic for me as I knew that Jack was disliked intensely by the faculty, and I did not think that he was a good fit for the college, but he was fairly appointed and not incompetent. From their remarks, I knew by the end of the conversation that Jack was going down.

However, the end of the era of Notar/Curto/Pawenski *et.al.* did not happen in 1978. For me, it ended 25 years later when I eulogized Dr. Notar at a memorial service held in the Ernest Notar Administration Building.

## Cross-section of Letters and Memos

### *To Whom It May Concern: Reference, Mary Ann Corieri, August 1, 1978*

Upon leaving Niagara County Community College, one of my greatest regrets is that I shall part company with Mary Ann Corieri, whom I have come to know and respect as an outstanding professional secretary and a very fine person. Her competence and loyalty have made her a strong asset to this college and invaluable in the office of academic affairs. Her knowledge of the community college is probably as good as that of most administrators and faculty members on-campus, and she certainly has been much help to students who appear in this office. In any administrative reorganization or transition, her presence will be a steadying influence.

Let this letter stand as my firm conviction that any administrator would be fortunate indeed to have her as an assistant. That fortune begins with her skills as secretary. She is an excellent word processor, thoroughly knowledgeable of office procedures, and highly efficient. Beyond these skills, however, she is a secretary who thinks and cares. Far more than a secretary she is an administrative assistant and office manager, *par excellence.*

Her personal approach has fit mine very well, but perhaps even more importantly she has that singular professional maturity that makes her a leader among other staff members as well. Over the years, she has consistently demonstrated a desire to grow professionally in her field, and this commitment has positively affected her colleagues. These are some of the reasons she is so well respected throughout the college community.

**Dr. John O. Hunter**

### *From: Eleanor Seminara, Director of Library Learning Center, Niagara County Community College, October 12, 1978*

God works mysteriously! He has prodded me to write to you and extend my earnest best wishes for your successful and happy tenure as president. The prod came today as I opened a file folder of correspondence marked "Student Reactions to College Services" and found the attached note to you. I can't begin to explain how my student help managed to secret it and keep it from you, but the humor of the situation cannot be ignored. I extend also my apologies for not having made sure that this charmer got to you earlier. My only excuse is that it has been a very "trying situation" since you left.

### To: Bob Kenyon and friends at NCCC, September 7, 1979

How I wish that I could be with you on this special occasion! I shall always remember you, Bob, as one of the originals and an outstanding chairman. I suggest you carry the NCCC banner to Arizona, contact Jim Pletcher, Brenda Webb and Min Jack to open a branch campus for retired faculty. Ernie Notar can serve as emeritus consultant.. Our sincerest best wishes to you and Betty and fondest regards to everyone.

John and Lyla Beth Hunter

### To: Board of Trustees, Niagara County Community College, November 1, 1982

Many thanks for the invitation to unveiling the Ernest Curto room on the 20th anniversary. Ernie Curto was one of the most outstanding trustees I have known; his contributions to NCCC are many and great. I regret very much that I cannot be with him and my former colleagues on this auspicious occasion. Best regards to all!

Dr. John Hunter, President, College of Lake County

### .From: Carol Jamieson, Acting Dean, Niagara County Community College, February 16, 1979

Ed O'Keefe gave me a copy of your talk at convocation which I read with pleasure. Your message was clear and direct. As I read the address, I sensed you have found a position which is challenging but not uncomfortably so. I sound like Miss Fidditch approving your writing, but that is not my intent, I just wanted to say how pleased I am that you are doing so well.

Carol Jamieson

**To Whom It May Concern: Reference, Carol Jamieson, November 10, 1981**

During my tenure as Dean at Niagara County community college, I had the pleasure of working closely with Carol Jamieson. Mrs. Jamieson was first a highly respected member of the English faculty, who was rapidly promoted through the ranks. She was an excellent communicator and served as an editor of college reports, including Middle States documents, as well as on various college commissions and committees. In 1975, she was appointed as chairman of the division of humanities. It was in connection with this position that I began to fully appreciate her organizational skills and academic leadership. I also understand that during a change of administration at NCCC, she served as interim Dean of academic affairs. Had I been present at the college at that time, I would have strongly endorsed her appointment to this key position.

The humanities division at NCCC blossomed under Carol's leadership. Among various innovative projects which she initiated were an integrative approach to the liberal arts and sciences, interdisciplinary approaches to courses in the humanities, the development of tutorial writing components, basic skills course development, and new curriculum studies.

Dr. John Hunter, President, College of Lake County

**From: Prof. Graham Millar, September 27, 2001**

John: The groundbreaking was yesterday, with most of the brief ceremony held in the gallery due to wet and cold weather. A lot of the old gang was there, including Clyde, Don Voisinet,Paul Power and me. Ernie got a louder and longer ovation than anyone else. As part of his remarks, he announced that his driver license had recently been renewed for another eight years. That would take him to age 102 and he plans to use it all.

**To: Anna Petrozie, NCCC, Message for Tony Gullo's Retirement Party, October 24, 2006 (Read by Clyde Tyson)**

Greetings to Tony Gullo and all of his colleagues and friends from one of them who would like to be there with you. I know this will be another great night of camaraderie and goodwill because we recognize the leadership and achievements of one of NCCC's titans. Tony should be honored not just by the social science department but by all at Niagara County

Community College who served with him, or depended upon him, or were touched by him.

Of all the faculty leaders I have known in higher education-- of whom there are many-- Tony was among the most deserving of the mantle of Distinguished Professor and Chair. Most of those present this evening can testify in specific ways better than I can how much Tony meant to the success of the department, the Faculty Association and the College at large. This trinity has been in my heart ever since I left in 1978, and I was always grateful to know that Tony was there. Like a rock.

I only worked with Tony up close when he was a young lion professor. He challenged me and, I believe vice versa. He stood strong from the beginning. I was responsible for bringing him into the department as a replacement for George DelGrosso. And, Tony, it was I who told Dr. Notar, when he asked why I was recommending your request without the usual justification, "let's go with him, he knows what he's doing." You may not remember but in that early period you thought that I was defenseless in daring to ask you for more documentation.

So the years have passed and now we say farewell to one of the best. I believe that with Tony and other colleagues from the social science department now retired, the NCCC that I knew has come to an end.

John Hunter

# Chapter III

## College of Lake County
### 1978 to 1986

Adventure was the pristine point for me:

Risking to find, and finding to embrace.

I fought the groove and galloped from the lull,

Rejoiced in jolts and reveled in suspense.

I am on fire with curiosity,

As eager as a petal to unfold

And taste the air of heaven as conceived,

To feel the synthesis of opposites,

The transformation of abuse, and know

What I had heretofore imagined only.

**(Rudolph Schirmer)**

There were major differences between the first two colleges I served as president-- College of Lake County and Alfred State College-- and the last two -- Cambria County Area Community College and West Virginia Northern Community College. CLC and Alfred were well established, healthy institutions, both troubled in different respects, but there was no threat to their survival. Definitely this was not the case with CCACC and WVNCC. Thus my presidential experiences were quite different between them.

When we first went to Lake County we had a marvelous reception from the Board which heightened my already considerable enthusiasm for leading this institution. Several years later after I had left the college, I discovered that I was not high on the original list of presidential prospects but gradually moved up as the search committee narrowed and focused on final candidates. Still I was not the immediate favorite; there was serious competition from sitting presidents. However, one trustee in particular fought for me-- J David "Mac" McCartney – and eventually convinced his colleagues. "Mac" left the board three years later, but we remained friends for the rest of his life, exchanging letters and consulting on poetry." Mac" was an excellent poet whom I have on my website.

There were seven elected trustees. They provided for the college a strong and caring board that compiled an excellent record of governance by policy. Two other members on our social list were Jim Lumber and his wife Barbara, and Art and Gen Katzenmaier. They were fine friends and companions. With Jim and Barb we discovered the American Ballet Theater in Chicago, and Jim was a generous host for dinner at five-star restaurants.

Art Katzenmaier was a retired school superintendent who handily won his board elections without campaigning. I had a special bond with Art that was not known: we were both afflicted with an hereditary condition called "benign familial purpose tremor" which causes the hands to shake slightly. I was never dysfunctional with it, but it was sometimes embarrassing if someone thought that I was nervous. I checked it out with a neurologist when I was 30 to ensure that I did not have Parkinson's disease, and learned that approximately 5 million other people in the country also have this benign tremor. Art asked me about it and shared his own experience with it. (For all I know, it may have helped me to win his support-- well, if so, I'm grateful, presidents have to take every bit of comfort they can.)

During my eight years as CLC president, from 1978 to 1986, we covered a lot of development ground and there were many significant votes. I am proud of my record of 7-0 votes on all of my recommendations with a couple of exceptions where Rich Bryan (who defeated Katzenmaier) cast a negative vote. (I think he was tired of seeing 7-0 scores.) The board elections were exciting affairs and colored our picture of activities with knowledge that here too politics are important. It was a sad occasion when Art Katzenmaier was defeated.

Another member I must mention twice is Rich Anderson, who was first elected as a young man and is now serving as a community college trustee with the longest record of service in Illinois, if not the country. Other members of this creative, energetic board included Millicent Berliant, Eleanor Rostron, Betty Jean Thompson, Nan Fairhurst, Nancy Block, Ron Johnson, Melody Brown and student trustees elected by the Student Senate.

The College of Lake County never faced the prospect of retrenchment or reduction in force for financial reasons, but it was obvious when I arrived that they were expecting action to reorganize the administration, which was fine with me. With the help of an experienced consultant, Irv Harlacher, we took a year for a pretty extensive analysis and presented recommendations to the Board.

The biggest changes were: a reduction from four to two vice presidents; reduction from five to four deans at primary level; addition of paraprofessional assistants; phasing out of developmental services as a separate entity; and a built in stress on open campus development, community needs assessment, and institutional research. Three years later, we had another major reorganization, so people got used to this kind of change.

Budget development of course required the usual careful attention, but we were always able to fund the major goals and strategies adopted. The college was very fortunate to be in a part of Illinois where there were several corporation campuses and steady population growth and real estate development. Along with reasonable tuition rates, the state and local tax appropriations were sufficient to carry our annual budgets and still provide a good balance in both operating and maintenance funds. By the time I left CLC eight years later, we had accumulated an operating fund balance of over $12 million. I never saw that condition again.

To give the Board and administrative staff clear understanding, as well as others interested, we developed a system of keeping financial data that served as a useful picture of how far we had come in financial administration. The data included year-to-year figures and graphs of assessed valuations, enrollments, tax rates and extensions, state apportionments, tuition costs, per capita costs and unit cost analysis.

Educational fund and Maintenance fund expenditures were also recorded along with yearly fund balances and projections. We had an aggressive investment strategy, using "repo's" and pursuing grants and contracts. The largest and most exciting of these was a contract with the U.S. Navy to provide technical instruction at the Great Lakes Naval Base. This was a sole source, cost reimbursement arrangement.(More on this innovative program below.)

The fullness and organic clarity of this method of compiling financial data in an historical context was unique; I was not able to replicate it exactly at any of my other colleges.

**Open Campus Development**

In my judgment, the most important strategy that the Board adopted was "open campus development", backed up with a comprehensive marketing plan. CLC was a premier community college, but in 1978 when I joined, its mission was too constrained. The Grayslake campus was isolated. Some faculty liked it that way, having pretensions of a small, elitist Harvard. The potential of an outward looking, adventurous community college was being wasted.

Once adopted by the Board, the "open campus" strategy quickly went into effect establishing outreach centers throughout the county, a stronger partnership agreement with the Area Vocational Center, and an innovative interstate agreement with the Gateway Technical Center in Wisconsin which allowed students in both states to enroll in courses at either institution paying in-state tuition. By the year I left, we had 25 outreach centers, including a permanent facility in south county-- the Highland Park Educational Center (Sheila Marks, Director.)

We had the horses, the resources, and the development was rapid and sweet.

However, and naturally, it was not all smooth. We faced some concern that this emphasis would neglect the main campus development in

Grayslake, but such was not the case. In these eight years we completed the Learning Resource Center (and named the Murphy Library), established the Community Gallery of Art, completed the Horticulture building, built the gymnasium (finally space large enough to hold commencement inside), established a Child Care Center on campus, did major facilities renovations for nursing, automotive technology, and refrigeration/air conditioning programs, and adopted a campus horticultural plan which included prairie restoration.

Through cooperation with the Area Vocational Center and major corporations we also established the state's first CAD/CAM Center and began a Software Development Center.

In this strategy, our first, and perhaps most important long-term effort was to bring the Waukegan/Zion/North Chicago lakeshore communities into the college identity, thus solving the Highway 41 psychological barrier problem. We bought the old Heins building in Waukegan and turned it into the Lakeshore Educational Center, which eventually was granted branch campus status by the Illinois Board of Higher Education (IBHE.) The Lakeshore Center's mission was focused on equal opportunity for minority students who needed ESL and other remedial programs. Watching these students thrive under the direction of Eleanor Murkey, Adena Staben (our Ingrid Bergman, 1985 Illinois Outstanding Adult Educator), Bill Vargas, Chuck Nystrom, Mary Dunn, Mary Charous, Rose Sajuan, Dr. Cotton and other such role models-- was an absolute delight. Our celebrations were glorious affairs.

In commemorating the Center, I tried to put its mission into context:

*… These are the poor, the black, the Spanish- speaking, the disenfranchised. I have met many of them, and they are very fine people -- intelligent, charming, deeply appreciative of the College. Talk to our faculty: they will give you some marvelous success stories…*

*Yet, here's where it becomes difficult to convey a balanced perspective, despite the efforts of the staff who have been directly involved in the development. We are not talking about a "separate but equal" doctrine here. If the Center were to become the minority branch campus of CLC, its promise would not be fulfilled. And we would lose something even more fundamental in the College potential. There is a lot of difficult work still ahead of us that may take several years, but it is solidly in line with the fundamental community college values of egalitarianism matched by educational excellence. This is, indeed, a big challenge of community development at the Lakeshore Educational Center.*

Several years later, we visited downtown Waukegan and saw how prominent the Center had become. Its success is, of course, due to many people, but I give special credit to Eleanor Murkey. I appointed her as director and she was later named campus Dean. Her life story is emblematic of victorious education. After a traumatic childhood and suffering abuse and low self-esteem in her teenage years, she began taking remedial courses at the College, and her self-confidence began to rise. She matriculated and earned an associate degree, then proceeded to a bachelor degree, and finally to a Master's degree. While pursuing degrees, she was employed by the College, first as a paraprofessional, and then promoted to position of director. She owes a lot to the college and vice versa. She was inspirational to many students who followed her.

The largest new project on the Grayslake campus was the construction of the Science building in the main quad. There was a lot of pessimism about getting this project off the ground at the beginning and ongoing criticism by the faculty during the planning stage. After a lot of consultation and analysis – – ICCB support but no funds from the state – – the project was finally enabled by a unique municipal revenue bond financing arrangement with the city of Waukegan in which the college was responsible for all repayments of the bonds. Monies earned through the college's contract with the U.S. Navy were also used.

Simultaneous with the approval of this project, the Board adopted a strategy and began to set aside funds in the budget annually for a Performing Arts Center, now beautifully constructed and appropriately named for Jim Lumber. Contrary to the notion of conflict between technical and liberal education, the intention was to balance support for science and technology programs with the humanities and fine arts, which in turn was supported by faculty/staff development.

The Lakeshore campus development and construction of the Performing Arts Center were outstanding achievements, both of which had dramatic impact on the college mission. This work could not have been accomplished without a collaborative team effort and community support.

Backing up the Board's strategic planning was the College Foundation with a high-profile membership. When I arrived, the Foundation chair was Alan Baske, who immediately convinced me to make a $500 donation. Shortly after, Alan was succeeded by Richard Kennedy, publisher of the Waukegan News Sun. Dick was an enthusiastic, very confident leader, and we did some good work together, particularly in the area of economic development. The Foundation was chiefly interested in contributing to the humanities and fine arts, particularly through the initiation of a Community Gallery of Art in the college library; but they also served as a conduit to the Navy for development of the CLC Naval Training School.

Some of the other members of the Foundation Board included John O'Meara, president of the Citizens Bank of Waukegan; Bob Wright, VP of Stenograph Corporation; Bill Schroeder, publisher of Lakeland Press; Ralph Edwards, chief personnel officer of Abbott Laboratories; Heinz Loeffler, a retired Navy admiral; Dennis Ryan, Lake County Attorney; Barbara Richardson, Lake County Treasurer, Jack Schaum, retired business man; and my college trustee friends Jim lumber and Dave McCartney. The executive directors were Frank Adams, followed by Kathleen Arns and Bill Class.

The Community Gallery of Art opened in 1981 and was immediately successful. During my time in Lake County, it sponsored juried exhibits by Lake County artists, a year-round calendar of musical performances, poetry readings, and other cultural events, such as Board receptions for our Illinois Outstanding Citizen Award honorees. In addition to the daily flow of students and community members through the Gallery, more than 5,000 people each year attended Gallery events.

The Board adopted its annual Illinois Outstanding Citizen Award, to be conferred each year at commencement, in 1981. The first recipient was Dr. William C. Petty, a highly respected, long-time superintendent of schools for Lake County. Dr. Petty was one of the most charming and erudite educators I have known whom I enjoyed immensely. During my time, other recipients included an esteemed, 85-year-old County judge, Warren Hulse, who happened to be my neighbor (had no bearing on the selection);

poet laureate and Pulitzer Prize winner Gwendolyn Brooks; the astronaut, James Lovell; and former board member Art Katzenmaier.

## Naval Training School

One of the most exciting projects I have experienced in my career was the founding of the CLC Naval Training School at Great Lakes Naval Base-- started with a contract of $400,000, ultimately grew to nearly $20 million, expanded courses to San Diego Naval Base and Pearl Harbor, Hawaii. It was a superb model for integrating community college and military instruction. The first contract was signed by the Board in September 1979, but we did not begin instruction until the end of the year. However, we needed to have the instructors (mostly retired Navy chief petty officers) on board before hand, and so I had about 120 of them on the college payroll while sweating out the Navy coming through on their end of the deal with contract funds-- probably the greatest monetary risk I have taken. My Navy pals kept telling me, "don't worry, it'll come through!" But I was monstrously aware that we were dealing with the federal government. Ultimately, we had 550 instructors on board teaching in 20 programs with approximately 30,000 cadets graduating each year.

In December 1983, I testified before the Senate Armed Services Committee in favor of a Senate bill which would provide training for enlistees in the military reserves through the nation's community colleges, the skilled Enlisted Reserve Training Act (SERTA):

*In summary, the programs that I have mentioned are the types of programs you will find in the spectrum of vocational/technical courses offered by community colleges. I do not mean to imply, of course, that community colleges have available ready-made programs like fire control technology geared to Navy fleet requirements. Such a curriculum results only from articulation with the Navy. The contract must precisely define the competencies and job requirements which set the instructional objectives. Such curriculum development is not alien to community colleges, and they could be engaged in permutations of this process as called for in SERTA. The main point I wish to make, however, is that the basic subjects which are essential to success in specialized training – – such as electrical technology, medical technology, computer science, mathematics and other vitally important subjects of general education – – are taught regularly in community colleges.*

*There are experienced professionals in the training field who wonder why partnerships have not been stimulated by public policy before now. The current Dean of the CLC Naval Training School, William Class, a retired Navy captain who is very knowledgeable of military and defense training needs, asks the primary question: " why do the community colleges, the military, and defense industries continue to duplicate each other in training programs? It is silly and wasteful and retards our ability to adapt to the new technologies."*

*It would be very difficult to duplicate instruction now being offered by CLC/ NTS through the Service School Command with all Navy personnel. The funding level to operate the school is just over half of previous Navy costs... An organizational development of considerable magnitude has occurred. The wisest course is to continue this development through the same cooperation evidenced so far. The college understands the Navy's need to contain costs and shares the conviction that quality and cost efficiency are parallel concerns...*

*The next step in this contractual relationship is to extend the model for credentialing purposes. The college has been exploring this possibility with the Illinois Community College Board and the Illinois Board of Higher Education. The creation of a Defense Occupational Institute may be the outcome.*

Unfortunately, the SERTA bill was not adopted by the Reagan administration, most likely because of the pressures from a mounting federal deficit. However, the Board took another step in fostering these concepts by authorizing me to submit a formal request to the Illinois Community College Board to establish an Institute for Special and Contractual Programs. The Institute was approved, only one in the state, which meant that I had to take it into consideration in an administrative reorganization which I was also conducting at that time.

None of this entrepreneurial action could have happened without some very good staff who had many duties to fulfill, some of them previously unexplored. We were working on a leading edge. I chose Jack Cote from the biology department to serve as the first Dean of the school because I wanted to have an experienced and loyal college person in that lead position. But we also had to recruit ex-Navy people, and in doing so, I gained great respect for Naval officers and became fascinated with their systems of instruction, which were every bit as successful, if not more so, as our own. We needed a happy blend, and I believe these mature professionals achieved it. Other officers who were instrumental in the success were Bill Class, Lee Hamilton and Frank Labasci, Navy vets, and Frank Adams, appointed as Provost for Contractual Programs in the reorganization. Class became Dean of the school when Côte resigned, and then Provost on the college staff. Yes, we had more than a few good men (and women.)

Due to my association with the Navy, I was made an honorary lifetime member of the Navy League. Although I no longer have active affiliation, I continue to hold this organization and the Navy in high regard.

## Faculty, Staff and Students

I have said that the main responsibility of administration is to lead and support an inspired faculty. Describe the institution anyway you like, the life blood is the faculty. At CLC, we had an outstanding faculty – – with a few bothersome exceptions – – who were very well supported. Even at the risk of slighting some who are equally deserving of mention, an honest depiction of the college requires me to stretch my memory for faculty citations:

Doug Sherman, geology, was a perennial student favorite, elected twice by students as "Outstanding Instructor." He was a very successful golf coach and served as acting chair of the Health/Physical Education/Recreation Department, but he could not win the search committee's support for permanent appointment. Later, I began to regret that I did not appoint him to the position anyway, but his move back to teaching turned out to be highly positive for him, his students and the college.

Without editorializing too much, I want to mention several others in the same category; they fed off each other's professional excellence:

Dr. John Mathwig, biology and an outstanding environmentalist; Ben Bruggen, history, Faculty Senate chairman, highly conscientious and caring; Jack Hudson, electronics, instigator of the Software Development Center; Tony Gundrum, also electronics, Faculty Senate chairman; Frank Harnisch, theater director and renowned enactor of Shakespeare; Eibleen Glennon, English and theater director following Harnisch, a published poet; Betty Becker and Judy Rosenberg, English (Judy was editor nonpareil of accreditation self-study; Steve Infantino, Ken Simonson and Brian Smith, philosophy, brought it wonderfully to life through role-playing in public performances; Ted Schaefer, English, published poet;

also, Dee Swan, Dr. Tana Durnbaugh, Ellen Powell and the rest of the Nursing Department; Bill Ballock, John Wilmot, Marv Johnson, Wing Park, our excellent Math Department; Ron Riepe, geology and another well respected environmentalist; Ruth Rickard and Liz Pirman, history; Dan Ryan, Donna Raymer, Jim Rominiuck, John Steinke, Bob Kerr, Bob Townsend, Dale Warnke—social science; Dr. Linda Wetherbe, human services; Tommie Ems, speech;

also, Marv Weiler, business, 1985 recipient of the state "Outstanding Instructor" award; Jim Paradiso, business, inventor of *"Adopt a Firm"* and Leavey Award winner for innovative enterprise; Sue Grove and Gary Thomas, business/accounting; Roger Weichman, chemistry; Toby Ward and John Shelton, physics; Doug Beitel and Jerry Lechman, technology; Judy Baron and Sister Susan Plevak, allied health; Sue Wunderlich, dental assisting, Faculty Senate chairperson;

and Warren Simpkins, Bruce Mack and Thomas Hoekstra, music; our award winning fine arts department – Ed Kanwischer, Dan Ziembo, Reg Coleman, Nancy Cook; coumselors Walt Peterson, Frank Nichols, Larry Whittier, also a winning cross-country coach; and my library pal, Cass McGovern.

The CLC biology department was an enthusiastic and adventurous crew : Mike Korn, Scott Hickman, Jerry Hinkley, Jack Côte, Rich Killen, Cheena Wade, Dick Meginnis. During recess, they were usually on the road somewhere with their students.

Hickman was well known as a lover of birds, an expert on warblers. Korn was a herpetologist who could not understand why others did not appreciate his exotic friends, including a caged cobra in the lab who struck at the glass as people walked by, and an innocent python that was lost for several days until it dropped from the ceiling onto the shoulder of the night custodian. Mike was an expert with snakes and certain he had control, but the situation made others uncomfortable so that the division chair, Dr. Virginia Thompson, ordered that there would be no more live serpents in the labs. This was done by her own initiative, but it was an action which I was also considering. Mike gave way gracefully; both he and Ginny were leaders.

Nor can I forget our administrative staff; we had an excellent team: Vice Presidents John Swalec, Hal Garner, Dan Webster, Pete Bakos, Vern Manke, Jim Doppke, Art Kent and Kathleen Arns (but not all at the same time!)

Also, there was a reliable and conscientious middle administration consisting of my executive assistant and then personnel officer, Christie Sobek; PR director Dorothy Regan (what a gem she was!); Deans Frank Adams, Wayne Haberkorn, Russ Peterson, Tom Buchta, Bill Class; academic associate deans-- Dr. Virginia Thompson, Russ Hamm(humanities; he fought for the Economic Development Director position and was appointed), John Lumber(social sciences), Don Holland(business), John Shelton succeeded by Carl Painter (technology); Directors Dan Petrosko (computer labs), Gary Churchill(computer center), Ed Snyder(student activities), Don Drake (audio-visual), Donna Palmieri (purchasing/business services), Pat Kerrcher (placement), and Gene Kulin (facilities manager);

superb and loyal administrative assistants Jovina Kazmer, Rose Peters, Linda Krueger, Linda Peterson, Virginia Hubbard, Joan Cejner, Joan Meginnis, Barb Oilschlager, Anne Allen, Adelaide Bannon.

Altogether, this was a very formidable team whose steady performance was vital to this rapidly expanding college.

One of the most brilliant students I have known was Christine Shoub. When I first met her, she was randomly taking courses across the whole curriculum without a degree orientation. Ultimately, she accumulated over 100 credit hours and a straight A average. I helped her to matriculate into a PhD program in pharmacology which she flew through and went on for a medical doctorate. She then conducted research on pork eating cultures in Central America.

Christine was exceptional, but there were many other students as well at CLC who proved the wisdom of Henry Adams' tribute, " a teacher never knows where his/her influence stops."

Other student leaders I remember are Melody Brown, who won a tough election to the board; Tim Burch; Marci Filler; Pat Sullivan; Heddy Abraham, senior student, organizer of the literary club; Delroy Bowen – – we helped him before he was deported – – even then we had illegal immigrant issues; Barbara Napper, technology student with a 4.0 QPA, named outstanding minority student; Dick Lyon, custodian and super student; Vernon Estes; Cindy Parker, Student Senate president; and the Student Treasurer-- her name was Suzan Hunter.

I had such confidence in CLC that I removed my youngest daughter, Elizabeth, from High School at the end of tenth grade and enrolled her full time in our liberal arts program. No problem! She was on the Dean's list and graduated two years later at age 16.

Though I have skipped over them here, we had our faculty/staff and student problems, of course, but CLC acted as a community and people were our priority. And though I have not seen most of the people named above in many years, and perhaps some are no longer with us, to mention them here I think is the most fitting part of this memoir.

My overall positive rating of the CLC faculty and staff is not meant to infer that they all held a similar regard for me. Some did; some didn't. And some were hard to read. On the day before I left the college I was visited by a serious lady professor who walked into the office and said, "well, John, here you are, forgotten but not gone?" Something there? *Je ne sais quoi.*

## Technology Growth

In my first semester at CLC, an electronics instructor, Jack Hudson, came to my office and requested approval to buy an early microcomputer, the TRS 80. My response was, "okay Jack, go ahead and we'll see what happens." Yeah, go ahead! The revolution was underway. Five years later we had 200 micro computers serving faculty and students. There was controversy about whether they should be Microsoft or Apple or some lesser platform, but there **was no** disagreement about going ahead with this strategy.

In 1983, we moved forward with a leveraging strategy, using seed money to attract major corporations, such as ComputerVision and Cincinnati

Milicron to create the first CAD/CAM Center in Illinois. The Area Vocational Center under director Merv Pillotte was also a partner in this enterprise. For a few years, until technology moved on as it always does, this automated industrial center was hugely attractive; it further enhanced CLC's leadership stature. At about the same time, we opened the Software Development Center, which did not take hold as quickly but was another advent of the future. Although we were not aware of it, this happened at the same time that Microsoft was making its historic bargain with IBM that ended up launching its empire at IBM's expense.

## Shift Happens

While on sabbatical at Harvard, I had taken a course in history of science and technology and continued with this interest when I came to Illinois. My technical skills were not high, in fact I was barely computer literate, but I had a good perspective on science and technology as a social movement. I also knew the importance of distinguishing three terms used in education: literacy, competency and excellence, as well as the differences between and the connections of science and technology. In an effort to stimulate discussion of these terms in our curriculum development, I published a series of articles on *Technological Literacy* in the Waukegan News Sun (and later in a journal on education technology.)

I thought it was important to view "technological literacy" as a liberal education concept. Some CLC faculty agreed with me. In the lead article of the News Sun series, I made the following points:

- There are no experts for technology as a social process. There are expert handlers of parts of technology – – but no one who is competent in technology as a whole, no universal man.

- Technological forecasting does not work. There is no way to predict the rate of technological change or what kinds of technology will break open next. The best "prediction" probably is that most of the technologies of the 21st century haven't been brought online yet. (This was well before I read Kurzweil.)

- The biggest issues surrounding technology are not technical questions, they are policy matters.

- Technologies are becoming more and more accessible to everyone, more transparent, easier to use.

I believe these points have been proven valid.

Since 1980, we have been caught up in a roaring current of technological change, a curve which Kurzweil believes is about to go straight up. The challenge for us then was that if students are to be prepared to function as citizens of a technological society, it would depend upon liberal education as well as technical training. Today, I do not know if we have made sufficient progress along these lines in whatever passes for the liberal arts. I fear not. As someone once said," technology is a queer thing... It will bring you great gifts with one hand and stab you in the back with the other." We face many warnings that we do not take seriously enough the backstabbing threat.

In the hands of instructors like Sherman, Mathwig et.al. our curriculum and driving forces were both technology and the liberal arts. CLC was indeed a comprehensive community college, the best that I have known.

## Legal Known Unknowns

There was a bureaucratic and legalistic framework, mostly hidden, for this multifaceted development that required some sturdy outside representation. Unusual for most community colleges, I think, but we employed four different batteries of attorneys. We used Fred Lifton for labor negotiations and he was the best I have known in that field. Another large Chicago firm was employed for Navy contracts. There was always some legal action going on, ranging from small and fairly inconsequential to large, obtrusive and very costly, and some in between.

The college was part of a consortium in court conflict with the Zion Nuclear Plant over assessed valuations. The consortium had employed a Chicago law firm to represent its interests. Despite the outlay of over a million dollars, nothing seemed to happen. I met the attorney in Springfield and was immediately repelled by his arrogance. It was apparent to me that we could go on paying his fees and the case could keep dragging on with no end in sight. So I suggested that we "sue for peace" by meeting directly with the Zion Nuclear authorities to negotiate a settlement. Our Foundation chairman, Dick Kennedy, who was publisher of the Waukegan News Sun, picked up on it and made the suggestion headline news. But our allies did not like it and resisted vigorously. I thought this was plain stubbornness, but in their defense there was much more at stake for them than for the college. When I left Illinois there was still no resolution.

At the lower end, but ethically bothersome, was the case of a woman with no business at the college, neither a student nor an associate, who drove into the parking lot, went immediately to the security office and reported that she had fallen because of a pothole. We never saw her again, but two months later received a summons from her attorney; she was suing the college for $25,000. Responsibility for settlement was given to our insurance company, and they decided to settle for $25,000 as the most cost efficient disposition. Apparently, it would have cost more to go to court.

At about this time I was reading Burns' *The Deil's Awa wi th' Exciseman*

> *The deil cam fiddlin' thro the town,*
> *And danc'd awa wi th' Exciseman'*
> *And ilka wife cries, 'Auld Mahoun,*
> *I wish you luck o the prize, man.'*

> *The deil's awa, the deil's awa,*
> *The deil's awa wi th' Exciseman,*
> *He's danc'd awa, he's danc'd awa,*
> *He's danc'd awa wi th' Exciseman.*

A case in the obtrusive category--very obtrusive -- was strange but compelling in the way it dragged us into the inner reaches of our juridical system. It involved an ex-employee who sued for wrongful dismissal. It was strange, to me at least, because it was totally frivolous, yet the zealotry of the grievant kept it going, to the extent that even though he lost at every turn, he spent a huge amount of money on his hopeless pursuit and ended up suing his own attorney. I almost felt sorry for him except that he had put me and others through hell for no good reason—unless that was the reason. I don't know now why this case bothered me so much, except that

I thought I may have perjured myself in my testimony during discovery. I remember crawling across the room at one point in my despondency.

However, the discovery process, which haunted me even after I left Illinois, was very enlightening on how our system works. It occurred to me that three such intense lawsuits could bring a small college to its knees. The case cost the college over half a million dollars in legal defense fees.

Through cases like these, I gained appreciation of legal machinery available at a price as weaponry aimed at anything, - - - only just maybe, justice.

In my presidencies, I continued to have experience with the courts but not like in Chicagoland. At Alfred State College I had a shift to local court cases involving students, preferable, even though more heavy laden with moral concern.

But not to end on a negative note, in the spirit of my colleagues and friends who gave so much initiative, here is a more fitting coda for College of Lake County from a line by John Keats: " There is an old saying, 'well begun is half done'—'tis not so! The truth is, not begun at all till half done."

When I left CLC, I made the following statement, which I believe can stand for all the colleges that I served as president:

"We can't bat 1000 all the time, but I think it's good to count our hits and errors. If we are honest and discerning, we can measure our victories and defeats as well as our developmental potential. Where did we succeed? Where did we fail? We succeeded where we cared enough to accept and respect the student for wherever he was when he came to us. We succeeded where we communicated the nature of the teaching – learning experience. We succeeded where we felt and made possible the feeling of joy in academic discovery. We succeeded where we made a friend.

Where did we fail? We failed where our caring was superficial. We failed where we permitted a false notion of freedom to reinforce an already critical lack of self-discipline and self-respect. We failed where rigid routines and organizational structure stood in the way of the faculty – student interaction. We failed where the whole of the mission was obscured by reductionist fallacy."

# Cross Section of Letters and Memos

## To: A.J. Katzenmaeir, Grayslake, Illinois, November 14, 1983

Dear Art: Taking pen in hand with you in mind now is a difficult task. As simply and sincerely as I can, I want to express deep gratitude to you for your service on the board, this on behalf of all the college administration.

Beyond that, there is an immeasurable sense of personal loss in the knowledge, still difficult to internalize, that your wisdom, guidance and support shall not be present in the new board. No election result has ever been so shocking to me.

Last night, two nights after the election, breaking one of those periods of silence common to husband and wife, Lyla Beth suddenly said, "John, it is still hard to believe that Art will not be on the board. He was such a wonderful board member. He never wavered, always so faithful. I think we should pray that the new board will be able to make up for this loss."

Art, in this spontaneous, heartfelt expression, I believe Lyla Beth echoes what many people are thinking. You remain with us.

John

## From: Peter Johnson, Executive Director, Illinois Council on Vocational Education, June 28, 1985

Thank you for sending me your publication on **technological change and educational reform**. It's an excellent publication and one that all educators need to read. This is the type of material I need to get to a number of people and specifically to the 13 members of our Illinois Council. Would it be possible to obtain about 25 copies? We would be glad to pay for them. I'm looking forward to a late summer or early fall visit with you. Your two/two plans – – articulation strategies with the AVC and other institutions are what it's all about.

**From: Leslie E. Malpass, President, Western Illinois University, July 1, 1985**

Thank you very much for sending me a copy of your recent publication, *Technological Change and Educational Reform*. After reading the document, I distributed it to relevant deans and department chairs on our campus. The section on New Strategies and Goals is especially helpful. Congratulations on a most illuminating and helpful document. All the best!

**From: Steve Infantino, Professor of Philosophy, 1984**

Dear John: Thanks for the article on Values Clarification. I agree with your statement," Judgment is not bigotry." One can be understanding and tolerant of a position while still believing or judging it to be wrong. On the other hand I think you could have been a little fairer to the values clarification approach by pointing out that there is nothing wrong in making a decision or choosing certain values as long as one is honestly in doubt. Often people choose values prematurely and the choice is usually in favor of personal expediency. I would love to discuss this with you. Give me a call when you're free.

**From: Brien Laing, Chief Executive Officer, American Hospital Supply Corporation, December 5, 1984**

This is just a quick note to thank you for sending along a copy of the 1983-84 Annual Report. I enjoyed every page – – it was stimulating reading.

'Striving for Excellence" is an outstanding description of the College of Lake County! It's my favorite word, and I use it often. A tip of the hat to you, John, for your excellent leadership and your fine guidance of this most important Lake County institution.

**From: Frank Mensel, Vice President for Federal Relations, AACJC, November 13, 1984**

Your comprehensive analysis of the complex challenges that community colleges face in providing the country with a better and more flexible delivery system for training military technicians is exactly what I bargained for. Your use of the term," thicket", is very apt.

The analysis will be very valuable to me in my informal negotiations with Congressional staff as we attempt to restructure SERTA. If we can come up with a new bill that our sponsors still like I will surely share with you in the draft stages. We consider your experience a great asset in this struggle.

### From: James R. Galloway, Assistant Superintendent, Illinois State Board of Education, December 27, 1985

The Automated Industrial Center sounds exciting and on the cutting edge for serving the private sector and educational needs of the citizens of that area of the state. Every time I turn around, you are out in front of the pack, John, with yet another exemplary activity. It is tremendous and I am confident that you will continue to lead in this way. Hopefully, if I could ever get up to Lake County your invitation would still be open. Best wishes for another successful year.

### From: Lt. Col. Theodore S. Clements, Commanding Officer, U.S. Army Recruiting Battalion Chicago

Dear Pres. Hunter: On behalf of the United States Army Recruiting Battalion Chicago, I would like to take this opportunity to extend to you my sincere gratitude for your cooperation with the United States Army. Your support and endorsement have provided prospective graduates viable programs and options on employment and educational opportunities. Especially noteworthy has been your relationship with Capt. Joseph M Naylor.

I am very pleased to be associated with your outstanding institution. In the short time since our relationship has been established, our cooperative initiative has been remarkably successful. I trust that we will continue to be staunch partners

### To: Northeastern Illinois University, Chicago, Illinois, May 22, 1986, Re: Student C. M. Reichert

Ms. Reichert was a student in a class which I taught during the spring semester 1986. I found her to be a serious and committed student who was always alert, participative, and capable of learning new and complex material quickly. I believe that her skills developed during the semester, and she was the principal author of an outstanding term paper for students at this level.

Dr. John Hunter, President, College of Lake County

## To: *Illinois Community College Presidents and David Pierce, ICCB Director, June 2, 1986*

Though I look forward to my return to SUNY, one of my regrets in leaving Illinois is that I shall not be able to fulfill my position as Chairman of the Presidents Council. I have enjoyed immensely the relationships on the Council and our work of the past eight years. The Presidents Council is one of the finest organizations I have experienced and certainly worthy of our commitment. It is a great asset and tribute to the excellence of the Illinois community college system, and I was honored to have been elected chairman. Dr. John Hunter

## From: *Ben Bruggen, Professor of History, College of Lake County, July 22, 1986*

Dear John: I wish to express my appreciation for your contributions to the development of the College Senate and to my professional development. In 1978 the College Senate was on the verge of disintegration. By your willingness to work with the Senate and your unselfish time commitment to it, the Senate is now on a firm footing and has an accepted place in the governance structure. As to my own growth, my association with you has fostered in me a different outlook on governance and its goals. Specifically, you have demonstrated that the "process" is very important and in the end will usually turn out a respectable product.

## To: *Ms. Eleanor Murkey, Director, Lakeshore Educational Center, Waukegan, IL, October 9, 1991*

I regret very much that we shall not be able to attend the 10th anniversary celebration. We had so looked forward to this event, but my father's memorial service will be held at the same time.

I believe now that during my administration at CLC, the most important strategy we adopted was to extend the college identity and service throughout Lake County, thus making us a truly comprehensive community college serving all clienteles within our jurisdiction. This strategy took hold most significantly when we began to develop the Lakeshore Educational Center after we purchased the Heins Building.

Of all the exciting projects in CLC's development during those years, my fondest memories are of the Lakeshore Center. This development erased Route 41 as a wall of separation between the Lakeshore communities and the College of Lake County.

To some degree, as you know, it was an uphill struggle, but the challenge of expanding our vision to include those folks who were in most need of our assistance turned out to be, literally, a labor of love. You and your staff provided the center stage for an expression of that love and purpose and commitment. Of course, there were many others from the Board of Trustees and throughout the college organization, as well as community leaders, who made this development possible.

John O. Hunter, President, Alfred State College

# CHAPTER IV

## Alfred State College
## 1986 to 1994

You've got to be brave, and you've got to be bold,

brave enough to take your chance on your own discrimination –

what's right and what's wrong, what's good and what's bad.

(Robert Frost)

I regarded the College of Lake County and Alfred State College as comparable institutions because of their academic quality, but the mission of Alfred was much different than I anticipated, primarily because it was a residential campus and the students were younger than the average community college student. However, it proved to be a refreshing experience working with students in the age group of 18 to 22 years. I liked them very much, and I believe they liked me. Lyla Beth and I especially enjoyed rooting for them at athletic contests and attending their choral concert and theater productions. Some are still my friends. I also enjoyed the faculty and staff who were very good at their jobs. Our mission and direction of development were excellent. Yet the Alfred culture was a microcosm of what was going on in the four year colleges and universities at the undergraduate level. It was not good, and I doubt that it has gotten better. I shall explain this opposite while unfolding the record of development year-by-year.

## 1986 – 87

Alfred was a strong institution with an experienced faculty and staff who were used to the challenge and the idiosyncrasies of the State University of New York, the largest university system in the country. Alfred was a two-year college of technology with an excellent reputation for its programs, including vocational "hands on" programs at a second campus in Wellsville.

When I arrived, however, I could immediately see the need for some administrative change and "tightening up." The first priority was to focus on college reorganization and creation of a strategic plan.

We operated without two vice presidents during this year, but challenges of the transition were picked up by some good people, and I was fairly confident we could make necessary adjustments administratively without too much controversy. I was half right. I also discovered early that Alfred, a beautiful and almost isolated place, was not the "Happy Valley" it was supposed to be.

By the end of the year with organization development as a continuing goal we had turned the corner to a new era of administration. Bob Granger, a veteran administrator, was appointed Vice President for Finance. Bill Mombert, a good financial associate, was appointed Director of Resources Development. Both were a big help in my orientation along with the presidential secretary, Lorraine Crandall, who proved to be an excellent listener and confidante, and our able office assistants Connie Pye and Mary Scholla.

Some other staff members who impressed me as experienced and competent were Gary Frazier, Dean of Engineering Technologies, whom I had first met while Dean at NCCC; Terry Weaver, Dean of Agriculture and Allied Health; Doug Barber, who became an assistant VP ; Jim Bassage and Tom Massara, leading residential life and auxiliary services, with duties and problems which I had not encountered before; Barry Lash, Director of Libraries; John Larson, Dan Neverette and Neil Benedict, Directors of Student Activities; Al VanderLinde, Dean of the Wellsville campus; Dr. Maurice Rucker, Dean of Business School;

also Deborah Clarke, Director of Public Relations, and her lively assistants Marilyn Lester and Don Manktelow; Dennis Kelsey, Director of Computer Center; Jerry Barrett, Director of Public Safety; Lois Weber, bookstore manager; Pat Argentieri, Mike Geidlin, Jeff Ahearn in Controller's office; Karen Canne, Dave Sengstock and Mike McCormick, dining services, and Jim Hawes, physical plant;

and Jim Grillo, VP for Enrollments Management (creator of "Alfred State Of Mind") who later wanted to transfer to teaching business -- a request I granted with tenure appointment.( Therein hangs an interesting tale.)

At the beginning, these folks were the core of my administrative staff which remained pretty much intact to the end of my administration. There were some other appointments and replacements along the way which I shall detail as we go along. These were good people, responsible and loyal to the college.

In the fall semester, I put out three major position papers: the first was on administrative reorganization, the second on enrollments management, and the third was titled "Computers and Strategic Planning." After some brief hesitation and legitimate concern about local department needs (again, it's a question of balance), we did adopt a campus wide strategy and pushed it aggressively as top priority. Yet, I can't say that the bottom line decisions to go with this strategy were difficult. As a leading college of technology, we needed first rank computing capability; on that point there was general agreement.

Although retrenchment loomed ahead, the college was never in a crisis of survival because of SUNY oversight and protection -- one of the advantages of this huge bureaucratic system -- but I did not like the sparing nature of local autonomy.

I reflect back on my first management staff meeting when we didn't know how much money we had and one of the vice presidents was trying to calculate on the back of an envelope how many positions we had filled. We had these oddities that people seemed to think were normal, like "split lines" and "permanent temporaries." (I saw this again at WVNCC.) We had no local financial reporting system and no administrative charters of responsibility. We had no uniform policy for search and selection and no affirmative action policy or plan. Other stated policies were obsolete, as I soon discovered when I took them seriously. I had two improper practice charges in my first semester. Policy wise, we just weren't in the game -- although some senior faculty thought my "new rules" would soon crumble. All of that was made straight.

During the winter of this first year, there was a tragic accident on the road between Alfred and Wellsville campuses which made it clear that student safety would have to be a major concern in all of our efforts regarding student welfare. This was number one on a list of critical events. I appointed a joint college/community team to investigate and make recommendations for safety improvement.

Then in midyear, the State announced a temporary freeze on expenditures and new hires, and we were facing shortfalls in both the state operating budget and the dormitory income fund reimbursable budget (DIFR). These two problems were addressed vigorously throughout the year and were successfully resolved. However, it was a first lesson in serious financial challenges to come. The Facilities Planning Council was created to assist in strategic planning and a list of ambitious projects was drawn up.

Evidence that the college mission was changing fundamentally was initial work done on a strategy to introduce Bachelor of Technology programs. This effort was broad-based, but the leaders were Gary Frazier, Dave Conde and some engineering technology faculty members.

Some other highlights of the year included:

*The Computing Graphics curriculum was the first in the nation to receive TAC/ABET accreditation;

*Julie Ogden, Nursing student, won the NJCAA women's cross-country championship;

*Erwin Kailbourne, CEO of Norstar Bank, was the first Alfred alumnus to receive an honorary doctorate degree from SUNY, conferred at the 1987 commencement.

## 1987 – 88

As the previous year was marked chiefly by college reorganization and planning, 1987 – 88 focused on several programmatic developments. It was very important to focus on the declining enrollments problem, and so an integrated approach by the entire college community was fostered. There were several specific accomplishments in this area during the year and we began to see a turnaround in admissions. Credit goes to a sharp and steady crew headed by Jim Grillo and including Deborah Goodrich, Val Nixon, Nancy Marino, Laura Giglio as well as admission counselors and student assistants.

More work was done on the strategy to introduce Bachelor of Technology programs; a relationship with SUNY Binghamton was established for this purpose. New programs in biotechnology and health services management were added to the curriculum.

Academic computing growth was measurable on both the Alfred and Wellsville campuses due to corporate assistance. It was clear that we had to focus on such assistance in order to upgrade and enhance our technologies and this became a major emphasis in facilities/financial planning.

Administrative appointments made during the year included vice presidents Lee Alley (Student Services) and Rolf Zerges (Academic Affairs), assistant VP Doug Barber, and Dean of Agriculture and Allied Health, Jim Thompson. Steve Babcock was appointed Director of Athletics; Sally Doty as Director of Personnel. We tried to focus on improving college governance and communication, an area where there are some interesting side stories. To improve exchange with the president's office, I appointed the President's Advisory Council on Excellence (PACE).

The first of several interesting trips to Central America occurred when I visited Nicaragua with Congressman Amo Houghton and other Southern Tier college presidents. We met with Pres. Daniel Ortega and members of the Sandinista government, one result of which was to establish scholarships from each of our colleges for Nicaraguan students. I remember our student, Julio Cardinale, because of his interest in a program called *Catecumical Way* and the risk he took in not being able to get back to the college when he returned home for a short but essential participation in it. This was not liberation technology, but there was evidence of this Marxist strain, for example a superimposed face of Karl Marx on a cross in downtown Manaqua.

Relationship with Congressman Houghton continued to be excellent throughout my administration.

The visit to Nicaragua led to a meeting with a private foundation in El Salvador and our eventual partnership, which is another story in itself.

Other highlights of this year:

*Alfred State was named a Farm Medic National Training Center to provide agricultural rescue and safety programs. The leader of this venture was one of the most enthusiastic, enterprising faculty members I have known. His name is Rich Hoffman.

*The Medical Records and Laboratory Technology programs were re-accredited with high marks for the maximum period. We had excellent faculty in the medical services curricula. Some of those I remember are the chairman, Glenn Fairchild, and Art Gaisser, Vickie Bolton, Michelle Bartholomew, Carol Lange, Janette Thomas, Ron Putnam, David Schwert, John Buckwalter, Wes McCrea. It was a genuine pleasure to spend time with these folks. Putnam and Schwert each served on the College Council, excellent faculty representatives.

*Eight members of the Alfred State chapter for Student Automotive Engineers won first prize in an SAE competition against stiff competition; runner-up was a team from RPI. Our team was led by Prof. Yogi Jonchhe.

*The Automotive Trades Department on the Wellsville campus was awarded "Best Post Secondary Training Program" in the state by the Motor Vehicle Manufacturers Association. Some of the faculty well deserving of this honor included the chairman, Lyman Savory, Skip Merrick, Mike Ronan (who also served as advisor for Sigma Tau, academic honorary fraternity ), Don Catino, Tom Jamison, Roland Granger, Gary Troutman, Dan Murray and a few others who should be added.

*The College Farm swine facility was built through a loan from the Alfred Educational Foundation. College students and staff did the construction.

* The Alfred Student Theater production of *"Night Watch"* earned the only award given to a college group at the 28th Annual New York State Theater Festival In Corning. Director was Barbara Larsen.

*Other outstanding performances during the year were the Alfred State Concert Choir, conducted by Anthony Cappadonia, and the college band, conducted by Mike Lester.

*A new student awards program was introduced by President Hunter honoring 30 outstanding seniors at a Presidents Recognition luncheon as the Leadership Class of 1988. This was an annual event during the years of my administration. The selection process was careful and gave me a lot of pleasure.

*A new program for savings and accountability in college development was introduced. Very important for the future, it included the installation of a new telephone system projecting annual savings of $230,000 per year.

## 1988 – 89

Again, I was preoccupied with the SUNY budget crisis, which prevented some of our objectives from being implemented, but overall this was an excellent year of progress, particularly in enrollments management and student development. The enrollments management system was strengthened by a new unit, Enrollments Management and Academic Services, headed by Doug Barber, which brought together all aspects. The College met all of its enrollment targets.

The strategic goal to establish college wide computing was also accomplished. This involved cable networking of the campus through fiber optics, including flexible computing access in the residence halls. The Academic Computing Services Center was established to provide professional development and assistance in the implementation of networking strategy as well as troubleshooting, repair and maintenance at all levels. SUNYSAT was made operational on campus during the year.

A new emphasis on the theme of Student Development was offered through some major restructuring in student services. This involved new approaches to the endemic problem of alcohol abuse. An administrative Student Development Council was formed along with a professional staff advisory group for Greek organizations. (The Greeks were catching my eye more and more often.)

Because of an unusually high number of incidents of violence in the fall semester, chiefly alcohol related, and a series of arson fires in the Mackenzie dormitory complex, I issued a demand for action and new leadership by staff and student leaders. There was an immediate, encouraging response, but the problem of alcohol never left us. Alcohol abuse brought an increasing number of rape allegations, which in my maverick mind were also due to SUNY's PC lax policy on residential life. (See my End Note for more on this losing battle.)

More positively, we had some brilliant academic success: nine engineering technology programs were reaccredited by TAC/ABET with high marks. Programs in Allied Health and Business Technologies were also reaccredited.

Some important facilities goals were reached, including the creation of the Physical Fitness Center, a high-priority project which had been promised to students two years earlier. The planning for a Student Development Center adjacent to the library was also completed. On the Wellsville campus the Food Service building addition was finished to be operational in 1989 – 90.

**Other highlights:**

*The 1989 Nursing class had a 100% success rate on the RN licensure exam. This was a great department! Some members I remember are the chairperson, Marilyn Lusk, and Joanne Daniels (who published that year), Kathy Decker (who sent me one of the most encouraging notes I have received), Rosemary Fischer, Therese LeGro, Cynthie Luehman and Mary Smith.

*Gov. Mario Cuomo visited the Alfred campus in August, hosted by members of the College Council. He toured the new Computer Integrated

Manufacturing Center (CIM) in the School of Engineering Technologies. At a later public gathering he announced that the college had been named as a Rural Services Institute.

*Delegates from El Salvador spent three days on campus as another step in exploring the possibility of building a twin college of technology in that country through partnership with Alfred.

*A conference on farm enterprise policy and marketing was sponsored by Congressman Amo Houghton who was very concerned with the plight of our farmers.

*Under coach Gary Moore, the men's cross country team won their sixth straight New York conference championship; both men's and women's teams won regional championships. Cross country had always been a strong sport at Alfred. Running the hills at home was an advantage – – as I knew from competing against Alfred as a member of the UB cross country team when I was an undergraduate. We always hated to run at Alfred.

*A five-year strategic plan for the future of Alfred State College-- the "Foundation Plan"-- was finished and adopted. We were commended for it by the SUNY Chancellor, Bruce Johnstone, and other members of his administration.

*Alfred State won the attendance award at the annual meeting of the Association of College Trustees with nine members from the College Council present for the Albany sessions. The nine, who paid their own transportation costs, won a sugar maple tree for the college. These were clearly very dedicated people. The College Council had been instrumental in the planning and development of the College since the beginning of my administration. I worked closely with the chairman, Dick Lippert, also a good friend, to ensure that we had a solid bond. Other colleagues on the Council, whom I also count as good friends to this very day, were Pat Fogarty (whom I believe is still serving), Dr. Jim Koller, Dr. Charles Orlando, Dr. Gerald Thorington, Betty Minemier, Jane Jamison and Caryll Goldberg. Dave Serbacki joined later. Dick Johnstone was an Alumni representative.

Another friend who is now my neighbor in Hornell served on the Council as a representative of the Educational Foundation – – his name is Bud McCarthy.

Bud was the first person I met when I arrived at the College on a sunny morning, and he was generous with his time escorting me on both campuses, providing my first orientation to what I would call my own.

## 1989 – 90

This was a year of self study. Nearly half of the faculty and staff were directly involved. The College Council was also actively involved in the process. It was also a year filled with controversy.

Curriculum evaluation led to some hard decisions to de-activate the Agricultural Power and Machinery program and to retrench several positions in other programs, with the benefit of shifting those positions to the schools of Engineering Technologies and Liberal Studies where enrollment growth was most notable.

Continued emphasis was placed on the theme of student wellness and development. The student conduct code was substantially revised, and strong new policies on sexual harassment and misconduct were adopted. The extent of these problems continued to worry me. The College Council was enormously helpful in these matters, along with the Student Life Committee of the Faculty Senate and the Student Senate. It was gratifying that no one wanted to ignore the problems. The Faculty Senate adopted a strong statement on professional obligations, especially as related to class cancellations.

A new athletic code, athletic academic honor roll, and mandatory study halls for athletes were introduced. The fitness center proved to be a shining resource for our students.

Phase 1 of the computer dormitory plan was completed with over 200 PCs tied into the fiber-optic network. Two new computer labs were established in Brown Hall for business students and linked to the dormitories via the network. Two other important construction projects had begun during the year: installation of a new campus lighting system, and the first phase of replacement of underground high temperature/hot water lines.

The College became involved in the low-level radioactive waste issue, dominant in the local area due to intense objections to the location of a site for radioactive waste in the Southern Tier. I visited Barnwell, South Carolina with Congressman Houghton to investigate the technology and logistics of its low-level radioactive waste storage site. We were impressed with the technology and Barnwell's acceptance of it, but it was an entirely mind-set back home. I had correspondence with the Governor's office and published articles on the issue.

Another major controversy during the year was the adoption of parking fees as a means to offset budget reductions. In the final analysis the College Council agreed with the faculty that the parking fees policy I wanted should be rejected. I considered a veto of their recommendation but then consented to the Council's advice. The issue was temporarily abated, but I knew that eventually parking fees would come.

A six-member delegation from the Foundation for the Promotion of Educational Development, FEPADE, El Salvador, visited both campuses in October to strengthen the group's relationship with the College for the establishment of a twin college of technology in El Salvador. In June and July consultation visits to El Salvador were made by President Hunter, Dean James Thompson, and professors Terry Tucker, Tom Burnard and Bob Sullivan from the Wellsville campus.

We took a major step forward in economic development by joining Corning, Inc. and the New York State College of Ceramics to establish an industry incubator on the Alfred State campus. A 20 year lease was executed with Alfred Technology Resources, Inc. on which I served as vice president.

Simultaneously, we had several exciting projects conducted by the School of Engineering Technologies, including the "stepless gear" transmission project of the Gleasman Corporation.

**Other highlights:**

*An enrollments management summer orientation program was adopted, and an Adult Education Services Center was established.

*Thanks to the Student Senate, senior citizens in the community were offered free transportation to the campus from the Senate's 15 passenger van.

*Eugene Jacobs of Hornell was reelected chairman of the Education Foundation Board for the 18th consecutive year.(Time for a change?) Dick Lippert was re-elected chairman of the College Council.

*Nearly 1000 artists, blacksmiths and their families from throughout the U.S. and several foreign countries came to the Alfred campus in June for the artist and blacksmiths Association of North America 1990 International Conference. Charles Orlando of the College Council was prominent in this undertaking.

*ASC athletic teams again won regional championships in men's cross country, women's indoor and outdoor track, and men's soccer. We had introduced soccer as a varsity sport the previous year.

**1990 – 91**

My annual report noted that this was a year of "crisis and renewal." It was an extraordinary year both in regard to crisis management and in the achievement of major institutional goals – – that "yin and yang" of my Alfred experience. It was, perhaps the best year of my administration. At the end of this year, the College stood on new ground.

The financial management crisis hit its peak as the state fiscal situation began to have paralytic effects. It looked like the College would lose 30 positions and over $1 million of its baseline allocation. The remarkability of the college to sustain programs and continue strongly with stated goals in the face of genuinely deeper austerity and a paralysis in Albany was a great tribute to the spirit of the Alfred faculty, staff and students.

Our first declaration, supported by the College Council, was that in its crisis management the college would resist any retrenchment by local decision-making. Probably for the first time in the history of the college, a coalition of the major constituent groups was achieved to support the College's political goals. It was indeed impressive and caught the attention of the SUNY central administration.

A major achievement was an amendment to the SUNY Master Plan which authorized Alfred to confer the Bachelor of Technology degree. This approval was hard fought for and full of political twists and turns. The addition of these programs gave Alfred a new mission. Ultimately, the mission change was endorsed by the Governor in a letter which cited "the academic excellence of Alfred programs."

Another significant achievement was Middle States reaccreditation for the maximum 10 year term, which came with strong endorsement of the College's direction of development, high marks for the placement of ASC graduates, and "the energetic and enthusiastic participation by the campus constituencies in the evaluation process." The event equaled the North Central laurels piled upon CLC in 1985.

Partnership agreements were signed with FEPADE in El Salvador; the Cattaraugus/ Allegany Board of Cooperative Education Services (BOCES); and the Allegany County Legislature for economic development purposes.

Construction began on the Student Development Center adjacent to the library. In order to accomplish this goal we had to diverge from the original plan of integrating it with the library because of asbestos problems. Major credit goes to my team of Bob Granger, Rolf Zerges, Doug Barber, John Anderson, Steve Lester. Anderson was newly appointed as Director of Student Development; Lester as Director of Facilities. With them, I worked hard on this project and was very pleased with the result. We had excellent cooperation from SUNY's Vice Chancellor Irv Freedman and the facilities administration. (I had no clue at the time that the building would later be named in my honor.)

*What they undertook to do,*
*they brought to pass.*
*All things hang like a drop of dew*
*upon a blade of grass.* (W. B. Yeats)

## Other highlights of 1990- 91:

*The College established a chapter of Phi Theta Kappa, my favorite student organization. The new chapter was advised by distinguished teaching professors Art Gaisser and Ruth Keyes.

*A $50,000 fund in support of the School of Vocational Technologies was established for recruiting students by Caterpillar, Inc.

*Engineering faculty members Rick Hardman and Bob Rees were awarded a $46,000 National Science Foundation grant.

*The Alfred State cheerleading team captured first place in Region Three cheerleading championship competition, the best of 10 teams.

*The Alumni Chorale returned again in April to help celebrate Prof. Cappadonia's 40th year as Director of the College Choir. (Ten years later, Lyla Beth and I returned to celebrate his 50th year.) "Mr. C" had a legacy like no other faculty member at this institution, interesting, the celebration of music in a college of technology.

*The 1991 graduation included six students from El Salvador.

## 1991 – 1992

The College continued in financial crisis throughout this year. However, bolstered by its new Bachelor of Technology degree programs, Alfred State continued to offer the most balanced array of high-quality technology programs in the SUNY system.

The College had also climbed into a leading position in respect to campus wide computing, a strategy which was maintained despite budget reductions, and in fact with considerable cost savings. This is testimony to the value of astute planning trade-offs in the technology sector.

Due to financial difficulties, it was necessary to move forward again with a retrenchment and reorganization plan. By this year the College had absorbed cuts of well over $2 million in its base operating budget. The options were not very attractive, but I was resolved that we must move decisively. The reorganization resulted in the deletion of several administrative positions, including the offices of academic deans for the schools. The Deans did not like the new set up, naturally enough, and the move was highly controversial. It was also a wrenching adjustment for the academic faculty and staff. However, it avoided the reduction of faculty positions. Curiously, at the time, this did not seem to matter much to the faculty; I think my stock was beginning to decline because of the emphasis on organizational change which nevertheless was squarely matched to the College's needs (in the president's opinion at least.)

On the positive side, the position of Dean of Student Development was created, and John Anderson was appointed to the position. John taught both physics and chemistry for us and had served as chairman of the Faculty Senate and representative to the College Council previously. I saw management potential in him and so presented him the opportunity to join the administration. . Following my departure, I was not surprised that John moved steadily forward gaining experience in both academic affairs and institutional development. He was the perfect choice for president of Alfred State College in 2007.

A joint faculty/student panel worked out a new system for Greek governance, including a new constitution. It seemed that a new spirit of camaraderie and support for the College within the Greek community had been achieved; but as it turned out later there were still problems to be addressed, mostly alcohol related.

The ITCA project, building a college of technology in El Salvador, was well underway in this year. Nine ITCA faculty members spent the spring semester at Alfred, and 16 faculty from Alfred spent the summer at ITCA. Through its relationship with ITCA, Alfred became well-known in El Salvador.

## Other Highlights:

*In May the administration building was formally dedicated to honor the College's seventh president, my predecessor, Dr. David H. Huntington.

*A new policy for faculty evaluation and recognition was worked out by the Faculty Senate in cooperation with academic administration.

*New academic programs were approved by SUNY, including Environmental Technology, AAS, and Teacher Education Transfer, AS.

*Prof. Rich Hoffman was selected for participation on a biotechnology panel in Dublin, Ireland. Rich was developing our biotechnology program as well as Farm Medic.

*The College was awarded a $400,000 federal grant to improve the effectiveness of emergency medical services in rural areas, to be provided through the Farm Medic Training Center.

*David Conde, Dean of the School of Engineering Technologies, was elected president of the NYS Council of Engineering.

*The Athletics program was featured in the January 1992 edition of JUCO Review. Lacrosse was introduced as a new intercollegiate sport.

## 1992 – 1993

The building of the Student Development Center was completed, and it was occupied in January, officially dedicated in May. Several other capital projects were placed on the SUNY agenda, including a contract to enclose the Mackenzie dormitory complex, enhancement of the Orvis Center and adjoining physical education areas, including a new track, new handball courts, roof replacements and renovations for handicapped compliance. Other roof replacements on the EJ Brown and Huntington buildings were scheduled, and the final phase of the replacement of the high-tech/ hot water lines was designed and approved. In the summer, the old math Annex building was demolished to provide additional parking – – just in time before this useful old building collapsed.

Even though we were still facing difficulty in the operating fund, overall I was pleased with what we were able to do in the facilities improvement. Again, I give credit to my administrative team, especially Bob Granger and Steve Lester. In academic development, distance learning was picked up as a new, important goal; a new "Student Contract For Learning" was adopted.

The campus wide computing strategy which had been strongly pushed over the past few years resulted in considerable savings due to the utilization of physical plant personnel to complete the objectives. This strategy served the campus present and future very well.

Strategic consideration of whether or not to move the School of Vocational Technologies from Wellsville to the Alfred can't campus was initiated – – even though I knew that the decision could not be made during my administration. I felt that an analysis of the pros and cons of the move was necessary for two main reasons: one, the drive from Alfred residence halls to Wellsville campus was still very dangerous for our students; and two, we were facing some serious environmental conditions on the Wellsville campus that could impede development there.

Somewhat offsetting the latter concern, however, we had made some progress with an agreement between former owner ARCO and SUNY to remove asbestos in the old power plant on this land, remove the oil/water separator, and alleviate the groundwater problem. ARCO had brought action against SUNY and the Alfred Foundation, but after much negotiation and cooperation with SUNY central administration and the Attorney General's Office a settlement was reached.

The possibility of a move was still on, however, which upset the Wellsville faculty mightily. I was now a "bad guy." Well, as the old saying goes, "some things come with the territory." My view was that for the sake of our students we needed a plan to integrate the two campuses, and there was more than sufficient land available in Alfred to do so if capital development was turned that way.

The task of remembering names of the "good guys" at Alfred is daunting because of the size of our workforce. In 1993, we had approximately 650 people on board. The School of Engineering Technologies by itself had 45 faculty members. Several of our stars I have already mentioned, but I would be remiss not to cite some others who have stayed in my memory.

I worked with two presidents of the faculty union. Both were leaders at the state as well as local level. Trudy Butera was always a pleasure to consult with; together we dimmed the Alfred long shone light of warning against compatibility of union and college interests. Trudy became a lifelong friend of both Lyla Beth and me. We recently celebrated her 90th birthday.

Before Trudy was Bob Albrecht who was tougher and we didn't always get along. However, when we left Alfred, Bob gave me a present that introduced me to Flannery O'Connor. I came to appreciate Bob highly for his integrity and his solid contributions to the college. I wish now that I had taken time to know him better because we could have been much better allies.

Some other colleagues high on my list of favorites and I still see occasionally since I live near Alfred include Dick Kellogg and Mike Cobb from the Social Sciences department; Terry Morgan, Annie Constantine and Joe Flynn from the English department; Ed McCamy, philosophy; Hal Hackett, Fred Harris, Dennis Johnson from Mathematics; Phil Stohlberg, Tom Burnard, Duane Chaffee, Rich Saupe, Bob Sanders, Clint James from the Wellsville school; also on the Wellsville campus, our highly rated Food Service program led by Bob Sullivan and John Santora;

John LeGro, Bob Rees, Rick Hardman, Yogi Jonchhe, Herb Ehrig, Walt Lang, Art McLaughlin, Phil Alesso, Bill Bruce, John Joyce, Don Weimar, Rick Carlo, Rex Simpson, Herb Zuchsin, Bill Sheeahn, -- all from Engineering;

Chuck Neal, Tom Stolberg, Bob McCormick, Sandra Gerling-Yelle, Dan Platania from the Business School; Jim Copenheaver, Lyle McCaffery and Ed Burns, physics;

Counselors John Meachem, Nadine Shardlow, Carol Woughter ;

and some sharp administrative assistants whom I remember: Lois Emerson, Donna Ellis, Mary Fagan, Bev Gilbert, Deb Putnam, Alice Willsey, Betty Aftuck, Ruthie Newell, Betty Burdick, Dee Ackerman, Sue Hunt (dorm director), Dom Klenchick (print shop manager), Bill Moss (security officer), Don Palmer ( maintenance supervisor and classified staff union president), and Lyla Beth's faithful house supervisor and friend Kay Holsopple.

Many others too numerous to name kept Alfred alive and stirring.

Two close colleagues now gone whom I depended upon for their loyalty and friendship were Dr. Khalid Ashraf, Chairman of Social Sciences for several years, and Ruth Keyes, Distinguished Professor of Business Management and our neighbor. Finally, another good friend who died during my Alfred presidency was Brian Gillespie, speech, another lonely professor.

**Other Highlights:**

*Alfred State College was featured on the cover of the spring 1993 issue of *Education*. President Hunter served as special editor of this journal.

*An independent audit of college safety, policy and student rights protection was ordered and released in January.

*A total of over $1 million in grants was obtained during the year; the School of Engineering Technologies received a half million dollar grant from Computer vision Corporation for CAD software.

*Assistant Vice President Doug Barber, one of my best lieutenants, was appointed as our on-site consultant in El Salvador for the creation of ITCA. Following my resignation effective July 1, 1993, I served as our on-site consultant for the balance of the year.

*Through Vice President Rolf Zerges, the draft of a new strategic plan to replace our Alfred Foundation Plan was prepared to present to the new president upon his arrival on campus which identified key strategic issues and major committees in place for dealing with them. I was not involved in its preparation. The new president was Dr. William Rezak.

## 1999

Six years after I left Alfred, the Student Development Center was named in my honor. I was deeply touched because this Center was the symbol of development during my administration and, even more, the constancy of our concern and care for students. Initiative for the dedication had been taken by the College Council, fostered by President Bill Rezak, and ultimately approved by the SUNY Board. It was an enthralling event as colleagues and friends from NCCC and CCACC and from my life-long association with Theta Chi joined with Alfred folks in celebration—the most auspicious occasion of my career and certainly finer than any inauguration.

## Value End Notes

### Student Life

I entered with full-blown naïveté into a culture changed by the powerful force of political correctness when I went to Alfred. I didn't know about coed dorms and how contemporary college students live on campus. I was amazed to discover that a policy we had barring cohabitation was a sham.

Fostered by its institutions of higher education, America was experiencing the onset of a new morality tossing aside the old puritanical values. Alfred had bent the knee to it as had all its sister institutions, and how could it do anything else? It was like a moral earthquake had struck and left standing only those who thought it was all quite normal. After all, *in loco parentis* was tagged dead and gone: students, both male and female, were free to make their own decisions and choices, including sleeping together and using the same bathroom. The PC matrix seemed to confuse both students and parents. I heard about a situation where a girl had been mistakenly assigned a male roommate, and her parents wondered if they should protest.

I had to wonder too if my surprise made me like a man from the moon who had no clue about how to govern.

But it would all work out: SUNY would not allow me to be cast adrift. When it was discovered that I was contemplating a reactionary move regarding dorm policy, a Vice Chancellor (actually a good friend) was sent to visit me and get my mind straight. I temporized as much as I could but in the end complied because I wanted to be a successful president. How

I would love the opportunity to fight that battle again! – easy enough to say now.

The most striking part of this change was how it all happened so quietly, without contention from faculty or parents or politicians. Coed dorms and the fact of cohabitation was something we had to manage without complaint. So too with other facts of life on a residential campus. Alcohol flowed like a river. Student Life staff were appointed to control a gathering rampage, and they did the best they could, but the odds were in favor of a culture already changed and adjusting to the damages.

I also took on the Greek fraternities, a perennial problem. It looked like we could make a positive difference with some structural moves and by enlisting positive role models as advisors, such as Bob Love, a retired Dean, highly respected. But Bob was betrayed by his fraternity officers, disheartening, because he wanted to help students as he always had. And so did many others, such as Bob Granger and Jim Grillo. We all knew they were really good kids who joined fraternities and sororities to fulfill their personal and social needs.

I had done the same thing as an undergraduate at the University of Buffalo when I joined Theta Chi fraternity. So I knew what it was all about, but I had to find ways to stop the binge drinking and the marijuana addiction and the violence. I wrote about these issues in my values column, and a few students responded in agreement. But I do not give myself high marks for leadership in this area.

A sad case in point was a young man whose back was badly injured in a hazing incident that would probably cause him pain for the rest of his life. I made it a test case: we encouraged him to sue the fraternity, and we had the judge's attention. But the young man declined. He did not become a member of the fraternity that had won his loyalty, and he did not remain in the college. He simply dropped out.

There were other such heartbreaking cases involving students who had come to the college hoping something good would happen for them. This is the ground on which higher education leaders walk with their students today. There are still rules, but they are easily ignored or thwarted because our university of values does not sustain them.

I hate to appear so pessimistic, but I don't believe a real renaissance of higher education values can occur as long as political correctness and other ideologies remain endemic.

## The ITCA Project

This was a *cause celebre* for the College. It was a gift for our professional development with approximately 25 members of our faculty and staff traveling to El Salvador as consultants. It broadened our perspective. Yet I was never satisfied that we had a good handle on the contract. The difficulty in our relationships with FEPADE and ITCA was the Spanish language. It was greater than I anticipated, and while we were able to provide significant assistance, our contribution fell short of a ground for long-term relationship. I felt sorry that we did not leave with the confidence and respect we had at the beginning.

Nevertheless, on both sides, we all learned a lot from the exchanges: to see your own country better look at it through the eyes of another.

El Salvador is an extraordinarily beautiful country. Sharp definitions and vivid colors in paintings by some Salvadoran artists capture its beauty and something more of clarity and life purpose that needs to be better appreciated. Salvadorans are used to a hard life and tend to be hard on themselves, but they also have an evergreen spirit that will help to keep them focused on the challenge of peace they so much desire. We in Alfred were privileged to be involved with them. Some lasting friendships were made.

## Obiter Dictum

Long after my Alfred presidency ended, when I returned from West Virginia to Hornell, I had one last intervention with the college that I regret. The president in office at that time was facing some serious problems with the faculty and staff. I was suggested as a possible ombudsman, and I responded confidently to the idea. There was a brief representation on my part, but I saw that I did not have the president's confidence. My motives were sincere, but it was a bad idea. I formally withdrew my candidacy through e-mail to the president and the SUNY Chancellor.

That was the end of my Alfred experience, except that I am called upon, delightfully so, to participate in an annual poetry recitation sponsored by the English department. The favorite choice for my recitation appears to be Tennyson's *Ulysses.*

# Cross Section of Letters and Memos

### From: Admiral Roger D. Aydt, U.S. Navy, Tongue Point, Astoria, Oregon, February 20, 1987

I was sorry to learn that you had departed from CLC and returned to New York State. Lake County, I am sure, misses you. I am pleased, however that you are again in New York where you want to be. I have now completed my PhD program and wanted to take this opportunity to thank you for your help and assistance in overseeing my internship. You were always very considerate in everything I did. Associating and working with you, both professionally and socially was always a pleasant relationship. My only regret is that it may be some time before we will meet again.

### From: Edward G. Coll, Jr. President, Alfred University, October 23, 1987

I appreciate very much your providing me with your thoughtful review of Allan Bloom's *The Closing Of the American Mind.* I complement you on the precision of your writing and your provocative interpretation of Prof. Bloom's book. I intend to share your piece with several of my colleagues.

### From: W. Gary McGuire, Vice President of Community Education, Niagara County Community College, October 14, 1987

I want to tell you how impressed I am with Alfred state. As you know my son Christopher is enrolled in the air-conditioning engineering technology program. He continues to be impressed by the program, instructors and the environment of the college itself. He said he is having a great time both in his studies and on the cross country team. He also has become involved in the student government and as a curriculum committee member. He tells me that he stops in to see you every now and then. He is a very sincere young man, and I know he would not be singing praises of Alfred unless he truly believed it. I know that some of what he is experiencing is due to your leadership, and I would like to personally thank you for that.

**To: Winifred Whalen, OSF, Graduate School of Theology, St. Bonaventure University, March 30, 1989**

Dear Sister Whalen: I am very sorry to have missed the discussion on "All My Sons."

For possible class use, I am enclosing copies of an excerpt from Arthur Miller's **Time Bends**, giving an author's viewpoint on his creation. He makes an interesting comment on the mother/wife. In toto, Miller's commentary reminds me of a Thomas Merton comment: "we who are poets know that the reason for a poem is not discovered until the poem itself exists." Also I am enclosing some material which outlines a systems framework for looking at developmental theory. It includes reference to some developmental theorists not covered by Moran, such as A. Maslow.

Dr. John Hunter

**To: Angelo F. Orazio, Chairman, NYS Low-Level Radioactive Waste Siting Commission, Albany, NY October 24, 1989**

If the commission insists on going ahead with a public forum at this time despite this counsel, I invite you to seek Alfred State College as a facility for it through State channels to SUNY. I shall cooperate with any request approved in this fashion. But I would like to offer an alternative which I hope you shall give serious consideration.

The most troubling aspect of this problem to me as an educator is that there has been little genuine education of the public on the issues involved. This is not meant as a criticism of the Commission; I also share the responsibility along with others.

In my view, the NIMBY syndrome does not fully explain the depth of real and legitimate opposition---exploited but not invented by the fringe. There are two fundamental questions that should be answered before, not after, the site is selected. The first and most important is: How will this site be resourced and managed? (Given the record of waste site management, how can people be expected to respect a process which does not address this critical factor?) The second is: What benefits and long term guarantees of state support shall be given to the community which is selected? (There is a widely held perception that selection brings with it economic disaster.)

I urge you to delay the forum until these aspects can be addressed by appropriate officials. In so urging, I realize that the structure and mission may require change which is beyond immediate authority of the Commission to make. The constraints on the Siting Commission and the public perception of it are too damaging for an effective implementation of decisions without re-structuring. Indeed, the whole concept of shared responsibility by several State agencies is too much akin to the traditional bureaucratic response which has so undermined public confidence in the handling of environmental matters. Surely, New York can do better in structuring the management and control of such a high visibility project if we put our minds to it.

There is a reservoir of good will always waiting to be tapped in any community, and this is true now of Allegany County. The current climate is causing an unhealthy tendency which many astute citizens can sense. Other public officials and business leaders have expressed to me their concern about coercion and intimidation and potential violence growing in our midst. The people here shall remain opposed to the Site, but I believe they would respond to efforts to broaden the approach and reassure fair treatment with less hostility. The alternative is a rather hopeless condition of constant fear and loathing, and no-one wants that.

Please do not regard this appeal as an affront to the Commission's dignity or integrity. Please consider if a public forum at this time would serve any purpose other than mechanical fulfillment of the statute. (It cannot be successful.) Then consider the effects of a pause in the action and a fresh start.

John O. Hunter, President

**From: Christine Z. Shoub, Graduate of CLC, April 11, 1988**

When I learned last year that you had left CLC, I felt sorry that they had lost someone who had accomplished so much. I was glad to learn that you would be closer to family there.

Time has passed so quickly. I am now about to receive the Doctor of Pharmacy degree. I will start the final clerkship on the 19th of April, and I will take the pharmacy boards at the end of June. I have decided to continue my education, and I have been accepted at the University of Illinois College of Medicine starting in the fall. That means that I will graduate Medical School and start internship when I am 40. I've definitely "come a long way" since I was a truck mechanic and welder!

Sometimes, though, I miss the simpler life.

### From: D. Bruce Johnstone, Chancellor, State University of New York, February 13, 1990

Thank you for sending me a copy of your remarks to faculty entitled *Our Mission and Future as a College of Technology* and for sending a copy of the final Alfred Foundation Plan. I admired the speech and the Foundation Plan for both their style and substance. They supply the vision and direction required to make your institution a distinctive college of technology that aspires to be the best in its field. Both your speech and the Foundation Plan demonstrate that you are obtaining the greatest possible benefit from the recommendations in the NCHEMS report on the role and mission of the Colleges of Technology. In many ways, Alfred is the archetype of a college of technology and, clearly, the most favorable comments in the NCHEMS report indicate that your campus was the model that they consistently most admired. Most of all, John, thank you for providing clear and creative leadership for the College of Technology at Alfred.

### From: SUNY Provost Joseph Burke, September 17, 1990

I read your remarks at the faculty convocation with admiration as well as interest. It was sincere and eloquent, as well as candid and courageous. You have shown a willingness to confront difficult problems and to admit short comings.

I am certain that you will solve the issue regarding clarification of policy and consensual decision making. I know that you were right to emphasize the importance of the Middle States accreditation---as a means that does not only win the endorsement of Middle States, but also enables the college as a whole to work as an integrated institution. I am proud to be the Provost of the University system which has a president with the focus and fortitude that you have displayed. If I can be of any assistance, please feel free to call on me. Joseph C. Burke, Provost, State University of New York

### From: Choichiro Yatani, Ph.D., Assistant Professor, September 30,1991

Thank you very much for your cordial letter of September 23, 1991 concerning my case---a five-year struggle with U.S. government which has been internationally notorious for one of the relics of the McCarthy era and the Cold War at home. I am very proud of my ultimate victory because, as you state, my case has contributed to the defense of the very American principles of freedom and justice. But, actually it is American people who brought about this victory: witness their support and help, family and I could not have got over that ordeal. We were very lucky and honored to meet those people who deeply value and fight for the principles.

I also thank you for your mentioning my wife, Nanako, in your letter. She was most subjected to the suffering and disgrace in that unjustified persecution. During my 44-day detention in a Federal jail Nanakoi was at a total loss with our two children who were too little to understand what was going on to their father. Even after I was released from the detention, she had been worried about my future status and career. When I showed your letter to her this evening, she was relieved and overcome with emotions and almost stopped breathing. She says she has no words to express her thanks for your thoughtfulness. Choichiro Yatani

### From Prof. David Law, Accounting/CIS Department, April 19, 1992

Dear President Hunter: Thank you for taking me to lunch on March 23, 1992( and last year and the year before that). I appreciate your concern for my situation and school related problems/opportunities. I know you are very busy and have many forces pulling at you. It is nice you always take time to listen to what my concerns are.

I have enjoyed working at Alfred from day one and have enjoyed knowing that a caring and concerned person is at the helm. I cannot tell you how nice it is to work in a department that has the best computer facilities of any college in NYS.

### From: Congressman John Edward Porter, 10th District of Illinois, May 19, 1993

Dear John: I received your letter and information about your great work promoting development in El Salvador in conjunction with FEPADE.

Clearly, after years of civil war El Salvador must focus on rebuilding its domestic capabilities, particularly its devastated human resources. The program you have fostered with FEPADE seems to have hit the nail on the head by matching the appropriate approach with a country most in need. It is innovative, timely programs like this that will help ensure the peace in El Salvador and improve the lives of the nearly 5.5 million Salvadoran people.

It is good to hear that you have continued with your work at Alfred State, John, and continue to look for innovative ways to promote higher education in the US and elsewhere. Please keep in touch.

### From: Congressman Amo Houghton, November 29, 1993

Dear John: What a nice guy you are to write, and a great letter at that! WOW! It's fascinating to find out what's happening in El Salvador. I hope you are getting some personal satisfaction. They are so lucky to have you! The sad thing, of course, as you say, "the unfolding chaos and tragedy in Nicaragua." What's going on there? I don't understand it, John. If you have any ideas, let me know because you know how devoted I am to Violetta Chamorro. Amo

### From: Prof. Ed McCamy, January 12, 1993

This is an example of what situation ethics is all about. The original letter indicated that a young man who was his grandparents' favorite, dying of aids, asked his brother to tell his grandparents, after he was dead, that he was gay.

The brother asked Abbey about it. He pointed out that the grandparents were old, would not understand, and would probably be terribly hurt by the revelation. Her advice was that it was a promise and the truth never hurt anyone. If you accept "truth" as a "absolute," she may have been right, although anyone who thinks the truth never hurt anyone shouldn't be an advice columnist, in my opinion. She's too stupid.

I thought you might be interested is seeing that the idea of situation ethics is at the heart of resolution of the moral dilemma here. Thus, this is not some off-beat idea; it is, mainstream.

However, whatever we say, I think we are all situation ethicists in a way. When we tell someone a hurtful and unnecessary truth, I'm not sure we are doing this from honorable or religious motives. You know as well as I know much malice lurks in protestations of absolute honesty and truthfulness.

### To: Prof. Ed McCamy, January 18, 1993

What a delight to hear from you again! Forgive this handwritten response (and my errors herewith).

Somewhat paradoxically, I think what blocks your belief in any "absolute beneath the relative" is the cornerstone of mine, but in this Abbey case, we do not disagree. My mother would have subjected it to this rule---"is it kind, is it true, is it necessary?" A more interesting dilemma would have been posed if the grandparents had specifically asked, "did your brother ask you to give us any dying message?" This would have moved it closer to the "categorical imperative". As it is, somehow the dispute reminds me of the difference between the social worker and the protagonist in Malamud's "The Pawnbroker"---Abbey, the social worker. But I don't think she's stupid---she just made an error. John Hunter

### From: Delores S. Cross, Chairman, Allegany County Board of Legislators, March 25, 1993

Dear John: Just a brief word to thank you for the pleasant lunch and outstanding program. The life experiences shared with us were moving and pointed out clearly what education, encouragement and determination can do. Each individual that addressed the gathering had been dramatically changed by the Alfred experience. How very proud you must be of all of them, John.

Interest in developing a working relationship between academia and local government is not common. Yet, you initiated a partnership between Allegany County and Alfred State urging us to work together to promote economic development and growth in the County. The Agreement signed on May 6, 1991 put in place the framework for future activities that will benefit both County and college.

Delores S. Cross, Chairman

### From: Bob Albrecht of Alfred State (no date)

John, thanks for your note. This must be a frustrating busy time, so it is all the more appreciated.

I'm encouraged and relieved that you are fully aware of the anomie persisting in pockets on campus. Might I suggest that your strategy of "ignoring it, going around it" is difficult, taking on qualities of an archetypal struggle. I'm not certain that enthusiasm, commitment, even professionalism can maintained by an individual who works within the pocket on a daily basis. The strength of vision falters—for me at least---in the face of daily challenges. I'm working to shore up that vision, at some loss of energy and vitality perhaps.

I'm glad that you will reassure the younger faculty I wrote of. They are not fragile, you're right. But the encouragement will help.

**From: Russell N. Cassel, Publisher, Education Journal, May 5,1993**

First, if you were here in San Diego today, you could come down town and dance with me in the streets. It is 5 May the day of independence for Mexico, and there is fiesta everywhere. Remember that 1 out of 4 persons in San Diego County are Hispanics.

Second, the issue of EDUCATION you have guest edited should be in your hands very soon. I am sending you 162 copies. I would appreciate receiving a critique of our project if you are so disposed.

Third, I am enclosing a merit award plaque, given by our merit award board. Typically this is presented by one's superior, but in the case of a college president, only God reigns, I am told.

Thanks for sharing your world with me for this project. Russell

**To: Kevin Doran, Radio Station WLEA, Hornell, NY, August 28,1992**

In our last radio conversation, you asked, "What are the major changes you see ahead for education?" It's an important question to discuss because schools and colleges are facing great challenges, some old and some unprecedented.

The problems fall into these categories:

1. Deteriorating health (wellness) of students
2. Loss of oral/spiritual values and clear ethical framework, (corresponding increase of violence)
3. Declining sapiential authority of the professoriate
4. Outmoded (failed) structures
5. Cultural decline/upheaval
6. Management uncertainty in face of financial crisis and increasing demands

From my perspective, these are the strategic changes coming at all levels of education which offer hope but need critical appraisal:

1. Increased reliance on information technology
2. Instructional re-design to capitalize on the marvels of multi-media and computer retrieval
3. Schools re-structuring combined with stronger policy for accountability
4. Emerging dominance of holistic environmental concerns
5. Stronger partnership between education and industry

Now this is where it gets really difficult. Which is more important---vision or perspective? Values aren't worth talking about if we can't communicate about a whole new way of thinking---a paradigm shift away from the modern world view. In both broadest and deepest terms, this is about the crisis of modernity. Best regards, John Hunter

# CHAPTER V

## *Pennsylvania: Founding CCACC*

" There is a tide in the affairs of men,

Which, taken at the flood, leads on to fortune;

On such a full sea are we now afloat,

And we must take the current when it serves,

Or lose our ventures." (Shakespeare)

My strong desire was to follow in the footsteps of my mentor, Dr. Ernest Notar, founding president of Niagara Community College,NY. By God's grace I was given this opportunity in the spring of 1994 as I was leaving El Salvador.

One month after a strange interview process in which I met individually with some Board members who had been delegated as the Search committee, I was offered the position of founding president of Cambria County Area Community College (CCACC) ,PA. They liked me, and I immediately liked them (or at least most of them.) A contract was presented to me, meant as "an offer I could not refuse."

But I hesitated. The problem: it was also an offer the fledgling college could not afford. I felt like a jerk, perversely negotiating the contract down by approximately 30%. Why? *noblesse oblige?* No, I wanted to succeed and I could tell immediately that we were going to have serious money problems; indeed, that was a mild forecast of the most difficult, stress-ridden days I've faced in my entire career. I worked harder in Pennsylvania, with Lyla Beth right alongside, than anywhere else I have been.

From the writing of start-up plans, policies, and staff procedures, to plagiarizing curriculum descriptions, to coaxing partnerships, to scrambling for facilities, to painting walls and floors, to writing grant proposals and pleading for county and state dollars, to constantly striving for better understanding and support of the community college mission, to dealing with treachery and theft—all these and some of the more mundane yet necessary activities since forgotten are indelible marks on my helter-skelter existence as a founding president.

Few have any idea of what it means to begin a college. In Cambria County's case the challenge was made even more demanding by unreasonable expectations and an unreasonable start-up budget. But I knew all this going in. I had a dream of building a college from ground up, not in my image but according to ideals and principles ensconced in the traditions of American higher education that I had learned from study and experience and that I was confident I could impart to a team of founders and hopeful associates.

## A College to Grow or Die

Cambria County, PA did not go the community college route when it should have , essentially because there was no need. High school graduates found high paying jobs in the steel mills and coal mines that had been anchor industries in the area for more than a century. For those who wanted to go to college there was the University of Pittsburgh at Johnstown. Then, of a sudden, the bottom dropped out of the material " good life" with the decline of these industries. A socio-economic depression with its breeding miasma became an awful challenge that finally was picked up by people who were not used to failure. Their economic development strategies included the startup, better late than never, of a community college—but not exactly, not predictedly.

In this chapter I will be earnestly faithful to my pledge not to raise a negative text of individuals by name. However, the true story cannot be told without reference to the actions of some people who were a negative influence (putting it mildly.) Those references will come up in the context of the struggle of CCACC to grow or die. I want to highlight the magnificent opposite: those folks whose steadfast commitment and personal kindness made the struggle possible and ultimately led to a successful end, even though we did not go the way they had been advised to go by others.

> "Two roads diverged in a yellow wood, And I—
>
> I took the one less traveled by—
>
> And that has made all the difference." (Robert Frost)

Actually, this poetic conceit is a slight misnomer. There were compelling reasons to follow an innovative path -- for example, I introduced "flexible learning methodology" as the cornerstone of our curriculum—but although our situation sometimes required a temporary departure from higher education norms, it was my intention from the beginning to meet all the standards for accreditation -- along with the important certification for student financial aid-- of this new institution. This was the crucial balancing act for which I needed Board support as I was also weaning them away from their original, even more radical vision that had no chance of gaining accreditation. ("College Without Walls"-- no faculty--brokerage of training courses without complete control.) I faced recalcitrance by a few, who soon left the Board, and by their Delta Dynamic consultant who attempted a sabotage that was casual, weak and easy to refute. My strength was that I knew what had to be done to raise the foundation for an approved, autonomous community college; their weakness, despite bluster of imagined power, was that they did not.

None of the issues of governance brought us to a point of crisis, save one which is detailed in a later section. We succeeded because of a board that measured up to the creation challenge and because of some wonderful partnerships and friendships that steadily grew and became a sustaining force for the new experimental college.

Foremost among this vitalizing company was the Hiram G. Andrews Rehabilitation Center (HGAC) in Johnstown and its Executive Director, Dr. Al Reynolds, who gave me valiant support without which we could not have started. I continue to count Dr. Reynolds (we called him "Prince Al") as one of the best friends I have known in my career. We tried hard to integrate the college curriculum with the rehabilitation program, with limited success. We did manage to merge our libraries for which the college assumed supervisory responsibility and invested $149,000 in capital improvement (almost all of the capital monies I had available.) The Center and the college cooperated in grants development as well as "one plus one" programs, student activities and staff development. Nevertheless, I regret that we did not find a way to credential the HGA courses because the Center gave us so much material and moral support. Before joining with HGAC I knew nothing about people with disabilities. Working with the HGAC was another of those blessed experiences I have had (similar to El Salvador) where I learned more from the people I was meant to serve than the service I gave.

Dr. Reynolds was more than our enabler: he was the principal architect of bringing a community college to Cambria County. To be sure, it could not have been done without major political support, but Dr. Reynolds, HGAC, and the State Department of Labor and Industry—which committed funds for renovating a wing of the HGAC to house college classrooms—had the substance of the first foundation. Though not alone, Reynolds was first in the initiative . As we progressed, I saw the cost in political shenanigans he endured.

Although there had been speculation for several years about a community college for Cambria county, it was not until this initiative, endorsed by the County Commissioners (Ted Baranik, Kathy Holtzman and Mark Wissinger, replaced by Dr. Fred Soisson) that it became a real adventure, and then things moved at lightning speed. On June 4, 1993, the commissioners voted to become the local sponsor for Cambria County Area Community College. On September 7, 1993, the State Board of Education approved of the establishment of a community college in Cambria county. On October 14, 1993, the commissioners approved the appointment of a 15 member board of trustees (Larry Caprous was elected the first chairman). On June 1, 1994, I took office as founding president, with a mandate starting from ground zero to begin classes in September.

There was a large room with glass exterior assigned to the college at the HGAC. This room, with temperatures reaching 90° that summer of 1994 became a buzzing, blooming scene of activity. There was a staggering amount of foundational work accomplished: office staff hired and oriented, location of facilities and lease arrangements made, class schedule developed, marketing and advertising work, student recruitment and registration, adopting provider agreements for hands-on- technology instruction, ordering of textbooks and setting up the bookstore, syllabus development for course offerings , business office setup, development of accounts/ payroll, hiring of adjunct faculty and orientation. In the first year we had no fulltime faculty, but I began laying plans for an academic organization to take effect in the second year.

On September 5, 1994, we began classes with 436 students in three "stipended" programs at 13 different locations, seven professional staff members, and 35 adjunct faculty. It was a miracle!

Ten years later I visited these environs where the initial burst of energy had occurred. The college had left and the room taken back by HGAC to serve as a computer resource center. I heard no echoes of Mary Fisher, Theresa Pelow, Carole Kraft, Patty Drugo, Linda Choby, Nick Bocher or others of that early time; none of the college ambience remained – except that when I left I saw one remaining symbol--the sign carved by my son, John, above the internal portal proclaiming the "CCACC—HGA Center Library."

> " This, this remains, but I record what's gone. A crowd
>
> Will gather, and not know it walks the very street
>
> Whereon a thing once walked that seemed a burning cloud."
>
> (W.B. Yeats)

The essentiality of beginning classes so quickly in 1994 was only partly because of my " mandate". The main reason was that we had to have state approved ("stipended") courses and student enrollments in order to qualify for the next fiscal year funding. The first evaluation of courses at semester end showed good results, and the college entered the spring semester 1995 with strong momentum. Staff and student morale was high: they were proud to be "present at the creation".

In late fall, 1994, another "minor miracle" was an agreement with Link Computers to acquire the college's first computers and lab installation in time for the spring semester. One of my biggest early worries was that we would not be able to obtain our own computers which meant that our wheels would fall off before we even got rolling. A lot of our results were "en passant" and I knew that our theme of "commitment" was paying off.

This was the anthem of the creation of CCACC:

" Concerning all acts of initiative and creation, there is one elementary truth,

the ignorance of which kills countless ideas and splendid plans:

That the moment one definitely commits oneself, then Providence moves too.

All sorts of things occur to help one that never otherwise would have occurred.

A whole stream of events issues from the decision, raising in one's favor all manner

of unforeseen incidents and meetings and material assistance which no one could have dreamt

would come their way." (Johanne Wolfgang von Goethe)

Other anchor industry partners included Concurrent Technologies Corporation(CTC), Kimball &Associates, HF Lenz, Inc, Laurel Highlands Chapter of American Banking Institute (AIB), Admiral Peary Area Vocational Center, Bishop Carroll High School, and virtually all of the area high schools. In respect to their importance to the founding of the college, I must describe briefly their contributions.

Second only to HGA Center was CTC. I relied heavily on their staff as consultants and faculty members for three of our main programs --Environmental Technology, Manufacturing Technology and Computer Information Technology -- and we used their classrooms. Daniel DeVos, CEO of CTC, was an original board member for the college. The vice president, Dr. Howard Kuhn, was instrumental in our programs development, as was Jack Cavanagh who was one of our first faculty members. Ultimately, both of these gentlemen and friends became Board members. Dr.Kuhn, who was also my hockey buddy, agreed to serve as Academic Director of Advanced Technology; he and Hugh Callihan from CTC were very helpful to me in crafting a grant proposal ,CAT/Excell, which did not succeed but the research taught me a lot.

Kimball &Associates was one of our advanced technology providers in Geographic Information Systems—sophisticated support and instruction unusual for a first level community college. The AIB partnership gave us readymade bank management courses. The Admiral Peary AVC , led by Superintendent Joe Berdomas, gave us much needed space in the north and strong support with the high schools. Bishop Carrol High School, principal Charles Koren (who later joined our Board),became a major site partner when we leased from the Diocese a large, unused building on their campus. HF Lenz was a partner in our Building Systems Technology program. All of these partnerships I negotiated in the first year.

Unfortunately, there were also some partnerships that failed. The court reporting program had begun with the support of Sargent Court Reporting as the main provider, but that arrangement became too costly and we separated although Sargent continued to employ our graduates. We also had an agreement with the Johnstown Area Vocational Center, which I first thought would be a principal partner, like HGAC and CTC, but it did not work out. Although we had great cooperation, especially from Board member Ben Root, a partnership with NORCAM to establish an instructional site in Barnesboro, northern tip of the county, foundered because we could not attract enough students.

Throughout my five years as founding president, college relations with the media, especially Johnstown Tribune Democrat, were excellent. We were also frequently on local television, primarily because of a relationship with the station by my staff assistant for public relations, Susan Clifton. In our first year Susan was very productive, and I am sorry now that I let her go when she failed to meet later expectations. Perhaps I was too hard on her. At the end of the year she designed and produced a very attractive catalog (I wrote the contents) that stunned everyone as we went into our second year. Board chair Caprous said to me," wow! this is just like a regular college."

## Faculty and Staff

In the hiring of my original staff, I made an error of judgment assuming that I could make up for lack of experience in young people through my training and example. Two of them were let go within a month, and another caused me chagrin when she went to one of the commissioners to report on my "tyrannical methods." Really, on their behalf, I just did not inspire them with the immediate task before us and the glory ahead of us.

113

My orientation sessions were long and tedious, and it was foolish to assume they could match my passion and intensity in their young blood.

All of my personnel mistakes were made with hiring young people, which seems beyond borders of irony to me now when I reflect that some of my best educational work has been done with young people. As we began to build I was able to recruit some older colleagues to whom I owe gratitude not only for their competency but their understanding of and dedication to the college mission and goals. Yes, experience does count.

At the top of this list is my second business manager, Jim Wagner, a longtime financial vice president for Sani-Dairy Corporation, a major milk distributor in Pennsylvania. I was very lucky to get him: he had decided to remain in Johnstown when the corporation left and I immediately recruited him. We remain friends to this day. What a relief it was to have him in charge, especially after a theft debacle involving the first business manager which became an embarrassing moment for me with the board -- an interesting cock-up but I knew we would survive it.

The main obstacle in recruiting qualified faculty and staff was that I could not offer them a competitive salary or benefits. So I appealed to their growth nature, assuring them that if we could bind together and do the job of building this college, the rewards would grow as the college grew. My statement to each was, " this is a lifetime opportunity," and I sincerely thought it to be true.

The birthing of a college is a rare experience—and a risky venture. The folks who joined me did not fully understand the challenge we were facing but joined freely and confidently. I knew that we had to move aggressively on several fronts at the same time, and with a few exceptions, unnamed, they responded beautifully. My pride in them grew as we progressed. They learned how a common purpose pursued with mutual respect and commitment can morph into colleagueship that may last a lifetime.

My second error of judgment was failure to see how someone to follow me could risk everything desirous and positive about the college and its people priority by trying to erase the mark of the founders and remake the institution in his/her own image. But that is what happened. The crisis of the college was down the line.

Here is the honor roll of original staff and faculty:

Administrative and Technical:

> Jim Wagner, Chief Financial Officer (my second CFO appointment)
>
> Mary Fisher, President's Secretary
>
> Chris Mahla, Director, Economic/Workforce Development
>
> Theresa Pelow, Office Manager
>
> Sharon Barto, Director of Public Relations (replacing Susan Kalcik)
>
> Don Shaver, Dean of Academic Affairs
>
> Jeff Maul, Director of Admissions
>
> Nick Bocher, Director of Computer Technology
>
> Brenda Coughenour, Director of Financial Aid
>
> Robin Humphrey, Assistant for Academic Affairs
>
> Patty Drugo, Admissions Counselor
>
> Mary Hattaway, Financial Aid Assistant
>
> Linda Choby, Registration and Matriculation
>
> Scott Beamer, Information Desk
>
> Julie Davis, Workforce Development Assistant
>
> Tim Berkebile, Maintenance Worker (Board Innovation Award)
>
> Stephanie Burgess, Bookstore Manager

Original Fulltime Faculty:

(All fulltime faculty were given 12months appointments and expected to work a 40 hour week)

> Susan Kalcik (appointed Coordinator of Liberal Arts)
>
> Sherry Shurin (first hired as admissions assistant, showed her maturity immediately)

Dave Dillman (volunteered to help first day, became cornerstone of our computer instruction)

Marilyn Danchanko (excellent lead math instructor; exemplary in her analytic reporting)

Barb Mitchell (Board "Creative Use of Technology" Award)

Bonnie Bakos ( solid)

Sandy Schrum ( solid)

Michelle Bills (solid)

Vickie Cope (solid)

Glen Elliott (how proud I was to hire him away from Johnstown Vo-Tech)

Jan Garrett (saved the court reporting program)

Stephanie Chapple (taught for long hours in our Computer HOT Center w/o complaint)

Joe Slifko and Chris Lint (I saw immediate signs of future leadership in these young guys)

How blessed the new found college was to have such faculty, among the best I have known. They renewed my confidence in the traditional values of the collegium.

Provided that a faculty member is competent in his subject area and loves teaching, the best that can be done is to give him/her freedom in the classroom and opportunity to express ideas in governance of the institution. Faculty cooperation in accountability measures should be a given expectation, but bureaucracy and laws heavily laden prove counter-intuitive and ineffective. If the institution truly values excellence, so routinely proclaimed in all catalogs, the faculty must have freedom for its creative pursuit in accord with their individual personalities and desires to serve students.

If the faculty member is not competent or becomes jaded along the way , disaster will ensue; that is what is happening in too many schools and colleges in our country today. But at CCACC we were in virgin territory, and it was marvelous to imagine the future possibilities. And so within our limited resources, I tried to give the faculty not only academic control but real involvement in policy development. At my behest, we formed a faculty senate, they elected officers, we adopted a professional rank system, appointment and evaluation procedures, an academic freedom and five-year tenure track policy. It was not a misplaced trust.

I also required from each member, both administrative and faculty, a confidential monthly status report to include comments on problems and needs. These were intended to allow the person to introspect as well as to give me information and perspective. It was time-consuming but I always read these reports (sometimes amused by the writing style differences.)

All of those folks listed above showed their professional integrity and leadership in various ways. Their collected reports could have been excellent documentation for historical observation; all were compiled and saved in a large notebook, but unfortunately it was destroyed. (Marilyn Danchanko's reports were exemplary; when I needed one to exemplify the system to another institution, she sent me a copy from her files and I was pleased to see again the excellence of this communication vehicle, faculty member to president.)

It took a while, but short, before the college took on a glow of certainty as a formidable new force in Cambria county. In early days I was almost humiliated by a few businessmen in Johnstown who doubted our success and shunned my enquiries. I remember also a young woman I tried to recruit as my secretary who said, "A lot of people don't think you can make it." Yet, I was always encouraged by others whose warmth and good will on many occasions was palpable—wonderful folks Lyla Beth and I shall always remember. In addition to those mentioned above, here is a partial list:

Ben Root, the wise and generous trustee from Barnesboro and his wife, Cheryl; my dentist, Dr. Jim and Julie Ference (great dinners conversing on poetry); Rev. and Mrs. Ray Streets of Emanuel Baptist Church (what an enthusiastic spokesman he was!); Pamela Mayer, publisher of Tribune Democrat and David Levine, Editor; Bill and Pam Lonsinger and Johnstown Area Life Underwriters (JALU), sponsored annual golf tournaments for us; Charles and Carol Neuhoff of HF Lenz; Sister Mary Ann Dillon, President, Mount Aloysuis College: Father Christian Oravec, President, St. Francis College; Bobbi Ream; Gail Landis; Donna Gambol; Ron Budash;

Bob MacIver; Joe Rizzo, HGAC; Superintendent Russ Strange, Penn Cambria School System; Sam Valenty; Jack Chricton; Dave Davis, Lee Hospital; Bob Eyer, Wessel Auditing Co.; Lou Guzzi, Dynamic Design; Ed and Rosemary Pawlowski; Skip and Adele Picking; Dr. Frank Carney; Pat Kiniry, College Attorney; Judge Tim Creany; Rev. Julius and Dee Porcher; Monsignor Gaus, Dorothy Polke, Ron Rufrano, Terry Havener, Paulette Vandzura, Joel Bowser, Eric Rummel, Barb Lehmeir, Dick Luprick –all trustees; Joe Mangarella, Board Chair, and Don Zucco, Board Chair/ Johnstown Mayor.

Our Board knew early on that the college would need a fund-raising organization and had already taken steps to establish a Foundation even before I arrived. The first chair was Sam Valenty, succeeded by Larry Caprous. The Foundation sponsored the annual Founders Day Celebration at which the college honored a principal partner or outstanding citizen. Those honored during my tenure included Concurrent Technologies Corp. (Dan DeVos), HGA Center (Dr. Al Reynolds),Area Banking Industry, Crown American Corp., and Johnny Butler of State Department of Labor and Industry.

In 1998, the Foundation held a "5 Years Strong" celebration honoring faculty and staff: Mary Fisher, Sherry Shurin and President Hunter, for full-time service; and adjunct faculty Dave Angeletti, Jack Cavanaugh, Dennis Grenell, Ron Kirshner, Mary Kline, Marjorie Mattis and Steve Pipan.

**Curriculum Innovation**

There is an old saying that "necessity is the mother of invention." This was certainly the case in trying to fashion, with scarce resources, a curriculum appropriate to the CCACC mission and goals.

The Latin root of curriculum is <u>currere</u>, " to run"_–the same root that underlies the idea of a process. We called the CCACC curriculum process, Flexible Learning Methodology(FLM). FLM is a continuous " running" process. Who does the running? Well, the faculty and administration, of course, but mainly, it's the student. He does not come empty to the college, to be filled up like a milk bottle on the assembly line. No, she is always engaged in learning experiences—on the job, through personal relationships, travel, entertainment, etc. The curriculum is another experience for him/ her and the challenge is to ensure that it is a solid and significant one. There should be agreed upon assumptions when entering into the process , for example, jobs. Students want to graduate into jobs—or get a better job—or upgrade skills for a current job. Some students may enroll in a course simply for personal satisfaction, which should be encouraged, but the reality facing schools and colleges is that students who are seeking a degree (or other credential) are interested in job opportunities. It is simply dishonest to recruit students for a program in which the job prospects are dim or nil. This philosophy was one of our foundations of learning.

But we had to be cognizant of another reality as well. All students face this fact: it is very likely that they may eventually become employed in jobs that do not exist today . Jobs are increasingly obsolescent. Therefore a combination of general and technical skills is important. For the college, it meant that the curriculum review and revision should be conducted in partnership with employers and other educational partners. Internships and job opportunities and transfer possibilities come from the partners, which means that the partnership agenda must be constantly addressed. Partnership in all of our programs was another foundation.

Through partnerships, the college strove to be competency- based. We pledged to stand behind the competency of our graduates if they were employed by the business/ industry partners involved in FLM . If they employed a graduate who did not demonstrate competency as defined by the student's program, the college was bound to retrain the student at no additional cost. It was another risk—one that I worried about –but we made Guaranteed Competencies our third foundation of learning.

I don't know why for sure, but we never had a claim for retraining from any of our partners during my presidency. Perhaps it was because of their "ownership"—after all, we drew heavily upon them for our faculty and sometimes their facilities--this was the only part of "college without walls" that made sense.

FLM was not full blown operationally until my final year. The principles and concepts of flexibility were outlined in our first catalog, 1995- 96, and it took effect in stages, program by program. Flexibility meant many things for both faculty and administration. Mrs. Danchanko provided this classroom example:

*"We tried several problems with and without the algebraic concepts. It was intriguing to the students that if I let them work on an everyday problem, they would eventually get an answer several hours later through trial and error . I could take that same problem and solve it in two or three minutes by using problem solving, logic and algebra."*

This is what a master teacher does. There were many favorable comments from students who began to see where the skills taught in our courses would help them at home and at work.

The last strand of FLM, Guaranteed Competencies, was made official board policy in 1998, when we also announced with CTC and HGAC creation of the Partnership Center for Excellence in Workforce Development (CEWD), coordinated by Chris Mahla, and which included training affiliations with Microsoft, CISCO, and Environmental Systems Research Institute (ESRI). The CEWD was also recognized as REAL Entrepreneurial Skills Training Center, the first in Pennsylvania. These were all important seeds for growth of the college's leadership position in workforce development. The Partnership --HGAC, CTC and the College-- received a half million dollars to strengthen its workforce development platform in 1999.

**Students and Facilities**

In its fifth year of operation, CCACC was serving approximately 2400 students (headcount), credit and noncredit. The annualized fulltime equivalent enrollment had grown exponentially from 205 in FY 95 to 1,010 in FY 99. We also had approximately 100 students in Indiana County through a partnership with Indiana Vo-Tech. The original expectation, as contained in the 120 Day Plan approved by the State Education Department, was that the new community college would serve approximately 400 students . We passed that mark in our second year, and why not?—the need was much greater. The faculty and staff adapted quickly to an enrollments management strategy – marketing and admissions as well student service – that imposed extra duty on everyone. *"A student is never an interruption of our work; he/she is the purpose of it."*

CCACC blitzed the entire region – Somerset, Indiana as well as Cambria – with its advertising and outreach efforts throughout the five years of its founding. Led by our PR Director, Sharon Barto, everyone participated, including "the college lady" who traveled up and down the county without any automobile expense reimbursement. We presented her the "37th College Employee Award." Her name was Mrs. Lyla Beth Hunter.

CCACC was approved for State and Federal financial aid in 1996. This was, of course, one of our defining moments: without this approval enrollments would not have taken off as they did. This is where Dr. Stuart Steiner and Robin Dasher- Alston of the Middle States Association(MSA) come into the story. Approval was granted because the college became a Candidate for Middle States Accreditation. MSA appointed Dr. Steiner, at my request, as our official consultant in the accreditation process. I knew Dr. Steiner as a colleague in the State University of New York system. He was/ still is highly respected by MSA as a long time, experienced consultant. I anticipated his frank professional assessments in a constructive context, and it was so.

I may be wrong because I have not much solid information about CCACC since I left in July 1999, but it is my impression that Dr. Steiner and Dr. John " Mac" Kingsmore, also well respected by MSA, who became CCACC acting president in 2001 -- after resignation at Board request of the second president, my successor—were vitally influential in the college's finally gaining accreditation.

Dr. Steiner was concerned about the connectivity problem in our far-flung enterprise using so many different instructional sites. I shared his concern that we faced desiccation if we did not solve the problem, but as the cliché goes, easier said than done: we had no unencumbered capital and no prospect of convincing our governing authorities to build a central campus. So in 1998 we settled on a strategy of finding permanent principal sites and relying on a VTEL video conferencing system, for which we had successfully pursued grants totaling $300,000 so far.

We called it the "four site configuration" identifying two sites in the Johnstown area -- HGAC and downtown in the old Glosser building-- one in Richland Township—the Rachel Hill school to be acquired from the Richland school district ,or CTC facility (uncertain which)--and one in

Ebensburgh covering the north/ central part of the county. These plans were not completely finalized when I left office but options were clearly laid out. I think Dr. Anna Weitz, third president, did an excellent job in fostering final resolution of this issue.

Always we counted on students as our ambassadors. We regularly posted a series of testimonials with photos of our star students and adjunct faculty in the area newspapers – CCACC Student Profiles and Faculty Profiles. Some of the students were: Todd Wonders, Chris Miller, Glen Raymond, Carl Michaels, Cheryl Klotz, Patricia Burns, Robin Betts, George Eason (also HGA student). I even used one of them, Todd Wonders, for teaching an accounting course when I fired the appointed instructor at mid- semester. These were exceptional people who helped to distinguish the college by their maturity and loyalty.

Part-time faculty profiles included Mary Kline (computer tech), Steve Pipan (algebra), George Muhlberg (contracts management), Bob MacIver (business),Tom Hood (environmental law), Suzanne Baranik(psychology), Kathleen Banks(math), Jim Matysik (banking), Marjorie Mattis(psychology).

The celebration of student achievement (and corresponding faculty achievement) was difficult without a student center and activities budget. Nevertheless there were celebrations in all of the five years of our foundational experience. At the end of the first year we actually had a graduation commencement, conferring eleven certificates for one year programs. At the end of the second year a Leadership Awards program was begun, honoring both faculty/staff and students. It was my hope that this program would become a strong tradition, much the same as commencement. Whether or not this is the case, I do not know..

An athletics program happened *by the grace of God.* (Of course, that could be said about most of the college's development.) From nowhere, Jack Loya appeared to give us an intercollegiate basketball team for both men and women. The CCACC Shawnee Cardinals came alive, to my great pleasure-- and surprise. It turned out that wild Jack needed some supervision but he and the Cardinals gave the college a great boost. Like me, he was willing to expend his own money to build a winner. Jack was a natural warrior, similar to Don Chamberlain of West Virginia Northern

College. I suspect all athletes have that blood. The men's team won about half their games, but the court ladies lost all of theirs and did not return in the second year. I remember them anyway. Two were also selected for a Leadership Award —Melissa Spaugie, number 10, and Misty Nicholson, number 15. Again, I wonder if the college is still trying with the Shawnee Cardinals? (named for the Shawnee Indians, with the tribe's blessings out of Oklahoma, one of the few CCACC letters I still possess.)

With the gracious assistance of Rod Risley and Phi Theta Kappa headquarters we were also able to initiate a CCACC chapter. Permission is usually not granted until accreditation, so this was a coup and another fine stimulus for our students. Marilyn Danchanko, Jan Garrett and Bonnie Bakos immediately signed on as advisors. Phi Theta Kappa is my favorite student organization because of its academic thrust.(Student nursing associations are a close second.) I have been involved in starting chapters at all of my colleges, which was noted when I received the Shirley B. Gordon Distinguished President award in 2004.

## Financial Trouble

By the end of FY 1999, the college had 30 approved credit and non-credit programs; 51 full-time faculty and staff, 115 to 125 adjunct faculty (varying by semester), and 25 student assistants were on board; 188 associate degrees and certificates had been conferred; transfer articulation agreements with 25 colleges and universities existed; and six consultation visits by Dr. Steiner had been performed for compliance with candidacy status by Middle States Association. In every part of this growth a Damoclean threat had hovered over the college. It was a complicated, stressful and ironic problem:

Essentially, the County Commissioners and early planners did not anticipate our immediate success or the exponential enrollment growth, three times greater than mandated. When the college was first enabled, the Commissioners pledged to support the college at the funding level of one mil. In the first year we did not use the full mil. However, after that, the budget increased significantly each year in accordance with enrollment increases. Yet the County did not see its way clear to increase its share despite all my appeals, backed up with data showing that the college was one of the most successful ventures they had ever undertaken. In my final year they did approve an additional $100,000, but the real need was to increase from one mil to two mils merely in order to maintain a percentage of approximately 15% of the total budget.

I liked the Commissioners, very much, but they were driving me crazy. What were we looking at – the stars out or lights out?

Nor was the state fertile in its support. We had a serious audit issue because of the way we counted FTE for state reimbursement claims. With other community college allies, we were successful in 1997, my third year, in winning the State Board of Education's approval of a regulation to count all credits earned by both part-time and full-time students (quite normal for community colleges) which removed an artificial barrier to our claims. However, the implementation of this change regulation was delayed, and we were still waiting for action when I left the college in July 1999.

In this work I enjoyed a mutually supportive relationship with two state administrators whom I was confident would continue to support the college. They were Lee Myers, Executive Director of the Community College Association, and Michael Poliakoff, Assistant Secretary for Higher Education. It was a sad occasion to return for Lee's funeral in November1999. He was a loyal and knowledgeable community college spokesman and a good man, a loving family man.

I continued my friendship with Dr. Poliakoff when he became Director of Education for the National Education Association, but to my great regret I did not serve him well when he called upon me as a reader for NEA grant proposals a few years later. By that time I was up to my belly button in alligators as president at WV Northern College. I did not have time to prepare adequately for jury review and should have notified NEA that I had to drop out. *Mea culpa.* I am afraid the episode damaged our relationship.

On top of these troubles there was a clumsy, inexplicable case of theft by my business manager in the middle of our second year. In November he suggested with some urgency (should have been my first clue) that we should get a line of credit established. The Board authorized it for $100,000. Less than a month later I discovered that the entire amount had been drawn down without my approval, and the business manager informed me that he was taking another position at a Diocesan school, one of our allies. The circumstances made me cold and I started to look for fraud. Board members were very concerned of course and I was embarrassed, but strangely perhaps, I did not see it in the same light of crisis as did our Board chair at the time. My embarrassment was turned to humiliation. I hold no grudge. Perhaps I deserved it. Even though I signed all checks, I had not paid sufficient attention to the functions of the business office. My predilection had always been for the academic side of the house, and I guess I was suborned by the alacrity and good credentials of the young guy I had hired, who obviously had larceny in his heart . (Within a short time he was also under investigation for similar fraud in his new position.)

With the aid of our auditor, Wessel & Co., the college attorney, and ultimately the County Attorney, I was fairly confident we could get on top of the problem. We did so, stolen money was recovered (approximately $30,000), accounts were reconciled, and we paid off the loan (which I considered to be fraudulent.)

Actually, there was another plus too: it led to the appointment of Jim Wagner. But of course the case made the newspapers—the only bad publicity I can recall. I remember Congressman John Murtha telling me, "Don't worry about it."

**End Game**

When I took the presidency in Pennsylvania I was in great shape thanks to my physical regimen and sunshine in El Salvador. I passed the required physical exam with "flying colors" as the cliché goes. Four years later I had a different result. When I applied to upgrade my insurance policy, my blood pressure was taken, and the nurse was so alarmed she insisted that I see a doctor immediately. Constant stress was taking its toll. So I decided to retire. The college was now well founded. I laid out options and strategies for managing unfinished business, such as the "four site configuration" and the FTE claims issue. I wanted to go back to Oxford University; maybe that was the motivation. Human motives are rarely pure and never simple.

In any case, the college foundation was strong. I was confident that with Steiner's help initial accreditation was assured, and confident too that the

Board and new president could call upon me for background analysis. I pledged my fealty. I was naïve.

My friend, Al Reynolds, told me it was a mistake to retire: blood pressure can be controlled—he was proof of it—and I still had a lot to offer. It wasn't long before I realized that Al's counsel was correct; I had made a mistake. Was it an act of betrayal? I should have requested a semester's leave of absence and placed Jim Wagner in office as acting president.

> *" But Mousie, thou art no thy lane,*
>
> *In proving foresight may be vain:*
>
> *The best laid plans o' mice an' men*
>
> *Gang aft agley,*
>
> *An' lea'e us nought but grief an' pain,*
>
> *For promis'd joy!"* (Robert Burns)

I was in Oxford taking a six-weeks course at Christ Church College when I began to get disturbing news. The first casualty was Mary Fisher, my nonpareil secretary, who resigned in great distress. Then fell Sharon Barto and young Tim Berkebile and Jack Loya. Then Jim Wagner. To letters and notes I received, I counseled patience and continuing commitment, but in Jim's case I felt that I had to say something: If he was being blamed for the rocky financial situation, it was not fair; on the contrary he was a steady hand at the wheel; at least the Board should have known that. I was torn, for I understand the protocol that obtains to ex-presidents.

There was an exchange of letters between me and the Board. I commended Jim for his integrity and his work, and explained again the genesis of the college's financial situation. I did not share my letter with Jim and discussed it with no one else. Nor did I challenge the authority of the president or board to make personnel decisions, but I did express hope that Jim's contributions would be recognized, not rudely dismissed. In response, a letter, presumably representing my former Board colleagues, said nothing about Jim; it was as if those Board meetings which had praised him were now overturned. I was asked, "do not permit yourself to be pulled into the governance or management of the college." The letter was copied to the college attorney.

I had another concern that I expressed to the Board Vice-Chair: "If it were known that a staff member called me even on a purely personal request, what interrogation would follow? If I do not want to play this game, which I do not, I must sever all connections with my Cambria colleagues and associates." So it was done, sadly . A young staff member/former student whom I had encouraged suggested that we meet when I was in Johnstown on another unhappy occasion, but I refused. I think the faculty and staff in those days must have been confounded and perhaps still are. Something was broken.

There was yet one more issue that devastated me. From day one to the last, I insisted on discipline in my office to compile and collect in a large notebook all correspondence, reports and documents pertaining to college development for each year in chronological order. We ended up with six such notebooks. We also filed in the usual manner all papers produced.

The cataloged notebooks were intended not only as background information for analysis of any problems or issues that might come up but as primary source material for a history of the founding of the college, which I intended to write. Literally, it was a treasure that could have expanded far beyond this poor chapter the technical analysis of issues, the opportunities won and lost, the political and social cross-currents, and the exploration of personalities and idiosyncrasies that inhere in any human endeavor but are soon muddled or forgotten.

The notebooks were placed in the library. ( A Board member told me later that I should have taken them home; he was right.) About six months later when I wrote the college to say that I was coming to scan the notebooks, I was told that I had no access to them—they were property of the college— any copies of documents I wanted would need to be specifically identified. At that point I knew the notebooks still existed and pressed the value of my use of them by going to the college. The notebooks had been removed from the library on the day before my visit. In follow up I was then told that the notebooks had been disassembled and each page document placed in the normal office files -- a huge task indeed—and why? Why were the notebooks destroyed?

The obtuseness was staggering.

*"Our capacity of reason is magnificent, but there are mysteries in human experience that transcend even reason's explanatory powers."* (Theodore Dalrymple)

Is this then a mystery? No, it falls far short of that. It was an act neither static nor dynamic, gratuitous, without logic, that had an effect akin to striking someone blind, but even then, for me, only momentarily. CCACC as a collegial institution lost much more.

Look again for symbols. As I was preparing to leave the college, my staff gave me a large framed portrait--CCACC Founding President—which we hung in our waiting room at the Central Park Complex site. During my notebooks visit I looked for the portrait. It was gone and no one knew where it was.

Despite the travails we experienced in the period of 1994 to 1999, never did I doubt that we would be successful in establishing CCACC (now Penn Highlands Community College). It was only after I left that I felt real crisis and feared the outcome: would the college make it? I thank God that it was meant to be. Any glory belongs to Him.

Post Script:

Tim Berkebile was one of the young entrepreneurs I promised security and gratitude and eventually greater monetary rewards if he would stick with the college and make it grow. Tim had no college degrees, but he was creative and conscientious well beyond the value of any degree. I would join him occasionally to admire a completed piece of his work assignment. Actually Tim needed very little direction. I felt that I knew his spirit. After I left the college I heard that he made a mistake and was punished for it in a way that would have humiliated him. Although I only have my imagination to go on, I think he tried to hang on, but then he saw that my promise to him was empty, and he quit. I wish that I could see him again to express my apology.

I really do not know what to think about the college now. There are some good folks who remain from the early days; a few of them have told me that under the current president the situation is much improved. I am glad to hear that. I am glad that the college exists to serve the people it was built for, but how much of it remains from what we started? Was that experience just a shooting star?

----------------

From a Fan, Jane Wood, for My Johnstown Inauguration (except I didn't have one) :

### The Builder's Tale

*Once upon a time there was happy little town in PA, but they felt something was missing. They needed a school house. So they searched far and wide for a builder and they found six people to choose from. But they still were not quite happy.*

*Now there was a fine young man living happily with his lovely family in Hornell, NY, but he felt something was missing. So he searched far and wide until he came to the little town in PA*

*So the townspeople all clapped and embraced him and made him their builder. And that is the story of how John found his town, "John's town" and Johnstown found John, their "Fearless Builder".*

*And they lived happily ever after.*

## Cross Section of Letters and Memos

### From: Sherry Shurin, Faculty Senate Chair, Cambria County Area Community College, June, 1999

In the words of Ralph Waldo Emerson, "Spiritual Laws", "Every action is measured by the depth of the sentiment from which it proceeds. " Dr. Hunter, you are a man of great depth. You knew in your heart that although such an undertaking as the creation of this college would be a great challenge and fraught with difficulty, yet you were willing to rise to the challenge.

From the day you came to our community, you have ceaselessly worked to build the structure of the community college. You worked hard and long to make this college a success, working alongside of us, doing what needed to be done, whether it was moving boxes, answering phones or stuffing envelopes. You became a teacher, instructing us on how to build a college. You were our mentor, moving us to heights we did not know we could achieve. You were our Advocate, working for our benefit. You were a parent moving us into what you alone knew we could become

Dr. Hunter, we thank you for your commitment to us, as faculty, and for your commitment to the College and to the Community and making the Cambria County Area Community College a reality.

### From: Chris Lint, Penn Highlands Community College

Dr Hunter, the heartfelt honesty and accuracy of your words is moving. I and my dear friend Joe still fondly remember the "Hunter Era". It was a time of urgency and solid dedication to our mission. Those of us who remain try, I know, to act with the integrity and purpose of that time. Joe and I have accepted many roles over the years. We and others have grown as educators and as individuals. Thank you for what you instilled in us. We are making a difference. I think that's what you want us to do.

# Chapter VI

## *West Virginia*

*These obstacles are the last between us*
*and where we have so longed to be.*
*We ought if we could to eat them up alive.*

**(Xenophon)**

Summer 2000: I failed retirement again, and Lyla Beth, without hesitation, said again, "whither thou guest I will go." So we moved to West Virginia for another experience of starting over. West Virginia Northern Community College (WVNCC) was within the 100 mile radius of our permanent home in Hornell, NY which we agreed would be a factor in any relocations. This allowed us to be within a few hours driving distance of the family.

I liked the idea of the presidency at West Virginia Northern Community College for two reasons: In June 2000 the West Virginia Legislature had adopted a higher education reform bill which, while surely needed, was very challenging; and the College itself was obviously facing its own challenge of survival, given serious enrollment decline and breeding financial crisis.

The story of WV Northern's Renaissance is about people and values. It could not have been accomplished without partnership, without commitment to the college by many people, without determination to overcome obstacles despite a nagging cynicism, and without the competency of professional team members and loyal students.

By the year 2000, following five years of steady enrollment decline and serious budget deficits WV Northern was at a critical point. As the least funded community college in the state -- 25% less than its sister institution, WV Southern -- the bottom was about to fall out.

The famous B&O building in Wheeling which the college had inherited was itself a sad daily reminder of the college depression, and the Hazel-Atlas building a few blocks away was no better, maybe worse. Dirty building exteriors, blighted campus grounds, unreliable heating/air-conditioning, major parking and security problems in a seedy downtown area, windows that could not be washed because they would fall out (I kid you not!),, a chemistry lab so neglected it had become dangerous, and totally inexplicable, a lack of signage: I recall first walking up to the B&O building entrance, thinking, " students could not have any pride of walking into this building –if they could find it."

But the crisis was more than this unconscionable neglect of facilities: we were facing a structural deficit of over $1 million, and there was a poor policy base and rewards system for faculty and staff. All of these conditions combined to create the worst crisis management situation I have seen in all of the colleges I served.

However, it was also a great opportunity. There was no way to go but up. This beautiful and great Northern Panhandle -- rich in heritage and strong in basic American values -- was entering a difficult new stage of economic change. A true "people's college" was exactly the kind of institution needed for the challenge, and so the direction was clear.

Lyla Beth and I could see immediately that there were good people to work with and befriend in the Northern Panhandle. By this time in my career we had concluded that there are good people wherever we go regardless of the personal stress of confronting in the office of president the antipathy of individuals who cannot understand the complexities of college development or are facing their own personal crises which must be someone else's fault. We put our faith in the good will of the majority of West Virginians and were not disappointed.

WVNCC was founded in 1972 to serve the six counties of the Northern Panhandle. The district had been hit hard by the decline of the steel industry and coal mining, much like Cambria County, PA. Hardworking people suddenly found themselves without work, some with dim prospects of ever working again.

There were three campuses: Wheeling(the largest), Weirton and New Martinsville. The founding president was Daniel B. Crowder. We honored Dr. Crowder and his wife, Wreatha, in 2002, a 30th anniversary celebration. I recognized in Dr. Crowder the missionary attitude and zeal similar to mine and many other community college builders I have known. The college had fallen on hard times since its founding years, but it was a pleasure to witness a reunion of those loyal citizens who had been with Dr. Crowder at the beginning. Dr. Crowder and I shared the unique title of "founding president" and became good friends.

The prospects of revitalization to become a community college of excellence did not take hold easily, however. There was a malaise due to past disappointments both within and outside the college that inhibited immediate support. But West Virginia has good people and gradually momentum began to build. Leaders stepped forward. The necessary alliances began to form.

**Governance Issues**

During my WVNCC presidency I spent a lot of time in Charleston, WV on the various issues of reform with my fellow presidents and the Higher Education Policy Commission (HEPC). I can't say that I enjoyed the long trips, but the sessions with HEPC Board were interesting -- partly because of the contrasting institutional interests. I was president of one of the smaller and certainly the poorest of the state's colleges, but I often sat next to David Hardesty, president of West Virginia University. (I told Dave he was Tyrannosaurus Rex, while I was one of those little Pleistocene creatures, hopefully nimble...)

I was the only community college representative at a major WVU event one time and felt honored that David was so gracious to me. There was an egalitarian ambience to these events which was fine. But it didn't ring true: the community college mission and development issues were much different than those of our four year college sisters. I did not like feigning an elitist role; I felt more like a plant manager than a corporate executive.

In my second year I addressed the HEPC Board on the need to recognize the different issues confronting our institutions. The performance indicators adopted for reform accountability were geared to a rigid university model, and the criterion references were wrong for community colleges. For example, there was not a due respect for developmental education which was essential in the community college mission. The state did not fund it. This was a hard core issue that needed to be addressed in a policy context, along with other qualitative issues such as support for work force development courses, flexible learning, degree standards, degree timetables, the distinctions and connections of technical and general education.

I shared testimony of a first-year nursing student who was also a young mother:

*"My income has decreased due to school expenses and the need to work only part-time in order to attend school. There is a decrease in time spent with my family. There is an increase of stress due to the need to get adequate grades, loss of quality time with my kids, decreased income, and a lot less sleep. Why then would anyone choose nursing school? I believe for most of us it is an internal desire to help people, and make their lives more fulfilling. By helping people, we increase our self-esteem."*

There are hundreds of testimonies like this from community college students. The number of students who dropped out in a given year is less important than the question of why they dropped out and how we could meet their needs more effectively; in other words, what happens to our students? Sometimes attrition is a positive in a community college. On the other hand, a student may come and go through the college like a bat through a garage, affected not at all by the experience. What number does he fall into?

The idea of penalizing an institution which is already struggling because it does not fit into the prescribed bureaucratic model does not make sense. It made even less sense to deny the resources for the learning assistance, such as developmental education programs, that would be the surest path to achieving some of the stated goals.

A community college is an organic entity living in a constantly changing environment-- socio-economic, political, cultural, and bureaucratic. Of course, there must be accountability, but there must also be freedom to address qualitative issues at the local level, allowing the college to adapt without endangering system support. In West Virginia even with the reform legislation, or perhaps because of it, there was too much threat of interference by the state policy boards with college management.

Not due to my influence, but there was a later follow-up to the reform legislation that created a separate Community College Board and Chancellor for the system. Jim Skidmore from the HEPC staff was appointed to that position and our attention shifted to the Community College Board agenda.

To me progress fell short of the promise. It was not Jim's fault -- he was a competent, experienced community college leader -- but the Board fell into an even more bureaucratic tone of governance. Although sincere in their sense of responsibility, they were pushing the same numbers agenda without awareness of the values of community college autonomy. I felt Board officers were trying to jump over a paper moon.

The WV reform bill along with the appointment of a new Chancellor for Higher Education, Mike Mullen, created a dynamic situation which became very interesting due to some legislators who seemed unwilling to give Mullen a decent chance to succeed. I had my own differences with Mullen and the HEPC in regard to their ambition to create a bureaucratic platform for measuring productivity, but I did not question the sincerity or integrity of the response to the mandates of the reform legislation.

In my view, the quality of education cannot be measured by the numbers even though I had no quarrel with reporting the numbers. I have always advocated strong evaluation policies and procedures, and it is useful to conduct them with the aid of a data retrieval system.

These quarrels do not diminish other significant improvements made by the WV reform legislation. It was actually an historic piece of work which stood, possibly, to correct entrenched apparatus and old methods of governance dominated by the state, such as statewide salary mandate, personnel classification system, and grievance adjudication -- which long had a firm grip with mission- negative results and unnecessarily high costs. Yet, in spite of good intentions, loosening the grip remained uncertain because of the influence of personnel associations protected by statute. West Virginia paid dearly to prevent collective bargaining in the public sector. I saw no policies put forward to maintain the status quo of the quasi-unions that could not easily, rationally be sundered; but they advanced anyway.

The reform legislation also established, at long last, a community college system, including local board authority that held real promise for the future – perhaps not exactly what Kaye McClenney, community college consultant and friend, had in mind, but close. This feature is what attracted me to West Virginia in the first place and I was eager to cooperate as a community college president "present at the creation."

The initial WVNCC Board appointed by the governor and installed in June 2001 was a great pleasure to work with—competent and quick to learn " governance by policy," completely apolitical, respectful of the college staff. We had good understanding of our respective duties and obligations. The establishment of these boards was a significant step forward for West Virginia education.

The college also had a very loyal contingent of supporters on all campuses; these were the three "Friends" organizations--wonderful lay supporters!— again typical of all college communities I have known. The same could be said of the College Foundation, a fund-raising board that played a pivotal role in external affairs. Other important support groups included the Alumni Association and Arts- Link in New Martinsville. The area newspapers, *Wheeling News-Register, Intelligencer,* and the *Weirton Daily Times* were strong in their public support of the college. I felt very fortunate to have this support ready and waiting to promote public understanding of the college mission and our marketing efforts.

There is something about an educational institution that attracts people's interest and commitment. I have seen occasions when a board would confuse its role or try to take over the administration of its policy, which can lead to serious disruption of college affairs. Some of these are "live by the sword, die by the sword" experiences. But in most cases, citizens attracted to a board are intelligent, well meaning and responsible.

## From Bach to Bluegrass

It is almost ironic that despite West Virginia poverty in some places, the culture was not misbegotten, certainly not in the Northern Panhandle. Appreciation for art and music in Wheeling, and in the small towns such as New Martinsville, was radiant – everything from Bach to Bluegrass! Wheeling was a center of country music – engagements at the Capitol Theater where we met George Jones, Loretta Lynn, and others – and heard the marvelous Wheeling Philharmonic and annual concerts of Wheeling High School bands and orchestras (remarkable to see the kids freely exchange instruments) – home of Brad Paisley – Victoria Theater every Friday night, where it was hard to distinguish amateurs from professionals -- and the Penny Royal Opry House just across the river ("here we play nothin' but Grass".)

These folks knew and loved music, and they were a blessing to meet and know.

Back to the demands of the state bureaucracy: WVNCC was ahead of most of its sister institutions in keeping up with State Compact goals. Some of the sessions to discuss data outcomes were delightful, especially when I could show that there was more than one kind of data to illuminate what was happening to students.

Generally speaking, my fellow presidents and HEPC staff colleagues were friends and allies. We were all caught on the bureaucratic treadmill, hoping that eventually some reasonable compromise could be found between the proclaimed objectivity of data (reams of it) and the admittedly subjective professional judgment in illuminative evaluation. Meantime we pushed ahead with the promise of the reform legislation.

But alas, Chancellor Mullen was a casualty. In retrospect, I believe that I could have helped him by being more assertive in the foreplay of legislative demands, but I lacked the will to do so. Mike was the most data-conscious high level administrator I have known, and he could spin a lap-top like no one else I have known. I respected him highly for his acumen and integrity, but he did not quite fit into the mold of other system heads I had known-- SUNY's Bruce Johnstone or Illinois' Dick Wagner—who did not adhere to the NCHEMS format so formally.

## College Square Project

Although we disagreed on elements of accountability, Chancellor Mullen was a reliable and bold supporter of the college's need for a reconstruction project on the Wheeling campus. Almost from our first meeting I began to witness to him about the former B&O Railroad building terminus in Wheeling which the college had inherited back in 1972. Years of neglect due to lack of maintenance funds had brought it to a critical point: restoration or abandonment --? The Hazel-Atlas, a few blocks away, I could see no alternative to selling. Chancellor Mullen was immediately encouraging about taking on the challenge of re-building the Wheeling campus and thereby creating a whole new image and identity for the college. Mike did not flinch in the face of a challenge.

One of the first private meetings I had in Wheeling about the college was with David McKinley, a prominent architect and ardent preservationist, who had rehabbed many buildings. David was well aware of Wheeling's needs. He asked me point blank if I was one of those guys who talked a lot about development but didn't actually accomplish much? I assured him of my disposition for action and that I had not left it behind me when I came to West Virginia. From that point on we had a relationship that led to commitment not only to restructure the campus but to revitalize the downtown area where the college is located.

Our preliminary discussions focused on building a second structure in the ugly lot that had not been properly despoiled behind the B&O building. But then, as a true preservationist, McKinley linked our need to a huge structure across the street, an eighty thousand square foot, four-story building that had once been a Wholesale Grocery distribution center built to withstand the shock of the trains entering into it. This building was one of the most massive I have ever seen and certainly was never intended for educational purposes, but to rehab it as an Education Center was a vision that made much sense both for the college and the City of Wheeling.

In September 2003, the College Board approved a plan to purchase the building and renovate it to house classrooms, labs and other facilities, including a multipurpose gymnasium and space for the culinary arts program. The plan included renovation of the B&O building, grounds improvement, lighting and sidewalks (with City cooperation), and the sale of the Hazel Atlas building. The projected cost was $11 million with completion expected in the fall of 2006. *The plan was dubbed the "College Square Project."*

Project success depended upon the support of the City of Wheeling, Higher Education Policy Commission, WV Community College Council, the State Legislature, and Governor's Office-- with positive recommendations from Higher Ed Chancellor Mullen and Community College Chancellor Jim Skidmore, both of whom had already come onboard.

I was pleased to report to our Board in April 2004, "They all are behind us." Funding was provided by state lottery revenue and tax exempt bonds. For funding we owed gratitude to several legislators, especially Senators Larry Edgel and Bob Plymale.

The project was launched. The strategic phase was over. There was still a great deal of work ahead, but I was convinced that the new building and the B&O building renovation would come to fruition as planned-- and it was so.

Leadership from then on was in the hands of VP Larry Bandi, Sue Pelley (appointed project coordinator), Dennis Gill representing McKinley and Associates, and members of the Deans Council as monitors. Some others instrumental in the project were Rich Donovan, HEPC staff member, and Project BEST, a labor-management consortium. Coliani Construction won the construction award.

I left WVNCC in July 2005. With the new president, Dr. Martin Olshinsky, we dedicated the new Wheeling campus in September 2006.

This last event in Wheeling was indeed climactic: I heard no bells ringing or violins playing, but I knew we were at the end of a splendid rehabilitation and simultaneously at the beginning of something very significant for the people of the Northern Panhandle. I could see the new parking lots filled and hundreds of new students turning their eyes at last to their community college. Yet as I looked out on the audience I also sensed an indescribable something missing. There were many local officials and citizens present – but very few college faculty. My mind was carried up to the curiosity of this, at best, Laodicean display of interest – no victory, no celebration, what were the faculty's hopes and aspirations for their new college, so vitally linked to their vocation?

Dave McKinley, now a U.S. Congressman, also brought to my attention the possibility of creating a National Civil War Memorial on the college campus. I was surprised to hear that there was no such Memorial in any state. We met with Gary Casteel, a sculptor and architect who had done many Civil War projects (including a union soldier statue in Johnstown) and had already linked up with a board of directors for the National Memorial. We invited the board to a discussion in Wheeling, and it was decided to execute the project in Wheeling on our campus, which is located just across the street from the WV State Archives building. A lot of preliminary work was done, but unfortunately, although we had support from Wheeling leaders, we could not convince the state to sponsor the project. Those who control the purse strings simply could not capture the vision. This was a great loss to the city of Wheeling and the state of West Virginia. The Memorial would have brought thousands of people into the downtown area, a major boost for economic development.

The only compensation was that I made friends with Gary Casteel and his wife Leslie. Gary had excellent vision, talent and strong leadership style. We still communicate occasionally.

## People and Programs

Similar to other colleges I have been privileged to serve, WV Northern was blessed to have several dedicated faculty and staff members who did not lose their resiliency even though they were sorely tested during the years of occupying an almost squalid campus and without even minimal resources for professional development and enrollments management.

Among the veterans, the obvious leaders were Garnet Persinger, Regina Jeannette, Don Chamberlain, Mike Koon, Janet Fike, Rita Yeager, and professors Bill Deibert, Ralph Lucki, Mike Sidon, Marian Grubor, Nancy Krupinski, Kathy Herrington, Shirley Richlicki, Tom Danford. (This list is not complete: I will bring others into the picture, who came on board later during my presidency.)

These associates made distinctive contributions. It is interesting that even in the worst of circumstances in a college, there is always a core of individuals who will somehow keep the faith and not yield to the grim negativity so prevalent.

There is a story about an old gentleman in Dayton, Ohio who, when told that the Wright brothers were building a flying machine, said," it will never happen, it's against God's will, and even if it could happen, it certainly would never happen in Dayton!"

This was more or less the attitude in the Northern Panhandle. I ran into it constantly during my WV Northern presidency. I also recognized later that there were some staff who had very low appreciation even of benefits they received, let alone institutional progress. The vision I brought to the college development was not something they shared; they had sunk into a seemingly irremediable condition of estrangement from the college development.

Yet, I reflect with a vague unease, the veiled melancholy as one looks back on difficult time. There was courage and compassion in the Northern Panhandle despite the onslaught of jobs and pensions lost. If I felt stress or exasperation, it was little to nothing compared to what those folks were going through. Our faculty were the bearers of their culture, but I do not remember a lack of dignity or integrity.

The faculty were weak on collegial governance, but some programs were excellent, on par with any other community college programs I have known. I marveled at this because the resources were so thin. Clearly, the programs were testimony to the high individual commitment of their faculty leaders.

Most outstanding in this regard were: Culinary Arts, the only nationally recognized one in West Virginia, led by Marian Grubor; Heating/ Refrieration/Air Conditioning, led by Mike Sidon (what a charger he was!); Nursing, led by Regina Jeannette; and Surgical Technology, led by Nancy Krupinski. There was also an excellent math department.

So the faculty were not really a threat to our progress; they just didn't like it or trust it, or me as the initiator of change. Or was it resentment respondent to my arrogance?

A big part of the problem of change we faced was that it had to come quickly. I will admit that in some cases I did not communicate effectively to the faculty even though I had solid support from the Board and my administrative team. I regret my obtuseness, but then neither were there many exchange volleys aimed at helping me in the game.

In retrospect, I think the problem of faculty/president relations was largely that we could not reach a level of professional understanding due to our different backgrounds and experiences in governance. I think they were puzzled about my approach, which may have seemed too aggressive or even elitist. I was certainly puzzled by their reluctance to engage.

For me, a dialectical process is the heart of meaningful collegial governance:-- argument/counter-argument (or agreement) /synthesis, resulting in commitment. Synthesis is not necessarily compromise, which may be a weak form of it, but arrival at a higher, better result than either party originally imagined. (There are examples of it throughout these chapters.) The dialectic need not foster disrespect or antagonism, often quite the opposite.

I confess that I did not adequately prepare the faculty for a strong action agenda at WVNCC. But we forged ahead anyway. This was not a time for soft-headed, indecisive sensitivity games.

And what an agenda we had! Indeed, the challenge was not just change but complete revitalization and transformation.. The prospect of retrenchment and reduction-in-force that could seriously damage the college mission as well as the welfare of students, faculty and staff was real.

From my first day at WV Northern, I relied upon the "acting president" during the search, Garnet Persinger. Garnet had a mature grasp of the college's predicament and was strongly supportive of my efforts to create new ground for development. It was not long before her professional and personal integrity became obvious to me. Because of her long association with the college and most of the faculty and staff who were her peers, she became an easy target for blame. Yet I thought she had the best insight and sense of commitment of any of the administrative staff.

Until she was brought to the Wheeling campus as "acting president" she had spent most of her career building the campus in New Martinsville where she was highly respected. I think it is fair to say, at least from what I heard and learned about her in that community, she was the true "founder" of that campus.

To make use of her skills and experience in the broadest possible way I appointed her as Provost. I lost her to retirement in 2003 -- at the same time, fortunately, that I hired Larry Bandi as Chief Financial Officer.

I also brought on board Bob DeFrancis ,long-time Editor of the Wheeling News-Register, as Dean of Community Relations and Institutional Development; and appointed Mike Koon as Vice President and Dean for Economic Development. Mike had done a good job developing the Center for Excellence in Workforce Education (CEWE) and seemed a good fit for VP because of his comprehensive knowledge of the college's development and WV higher ed dynamics. Mike was a help to me in political analysis.

We also had Janet Fike and John Jones, and I appointed Mike Smith as Director of Institutional Research , and Sue Pelley as Director of Facilities. Janet Fike was Director of Financial Aid when I appointed her as Associate Dean and then Dean, one of the best Dean appointments I have made.

So that was our core management team, the "President's Cabinet." There was also a second administrative group of classified directors that I met with monthly we called the "A Team."

I make no reference to another position, Dean of Academic Affairs, because I made two separate appointments to that position after Garnet left and both were failures. Administration of academic affairs remained sclerotic throughout my presidency at WV Northern.

In my second year I pondered the need for more administrative positions, but by this time I also had begun to wonder if that would make any difference to the quality of college development?

The real problem was not our lack of administrative positions so much as it was our lack of resources for professional/ curriculum/ technological development based on clear strategies and objectives.

Then, because of excellent work by Garnet Persinger in developing a proposal for a "Strengthening Institutions" grant, we got lucky. The college received a five-year 1.5 million dollars [1]award for these purposes. It made an immediate difference

## Technology Challenge

The technology challenge at WV Northern was enormous. I was astonished that some faculty did not even have a PC and were not using e-mail. The basic problem was inadequate funding for the tech development . There was a unique problem because of three campuses widely separated in the Northern Panhandle. A lot depended upon finding a way to communicate effectively between the three campuses with voice, data and video. Most of the faculty were still using the old lecture, lecture, test method. Learning systems support was sadly lacking.

So it was very important to develop a strategic technology plan -- actually, a blitz-- undergirding operational objectives at the academic department level as well as for administrative offices and campus integration purposes-- a huge challenge for this college that many thought was insurmountable. Ultimately, we made a great deal of progress.

Five years later the college was set up in entirely different circumstances and actually began to lead in several aspects of development in the state of West Virginia.

In an administrative reorganization during my first semester, I created the position of Dean of Computer Information and Communications Technology and appointed Dr. John Jones, a minority staff member who was serving as Director of Technology to the position. John was very enthusiastic and we did a lot of good work together; but to be honest I was never entirely satisfied with our mutual understanding – maybe my fault-- and continued to monitor affairs closely. This was not the case with Garnet Persinger or Larry Bandi whom I trusted completely. Yet in fairness, John deserves major credit for our technology planning and accomplishments. Following are some of the major areas of development we pursued:

In connection with the "College Square project" an important goal was to create technology enhanced classrooms (" smart classrooms"), a strategy that extended to the other campuses as well. To accomplish this goal required an outlay of a half million dollars. The basic format for each classroom was an electronic podium with desktop PC, ceiling LCD, "Elmo" for document projection and VCR (no longer necessary of course). We created over 50 of these classrooms and conducted orientation classes for all faculty in their use. Also important was the creation of computer labs needed on all campuses; when I first arrived there were some labs but containing only 486 PC's.

Again, the interconnectivity was major-- very expensive but absolutely essential given the distances between the campuses. At first, we relied upon Verizon as our technology partner. Verizon had virtually a monopoly in WV Higher Education as a result of a state contract. Immediately, I could see serious problems in our relationship with Verizon. Inexplicably, the college had contracted for three DSIII and three T-1 lines, far more capacity than could ever possibly be used.

Two months after I arrived I met with Gail Given, Verizon Eastern Territory VP, and she agreed with me that the lines were too capacious.. However, it was several months before we rectified the situation; meanwhile we were being charged for what had been installed. Ultimately, we refused to pay some of these charges, and that controversy was still unresolved when I left the college.

In any case, we reduced to one DSIII and one T-1 lines, and began searching for alternatives to Verizon. Later, after State legislative action freed up higher education, the college shifted from Verizon to Stratus-Wave. The objective to establish a digital phone system using a PRI card in a desk top server along with a bundle of phone numbers which allowed more direct communication was an important part of this new strategy. We were paying approximately $3000 a month for analog service and it was not doing the job. We were also experiencing high bandwidth cost of $5700 per month, which we again felt was unjust because it helped to subsidize other colleges in the state-- a complication due again to state contract. These were very difficult issues but we persisted and ultimately prevailed so that by the time I left the college had a much better, more cost-effective technology configuration.

Another major development during my administration was SCT Banner system development, mandated by the state, which was supposed to unite the colleges with central offices. Again, there were complications, but we did successfully install a student service system-- enrollment, registration, etc.( for which I give high marks to Janet Fike.) We also began the deployment of a finance module. (again, Larry Bandi). We tried to work harmoniously with our colleagues at the state level engaged in Banner development, and I believe there was mutual respect and understanding despite the disagreements.

An internal need that was never off the agenda was a disaster recovery system, the lack of which made everyone nervous. While recognizing and pushing this need, personally I was more interested in integrating our technology with curriculum and instruction. In 2000 most of our faculty did not have the skills to develop a website. Fortunately, we had a few faculty leaders to lead the way: Most prominent in my recollection were Don Poffenberger, Pam Sharma, Terry Craig, Tom Danford , Dave Naegele and Dave Goeddel.

For the sake of fairness, I must also mention my daughter, Suzanne Hunter, who was Director of Technology in a New York school system, and my son John Hunter, who was a webmaster and taught web applications. They were a big help to me in my own professional development at that time, and both contributed directly to the college.

To cut across all departments and disciplines, we began in a simple way: I personally introduced a low level program, *Teacher Web*, at a faculty meeting and indicated it would be required unless there was a preferable alternative. I confess this was a ploy. The strategic goal was to wean everyone to Web CT, which ultimately was completed. Once stimulated, faculty who had lagged made rapid progress. Through the professional development program, we also introduced Knowledge Dispatch. Again, Professors Poffenberger and Sharma and Dave Naegele led in this transition.

## Politics of Funding

Pressed to explain why the pessimism was so deep at WVNCC-- Mike Koon, a long time administrator, called it a "general malaise"-- I believe one major cause was the neglect of the campus facilities. The campus was an unbelievable eyesore in downtown Wheeling. Another was the lack of support for the normal expenditures in maintaining and developing programs.

As always, there are layers of the onion. For the past ten years before I took office, the college had been egregiously and unfairly underfunded by the state.

Now, of course, all administrators will make the case for inadequate funding, but it is not difficult to assemble the facts to back up this argument for WV Northern.

During the five years of my administration our state revenue was flat-lined despite the unmatched big growth in our enrollments. The funding mechanism was tipped against us and in favor of institutions with greater political support-- not an unusual situation perhaps, but in West Virginia the decision-making for institutional budgets was overtly political though masked by sophisticated formulae. Here is a revealing set of facts (taken from official state documents) amidst the political circumstances:

Among the state's community colleges, two had a similar history, Both were "free-standing" (i.e., not connected to a four-year college), same mission, and serving the same size populations. These colleges are WV Northern Community College and Southern WV Community College.

Does it not seem logical that state support for these twin institutions would be approximately equal, or at least not a marked contrast?

Such was not our situation. In 2005, Northern's base budget appropriation was two million dollars less than Southern's, while our Fulltime Equivalent Enrollment was 300 more than Southern's.

Nor do these figures tell the whole story. When " supplemental funding" is brought into the picture, the differences are even higher. The reform legislation adopted in 2000 created four " funding pools" separate from the base budget appropriations. From 2002 to 2005 Northern's allocations from these pools was $455,000 less than Southern's. During these years Northern's FTE enrollment increased by 28%; Southern's increased by 5%.

We had 100 fewer personnel positions than Southern had.

Not much to say for productivity reward, is there?

Do these comparisons tell the story? Not yet. There are also lottery funds. Here's where the scale tipped in Southern's favor becomes radiantly clear. For the years recorded, Southern's lottery revenue was between $ 220,000 and $250,000. Northern's share was $0.00.

This is really interesting. 41% of the state's lottery revenue is produced in the Northern Panhandle (mainly by Mountaineer and Wheeling Island gaming centers/racetracks.)There was an historical pattern of neglect of the institutions and people of the Panhandle area where most lottery funds were produced. It is a classic case of political redistribution of wealth.

Could there be justification for it? If so it was never explained. In fact, I never heard an explanation for the system of appropriations even though I asked for it.

No, let's face it honestly and frankly: Southern West Virginia had the power. The legislature's majority leader lived in the district of Southern Community College, and his wife was the college president. Several of the legislature's chairs were from the south. Upon his retirement as executive director of the American Association of Community Colleges, David Pierce (whom I knew well from my Illinois days) was recruited and appointed to Southern's board.

So was this blatant corruption? No, I wouldn't go that far. These were decent and amiable folks, but they had become inured to a situation where their political power was naturally rewarded. I doubt that most were even aware of the derivative negative impact on Northern.(Of course, maybe I am naïve.)

I saw it clearly as inequitable, unfair treatment of my college--in a system of colleges which were expected to pull together for the cause of higher education serving the people of West Virginia -- that I had not seen anywhere else in the same degree. I soon learned that others in the Northern Panhandle were well aware of the inequities imposed upon their community college, but they too had become inured to the situation. If I thought about it too long, it became more than frustrating—infuriating!

So we began the campaign, "Stand Up for Northern", which we hoped to spread throughout the district, and I believe we were at least partially successful, certainly with our students who joined in valiantly. I was very proud of them.

Ultimately, the case went beyond Northern. It was important to bring fairness into play as a guiding principle in the reform effort by ending the conflict between north and south, beginning to balance the needs and rewards for all regions of the state, and finding the political path for governance that would advance the state's integrity and synergistic development. A philosophical agreement with the Wheeling News-Register led to a series of op-ed articles in which I expressed these points. I also outlined four proposals for funding formula revision that the WVNCC Board had adopted for recommendation.

Hopefully, the funding dynamics have changed since I left WV Northern. There were signs that a change was on the way when we received the College Square funds—which was a splendid catharsis.

There may be a variety of arguments to be engendered by these statistics, and in any case, we had to find a path of reasonable adjustment.

Because of our growing financial deficit problem, we had to do our assessment in the management context of retrenchment, which actually had begun in my first semester.

**Administrative Reorganization**

Another aspect of the challenge was that stagnancy had crept into the organization, and it was time to begin to afflict the comfortable. So we began a radical reorganization based on a functional analysis of all positions. Naturally, some members of the college community expressed their dissatisfaction.

Knowing the capacity for sabotage by an angry faculty to be infinite, I expected to face some of it. However, while we did not get complete cooperation, the reaction was a curious blend of resentment and passivity.

At a meeting to discuss need for change there were many complaints about past administrative mistakes and shortfalls before I came on board. Questions about my responsibility for them seemed to me a bit unusual, but I also realized that the organization had hit bottom and maybe others realized that as well. It was time to start over.

Reorganization yielded several significant outcomes: I was well pleased that the reorganization process successfully laid some basic principles of governance that I insisted upon: each administrator had a charter of responsibility outlining duties and specific authority, and each other staff member had a job description. Evaluation policy and procedures were adopted as well as strategic and operational (action) planning protocols; and a monthly administrative reporting protocol was begun.

We eliminated twenty-five positions over the next two years--going from 148 to 123 approved positions.(Some positions were recovered when the revenue stream improved.) More positively, at the same time, we reclassified twelve "temporary lecturer" positions held by staff for over five years to professional rank status. Most significantly, twenty two classified staff and seven faculty members were upgraded or promoted in the second year with very significant salary increases of 10% t0 45%.

Yes, that number is correct! One female professor's salary was increased by half in a single year. Never had I seen that before, but it was deserved and fairly given. A by-product of the process was Board adoption of a new salary schedule for faculty which finally lent some rationale to rank/reward differentials. Promotions continued throughout my presidency, even though a large percentage of faculty had already reached full professor rank. Over five years there were a total of 31 promotions and upgrades.

Perhaps these outcomes helped to assuage the feelings of turmoil over change; I don't really know, because I never received any word of satisfaction from anyone other than my core administrative staff.

Quite the opposite, on a return visit in 2006, two administrative secretaries, both of whom I had upgraded with significant salary increases, told me that they preferred the "old days in the Hazel-Atlas building."

I remain benighted.

## WVNCC Student Memories

In my administration at all of my colleges, the watchword was always, "people are our priority," applied to all groups associated with the college. I also insisted that, as a teaching institution, our mission—"raison d'etre"— focused on students first. Student development and leadership were my constant themes.

At WVNCC, Lyla Beth and I followed our usual path of meeting as many students as we could by attending all of the college events. Striving to develop the relationships among student organizations--- especially the student senates on all three campuses, intra- mural sports teams, and academic clubs, such as Student Nursing Association and Phi Theta Kappa-- was a major goal of my office as president. In this goal, certainly not by my own efforts, we had major success. Despite its poverty, the college environment was already charged with student enthusiasm for their activities.

One organization that was new to me was the Community Outreach Opportunity Program (COOP) , which had already established a fine tradition of service and assistance to community organizations, groups, and individuals in need. The need was great, and the response by this organization time and again was enthralling. In our 2004 re- accreditation report by the North Central Higher Learning Commission, granting the full ten years of re-accreditation, the college was cited for exceptional participation in community volunteerism.

Also in this category was the continuing achievement of the WVNCC Military Mail Call, which was number one among all the nation's colleges and universities for all five years of my administration and I believe several years before. In 2005, over 20,000 cards were sent to members of our military services, more than twice as many as the next closest college--which I believe was Notre Dame University.

These remarkable achievements of reaching out and giving belonged to the WVNCC students, but there was one staff member in particular whose leadership was indispensable. He was the Director of Student Activities, Don Chamberlain. Don was everywhere and did everything. He ran the sports program and participated with the students (in basketball he was usually a leading scorer). I felt honored when he called upon me to assist in student senate orientations; his orientation program was already excellent. At my request, he began to publish the student newspaper, "Northern Star."

In 2003, Don told me that he would like the college to sponsor the U.S. Flag Football National Championship. I was duly impressed with his ambition, and I knew he could do it. The games brought 28 teams and over 700 participants to the Northern Panhandle, first time in West Virginia. I loved Don's confidence and exuberance. He had a great ability to organize student leaders, which served him well because he had no professional staff assistants.

With pleasure, I remember how equally surprised Don was when I told him that we were going to build a gym on the Wheeling campus. It stunned him because he never expected to get free of using borrowed facilities for his program.

The only disagreement, soft, I had with Don concerned the college mascot adopted several years back—the "Thundering Chickens." It had received popular press at the time, but I felt that it lacked dignity, especially considering that we were going public with varsity basketball. However (life is full of howevers), the students voted to keep it, so I let it slide. I felt that the "Red Tail Hawk", a bird native to West Virginia, would have been a better choice, but (full of buts too) a president does not always get his way. At least we had some fun.

I had contributed over $25,000 to the College Foundation by the time I left. With that in mind I considered asking the Board to name the multipurpose center (gymnasium) in the new Education building in my honor, which I believe they would have done. But then I thought of Don and dissuaded myself.

I wish now that I had suggested naming it the Chamberlain-Hunter gymnasium in celebration of our synergic partnership. Every college needs these artifacts of identity.

There were some new faculty members who began to step up bringing new vitality to the co-curriculum: Delilah Board, Katie Freeman, Frank Decaria, Crystal Harbart ; I was delighted with these "recruits" because they brought the teaching-learning ethic I was always looking for. And there were three veteran faculty leaders -- Sandy Beck, Shirley Richlicki, Mark Goldstein -- who committed themselves to helping Phi Theta Kappa make a comeback on the three campuses.

This is also one of my fondest memories of my last presidency – watching this academic fraternity that I had favored throughout my career brilliantly revitalize its chapter at WV Northern. I enjoyed working with advisers and student officers as the Omega Epsilon chapter began to establish its prominence in the Ohio/WV region, winning Most Improved Chapter and several International Hallmark awards.

There were too many outstanding students to list them all here, but I will cite two who were exemplary of student leadership at its best:

The first is Mary Dudley, an older student with grown family, graduated in 2004 with AAS degree, elected regional president, and represented West Virginia as official flag bearer during opening ceremonies at Phi Theta Kappa's 2004 International Convention held in Minnesota. At that convention I was honored to receive Phi Theta Kappa's distinguished president award.

The second is Tina Cooper, worked a fulltime job and the mother of two children, whose classroom excellence earned her West Virginia's designation as New Century Scholar (only one award presented for each of the 50 states). Tina represented West Virginia at the 2003 AACC convention in Dallas.

I must also mention a Weirton retired citizen, Joseph E. Francis, who graduated in 2003 at the age of 79 years. Yes, a lot of community college students know that," you are never too old to learn."

My last reminisce of WVNCC: She was a black girl, I don't know if she was a student or part-time staff member, maybe both; I think her name was Gloria. I saw her in the parking lot as I was coming into the building, late for a meeting. She was obviously distraught, so I stopped to ask if I could be of assistance. She had lost her keys. We looked all over her walkway and parking space, but couldn't find them. So I was of no help to her, but next day I received a note from her that touched me with its charming sincerity. Apparently I had removed the stinger of her anxiety; someone had cared and that someone was the president. (P.S. She found her keys.)

**Commencement**

I did not allow an inauguration for any my four presidencies, but Commencement exercises were always a special occasion of celebration.

The following message at my final commencement was also published in the Register Wheeling News-Register and Weirton Daily Times: "Your Life Story"

Honored Graduates:

Three times I have stood where you stand today, and each time I remember commencement as an occasion of completeness---a positive mark on my personal record of goals achieved. At that stage of my life, when it was important to obtain credentials, I looked at life as a destiny to be created by intelligence, rational decisions and clear judgments. Life was a matter of choice.

As the years passed, I encountered pressures and problems I could not solve and began to realize, as Walt Whitman did, that even in the solution of problems there are the seeds of still greater problems. On the other hand, sometimes those new problems also carry the seeds of new ideas and possibilities. It began to occur to me that life is not according to my earlier rational vision. Rather, slowly I see, that each personal life is a story---not <u>like </u>a story---it <u>is</u> a story. And so I dare to suggest to you that the fundamental question confronting you on this occasion of your recognition is, "What is the story of my life? How does it unfold from here?"

The philosopher Alasdair MacIntyre writes, "The unity of a human life is the unity of a narrative quest." And, again, "I can only answer the question, 'what am I to do?' if I can answer the prior question, 'of what story or stories do I find myself a part?'" And yet again, "When someone complains that his or her life is meaningless, he or she is characteristically complaining that the narrative (the story) of their life has become unintelligible to them, that it lacks any point, any movement toward a climax. Hence the point of doing any one thing rather than another at crucial junctures in their lives seems to such a person to have been lost."

I believe the most profound task of education is to teach this narrative quest. As another philosopher, Victor Frankl, explains it, "man's search for meaning is the primary motivation in his life." This will to meaning is unique and specific in each one of us.

I congratulate you on your goal achieved. Undoubtedly, for you as it was for me, the credentials you have earned are important. But I also hope that you will take from this place in your life on understanding that new and different challenges lie ahead which are the next chapters in your story and can be woven meaningfully with all that has gone before.

There will be many more achievements for you, but there may also be disappointments, hardship, even sorrow. These need not defeat you. They are also the stuff of meaning. It is an illusion to think that life can be problem-free; what counts is how we react to problems. With this perspective , it is possible to weave the story in such a way as to be lifted out of those dark clouds which sometimes descend. Thereby, we evoke and deepen further our understanding of how life unfolds; "This is my story, this is my song; I was blind but now I see."

Finally, I would like to share with you at this point of departure the belief that we do not face challenges alone, however separate and existential our lives may seen. The victorious life becomes oriented to a sustaining source of power. Without this power to lean on, the man or woman is alienated. Whatever the power chosen goes far to create our personal stories.

Think of that children's game in which you look for a hidden picture, perhaps a face in a tree. If you look at it in one way, all you see is a tree, but if you change your perspective in the right way it becomes apparent that there is a face in the tree.

Education---this life-long process in which we are engaged---should help us to develop that perspective so that we see both the tree and the face. The face was there all along, of course. The picture never made sense without it.

I always concluded my commencement remarks with this scripture:

"Finally, my friends, whatsoever things are true, whatsoever things are honest, whatsoever things are just, whatsoever things are pure, whatsoever things are lovely, whatsoever things are of good report, if there be any virtue, and if there be any praise, think on these things." (Philippians IV)

# Cross Section of Letters and Memos

## To: J. David McCartney, Windbounds, Texas, January 28, 2001

Mac, I met an English professor here who has a precocious son -- in Princeton grad school at 17 -- which made me wonder about the professor. So I took him to lunch and we discussed the teaching of literature. He told me today's youth can't handle long novels, so Moby Dick is fading fast. Then I noticed Melville isn't on a list of the 100 greatest. I feel that I am becoming more alienated from current aesthetics. But then I discovered bluegrass in redneck country, wonderful, and our local symphony orchestra still performs Dvorck – – who always said that he was a peasant. So it is hard to judge. Where are we with real people?

The professor told me he is resigned to a remedial role but misses teaching literature. He can assign Conrad's *The Secret Sharer* because it's short, and he discusses John Updike. Well, again, I don't know what to make of that. I told the professor that I thought Updike's last line in his first novel, *Rabbit Run*, was perfect -- when Rabbit was running away finally from all responsibility -- "he runs, runs. Runs. Ah, runs." The professor nodded, but didn't say anything. What do you think?

## From: Judith U. Hoyt, Parent of WVNCC Student Rebecca L. Hoyt, May 12, 2003

I would like to say thank you for many things, I will start with your speech on graduation day. Thank you for your kind, caring and generous words to the students. My daughter was one of the graduates that day. I looked over at the most precious gift I had ever received and saw my little girl who had grown into a beautiful woman. I then realized my daughter was entering a world of many challenges and had just completed one of many.

I thank you for the support and guidance you have given to the students at WVNCC. I had the pleasure of meeting you a few times briefly. My first acquaintance with you was with Mr. Zervos the night the governor was visiting the school. The second time I met you was graduation night. Listening to your speech gave me a chance to understand why you are a well respected, positive influence in the many lives you encounter. You **are** a true advocate of education.

Thank you for your hard work and dedication, but most of all for believing in our children. You are most definitely a man of excellent leadership. Thank you for being a positive role model in my daughter's life as well as many others. God bless you always.

### From: Darryl Ruth, President, WVNCC Alumni Association, March 4, 2004

I speak for all Alumni Association members when I say that we are very pleased with the tremendous support that you continually give to the Association's activities. The most recent project, the Black History Month Celebration, is a wonderful example of your insight and your recognition of the importance of such events. As you know, the Alumni Board has set the goal of generating positive responses from the community that will reflect well on the college. Even though the Association has achieved that in the past, we have not always had the backing of past administrations. Your presence at these events and your personal support has meant a great deal to those of us who have worked so hard toward these ends. Therefore, I speak for all when I say we are very grateful for the recognition you continually give to the alumni.

Sincerely, Darryl

### From: Dorothy Jones, Professor of Psychology, May 25, 2005

Dr. Hunter, it is important to me that I express to you my appreciation of so many of your accomplishments during your time here at Northern. I'm sure I am not familiar with all of them, but what I know of is indeed remarkable. Much of what you have done was once said to be undoable. Most of *us* now see differently.

I must add that you have assisted me personally. You have demonstrated personal attributes and ways of dealing *with* people and situations that I will continue to emulate. Growth never ends and you have added to mine.

Dorothy Jones

**From: Daniel B. Crowder, Founding President, West Virginia Northern Community College, May 12, 2005**

Thanks for continuing to share **Liaisons** with me. From the latest edition, it is clear that you still have your capital development projects well on track. The progress Northern has made under your leadership during the past five years is truly remarkable, and the era will doubtless be remembered as one of the most significant in the history of the college. Your visionary insight, coupled with exceptional management skills, have made an indelible impact on the people of the upper Ohio Valley, and indeed the state of West Virginia. Those who have benefited, and will continue to benefit, from your service will doubtless remember you kindly in the years ahead.

In addition to progressive increases in student FTE, there have also been improvements in the curriculum, and governance structure, and doubtless in the overall morale of the community the college serves. As founding president I am grateful for all you have done to make West Virginia Northern a shining example of what an American community college can and ought to be. This was a dream widely shared by the founders of the school, and you have effectively carried that dream forward during the years that you have served.

In closing, I would also like to thank you for inviting my wife and me to the college's 30 year anniversary celebration, and for all the kindnesses you and your wife Lyla and your staff showed me and Wreatha during our visit in 2002. Dan Crowder

**Memo To: Terry Gernstein, Board of Directors, National Civil War Museum, January 10, 2006**

Terry, even though I am no longer in Wheeling I feel very badly about this. At WVNCC I pushed very strongly for the museum and felt that it was mainly a matter of communicating the vision. But now I'm not sure. The Governor's office shows no capacity for leadership in this project, which like you and Gary I felt was so compelling. Without commitment to a strategic financial plan from state leaders Wheeling's and seed money will not be enough to sustain momentum. So I think the project is in jeopardy on all fronts. I can't understand it, but certainly agree that the next Board meeting will be a decisive moment. I have suggested that Pres. Olshinsky replace me on the Board but have heard nothing back. I will stay committed to the Wheeling campus project as long as Gary does, but my frustration matches your own.

Best regards, John Hunter

### E-mail exchange: From Associate Dean Michael Stenger to Lyla Beth Hunter, July 5, 2006

Dear Lyla Beth, I was a student at Alfred State College. I have considered Dr. Hunter very fondly since I graduated in 1991. As time goes by we lose touch of important people in our lives. I would like to be able to write Dr. Hunter a letter of appreciation. Thank God I remembered that you were a singer, and sure enough with the wonder of technology I found your website.

Reply from Dr. Hunter: Michael, yes, I remember you and delighted to hear from you through Lyla Beth. I'm especially glad to know that you also went into higher ed administration. Up With People was a great program. I wonder if it still exists? Thank you very much for your kind comments, Michael.

Reply from Michael: Up With People still exists! They fell on tough times and closed doors. However it's back and will grow again. I have my 15 year reunion in Tucson, AZ next week-- and I cannot wait. I am very happy to get an e-mail from you. Can you believe that when we first knew each other we still had to write letters??

### From: Melissa Maher, President of Phi Theta Kappa chapter at WVNCC, August 17, 2007

Dear Dr. Hunter: I experienced your generosity as the 2007 Omega Epsilon chapter president of Phi Theta Kappa, and I wanted to take a moment to thank you for the president's stipend you provided. It certainly came in handy as I traveled to three Ohio regional events and the international convention in Nashville, TN. As you know, Phi Theta Kappa is an organization full of opportunities. I have grown in so many ways. Our chapter was able to make an impact on the community through our voluntarism, and many of our efforts were recognized in the Ohio region. I was named West Virginia's New Century Scholar, and I made the all USA academic team. I am sure that these accomplishments would not have been possible without my involvement with Phi Theta Kappa. Sincerely, Melissa

## Prayer for Nurse Pinning Ceremony

Almighty God, we thank you for this opportunity of coming together on this special occasion of recognizing our nursing graduates. We ask that this significant moment in the lives of these graduates shall be remembered and serve as a reminder of the best ideals of the nursing and teaching professions. In humility, Father, we recognize that our achievements and our lives, in order to be truly fulfilled, must draw upon love and reach toward your power and grace. Lead us according to thy truth and teach us, for you are the light that never goes out, you are the eye that never closes, you are the ear that is never shut, you are the mind that never gives up, you are the heart that never grows cold, and you are the hand that never stops reaching.

Niagara County Community College President and
Mrs. Ernest Notar with Mrs. Lyla Beth Hunter

First Officers of the NCCC Faculty Association - 1968
Jeanette Lencyk, Gern Jeager, and John Hunter

NCCC Deans: Norm Shea, John Hunter, and Pete Anderson

College of Lake County Board of Trustees - 1980
Left to Right Standing: James Welton (student), Nancy Block, Art Katzenmaier, Eleanor Rostron, Richard Anderson.  Seated: Milliceat Berliant (Vice-Chair), Jim  Lumber (Chairman).

Signing of Federal Contract to establish CLC Naval Training School at Great Lakes

Ground breaking for CLC Science building
Left to right: V.P. Vern Manke, V.P. Jim Doppke,
Waukegan Mayor Bill Morris, President Hunter

CLS Reception for Poet Laureates with Gwendolyn Brooks.

ASC College Council 1988-89

Governor Mario Como welcomed by Dick Lippert, College Council Chairman, and President Hunter.

During visit to Alfred, Governor Como surrounded by protestors against proposed low level radioactive site in Allegany Country.

Alfred State Cheerleading Team
1990 Campions

1992 Alfred State Black Student Union
Reception at President's House

Association of Women Officers at Alfred State College
Seated: Carol Woughter (Chair), Jeanne Lester, Lyla Beth Hunter
Standing: Kathy Lester, Sue Hunt

CLC Faculty with ITCA Colleagues, El Salvador - 1993

Inauguration of Alfred Farm Medic Center - 1992
Left to Right: Professor Richard Hoffman (Director),
Congressman Amo Houghton, and President Hunter

Lyla Beth & Dr. Hunter with Violetta Chamorro, President of Nicaragua, 1989.
Amo Houghton on left at Blair House, Washington DC.

Hosting John and Angie Ninos, Owners of Alfred's Collegiate Restaurant, "The Jet," with Fraternity/Sorority Leaders - 1993

*Albert R. Reynolds, Ph.D. ...Explaining HGA's role with CCACC*

**Charter Faculty Members Spring 1996**

Left to right: Dave Dillman, Marge Ulery, Sheri Shurin,
Lorraine James, Sandy Schrum, Dr. John Hunter,
Marilynn Danchanko, Dory Leahey, Don Shaver

CCACC Staff Party at VP Jim Wagner's House - 1999

**PETE VIZZA**/THE TRIBUNE-DEMOCRAT

John O. Hunter (second from right), retiring president of Cambria County Area Community College, is joined in a celebration at UPJ Sunday night by (from left), Joe Mangarella, CCACC board chairman; Lyla Beth Hunter, his wife; and state Rep. Edward P. Wojnaroski, D-Johnstown.

Garnet Persinger with Founding President and Mrs. Dan Crowder at
30th College Anniversary
2003

Commencement 2002
Honoring Darryl Ruth, Larry Bandi
CFO Banda was an early graduate of WVNCC

The Hunter Grandchildren Christine, AJ and TJ
at Dedication of Hunter Student Development Center

# CHAPTER VII

## *Burns and Yeats*

There are many names of poets and writers in these chapters, as well as many others who have impressed me during my career as an educator and to whom I am indebted because they have touched my soul in some way or brought me to a truth that I would not have discovered on my own. I gladly proclaim my allegiance .

If I were asked to make a list of the best, the names would vary on a given day, but two would always be at or near the top: Robert Burns and William Butler Yeats. Paying my respects to them in this brief outline I shall attempt to explain why.

When I go to Burns and Yeats, each will affect me in a different way and register for me in my hour something different to contemplate. Well, of course, that may be so about any writer. But these two draw me because of their life stories as well as the originality and distinction of their works. They are very separate in their lives yet bring to me an image of mutual elegance. Both were romanticists. Of the two, Burns was immediately closer to genius and more natural; Yeats was the superior lyricist and more mystical and binary both. Really it is foolish to try to compare them any further, but I would rather try to compare their greatness than to probe for their faults and weaknesses. To paraphrase another genius, "take them for all in all, we shall not look upon their likes again."

**Burns**

In the year 2000, the people of Scotland voted Robert Burns the greatest Scotsman who ever lived– – an extraordinary election considering the deeds and fame of so many Scots in world history. But such recognition is really minor to his true worth as a poet for the world.

The memory of Robert Burns has been fondly proclaimed at suppers on his birthday for the past 250 years. He is the only poet honored in this way; even Shakespeare does not get this annual attention.

In Burns' short turbulent life he produced poems now universally admired, published a book of poetry in the Scots dialect, thus preserving an ancient tongue, revised and wrote over 300 Scots songs, including what has become the world's anthem, *Auld Lang Syne*, wrote over 700 letters in superb standard English, including some of the most beautiful love letters ever written.

Even though he wrote mostly in Scots dialect, there are familiar Burns lines translated in many languages. Many of these lines are used by people in every day conversation without knowing who wrote them, just as they use Shakespeare and scriptural references. His lyrical legacy is all the more remarkable because many of his writings were inspired when he was working the land, filling a life of hardship which he described most aptly as, " the cheerless gloom of a hermit... with the unceasing toil of a galley slave."

Does it not make us wonder how a peasant farmer, who lived all his life in the harsh environment of Ayrshire, Scotland could leave us with such a magnificent body of literary works that continue to inspire people of every culture? What explains Robert Burns?

By the time he was 16, he had read his way through much of the classical literature – – Shakespeare, Alexander Pope, John Locke and Scottish poets who had preceded him – – and he learned Latin, all with not much more than a year of formal schooling. Yes, he was naturally bright, and he was a dedicated scholar, but that does not quite explain him.

The first key to understanding his growth and development is that he had been taught to read! Indeed, as with all boys of his age in Scotland -- unlike in other lands-- it was demanded of him by the church established during the Scottish Reformation led by the religious radical, John Knox, a preacher of truly terrifying power, who insisted that all boys (and girls) must be taught to read Holy Scripture and Knox's book of discipline. As a result, Scotland's literacy rate by the end of the 18th century would be the highest in all of Europe – – astonishing! In Burns' time Scotland was one of the poorest of countries, with a population of about two million people, yet the value placed on basic reading and writing for religious reasons turned it into a remarkably literate culture. What old John Knox did not foresee is that once an individual is taught to read, his mind is free, and he may begin to make his own decisions about what to read and write and think. The expression, "free to think for oursel's" has origins in Scotland.

And Burns pushed it to the limit, sometimes beyond, which would land him in trouble with the kirk or the court. Burns was always a beacon of controversy. As the saying goes, he was far ahead of his time. Among his immortal poems, "A Man's a Man" is one of the most powerful statements ever written on the fundamental dignity and integrity of all men everywhere.

> *What tho' on hamely fare we dine,*
> *Wear hodding grey, and a' that,*
> *Gie fools their silks, and knaves their wine—*
> *A man's a man for a' that.*
> *For a' that and a'that,*
> *Their tinsel show, and a' that,*
> *The honest man, tho' e'er sae poor,*
> *Is King o' men for a' that.* (Burns excerpt)

In the late 18th century when the ideal of individual freedom was still birthing, this poem was uniquely ennobling, verile and joyful -- but also revolutionary!

Nor did Burns neglect the majesty of women. Long before our shallow era of political correctness, at a time when Thomas Paine's revolutionary pamphlet, "The Rights of Man," was flooding Europe, Burns wrote his poem, "The Rights of Women."

Burns had a rare insight into the hearts and minds of his fellow Scots that he learned to apply to all people everywhere regardless of class distinctions or stations in society, rich or poor. Perhaps the best way to explain it is that he believed and lived by the words of our Declaration of Independence: *"All men are created equal, and are endowed by their Creator with certain unalienable rights."*

Burns had not much trust in government, but he was a true Scot, and vigorous, as his poems "Scots Wha Hae," " There'll Never Be Peace 'Til Jamie Comes Home," and even "Scotch Drink" testify.

Yes, Burns was a serious man -- a man of integrity and wisdom. But he was also a man who loved to party and " he dearly loved the lassies o".

> *Green grow the rashes, O;*
> *The sweetest hours that e'er I spend,*
> *Are spent among the lasses, O.*
> *Auld Nature swears, the lovely dears*
> *Her noblest work she classes, O.*
> *Her prentice han' she try'd on man,*
> *An' then she made the lasses, O.* (Excerpt)

Again we see the greater dignity and majesty he gives to women.

It's notable and interesting that among his critics— he had many—we cannot count any of the women he knew and loved. His love for women was sincere! and his ability to express his love, unequaled. Truly, he was capable of loving more than one woman at the same time, even though the circumstances often brought him torment. He said of himself that he was "possessed by a social and amorous madness." Or we could simply say that he had an intensely romantic spirit. And so he gave us " love at its sweetest, love at its saddest, love beyond realization."

Jean Armour/Burns was the steady love in Burns' life to the end. She accepted his 'sins' and it was to her he always returned. Jean bore him nine children.

Robert Burns died too soon, much too soon-- he knew that himself—he died at the age of 37. He told his wife at the end, "Don't be afraid: I'll be more respected in 100 years after I am dead than I am now." He was not and does not need to be made into a poet superhero, but through his poems and songs he brought wisdom and grace that made him a legend in his time and likely will continue on for many generations to come.

I grew up in a Scottish family. My parents and grandparents and uncles and aunts on both sides were all Scots from a long line of Scots. Perhaps this is a reason I admire Burns , but I would rather think it is because I recognize his profound insight to the human condition and his ability immediately to turn a rhyme. But what surpasses all a' that and a'that is that he was a wonderful human being. I say this not as a scholar of Burns but as a friend I have come to know. For truth is in the heart as well as in the mind.

*********************************

**Yeats**

William_Butler Yeats was born in Dublin, Ireland into a sophisticated but not wealthy Anglo- Irish family well known in art and religious circles. His grandfather, the Rev. William Butler Yeats(1806 – 1862) was a very orthodox rector of the Church of Ireland. His father, John Butler Yeats (1839 – 1922) was a complete skeptic, rejecting religious belief entirely, fiercely intellectual, and a prominent artist. Yeats' younger brother, Jack, was also a well-known painter.

Yeats, the poet, was influenced both positively and negatively by his father. Out of his own need for belief in revelation and a higher power, he rejected his father's intellectual skepticism but he did not turn back to his grandfather's church.

He was a dramatist as well as a poet, having only partial success with his plays and stories which ironically occupied the greater portion of his time. His poems are immortal. I think of him as the Mozart of poetry. His metaphorical imagery is clear, crystalline, sometimes hard, sometimes soft, often brilliant.

There are two convoluted terms that we need to get a start on understanding Yeats. These are "dialectical thinking" and "antinomies". Essentially, the "dialectic" is the notion that for every force(thesis), there is a counter force(anti- thesis), but these opposites can move us to a higher plain(synthesis)."Antinomies" are contradictions between inferences or principles that seem equally necessary and reasonable.(To a hardened rationalist, it may be unseemly that Truth should act in this way, but She does.)

These combine as the best description of Yeats' approach in all his roles-- as poet, dramatist, theater founder and director, Irish Senator and political leader (reluctantly undertaken), Nobel Laureate, and lecturer of world renown. His thought was profoundly dialectical. For every truth he looked for a counter-truth-- a truth that contradicted the first truth.

Yeats blamed himself for being too shy, yet he was always ready for conflict. He loved going into debate. If it were possible to engage him, he would expect you to present a strong case. If you did not, in the end he might frame it for you.

Truth and beauty in the end are all that matter, and they are always elusive. Knowing that all that is known fights with all that is unknown and that he could not avoid combat, Yeats' stance was always heroic--Promethean-- even facing certain defeat. His tenacity sprang from a strong belief in the value of Celtic tradition and his commitment to heroic art. He worked through his philosophy and belief to creative, mystical vision.

He tried to create his own religion, resorting to various occult forms, including his wife's automatic writing. This fascinating effort is most reflected in his long prose piece, "The Vision," published finally in 1926 at his age of 61.

In the end, Yeats failed in his quest for a spiritual framework. He failed in my view for the reasons that Alexander Solzhenitsyn articulated many years later in his Nobel address: an artist who attempts to create an independent spiritual world simply "breaks down… because no mortal man, even a genius, is capable of bearing such a burden-- the whole irrationality of Art, it's blinding convolutions, it's unpredictable discoveries, it's shattering impact on people, are too magical to be exhausted by the philosophy of anyone artist."

With enormous creative energy, Yeats throughout his life, even more passionately in old age, pursued this impossibility. Yet where he may have failed philosophically in his system, he created a body of poems of the greatest power and beauty. They are nothing less than miraculous in their aesthetic revelation. In my opinion, *The Wild Swans at Coole* is the most beautiful lyrical poem ever written.

Yeats was romantically and politically involved with Maud Gonne for most of his life. Maud Gonne was six feet tall and beautiful-- some said the greatest beauty in Ireland-- of regal bearing, politically very intense. She was a passionate and fearless speaker and campaigner. Yeats thought that she could be Ireland's Joan of Arc. In the Victorian age, long before women's liberation, she was indeed a liberated woman.

He first met Maud when he was 23. At 25 he proposed to her and she refused him. At 33 he proposed to her again and she refused him. When he was 37, Maud married John McBride, an equally intense revolutionary. Yeats was stunned. However, the marriage lasted only two years.

Yeats had other love affairs and many women as friends, but it was always Maud Gonne to whom he returned. She favored him frequently with letters expressing devotion to their spiritual love but warned against seeking physical consummation. But Maud played a double game: during the years of her "spiritual marriage" to Yeats, she carried on a secret relationship with a French politician and had two illegitimate children.

His unrequited love for Maud is woven in different ways into many of Yeats' love poems. Years later they did have a sexual encounter-- and he was disappointed.

Politically, Yeats was a "right winger." His problem with Maud was that she was too radical for him. For Maud, Yeats lacked the manly militancy of other comrades such as Major John McBride, far less talented and in the end far less heroic. All three believed in the Irish nationalist movement, but Yeats was too much of the poet rejecting violence to be a revolutionary fighter. Still he could not escape becoming involved in the politics of Ireland and England during the phases of Home Rule for Ireland, then the Easter Rebellion of 1916, and the ensuing struggle for complete independence. Throughout this period, he demonstrated that he was on top of the issues but also how conflicted he was by the violence.

He felt some sympathy for the good intentions behind England's Home Rule effort, but it vanished after the defeat and disgrace of Parnell, the Irish statesman about whom Yeats wrote some poems. Yeats saw that the blood of Easter 1916 tragically changed everything:

> *All's changed, changed utterly:*
> *A terrible beauty is born.*

Murder, rape and mayhem descended upon Ireland. Yeats' poem, *Nineteen Hundred and Nineteen*, is a devastating political comment. He writes of an incident of a murdered mother that happened in Yeats' neighborhood. But this poem also includes a stanza highly critical of the Irish revolutionaries:

> *We who seven years ago—*
> *spoke of honor and of truth*
> *shriek with pleasure if we show*
> *the weasel's twist, the weasel's tooth.*

The political poems show how torn Yeats was in his loyalties: he is an Irish nationalist

--he loves Ireland -- but he also loves England because it is in his blood.

In 1919, when Ireland was in Civil War and World War I was raging in Europe, Yeats' vision turned apocalyptic. The result was a poem of great power -- *The Second Coming*-- one of the most remarkable poems ever written, with lines marmolean and unforgettable that seem to fit every generation:

> *The blood- dimmed tide is loosed, and everywhere*
> *The ceremony of innocence is drowned;*
> *The best lack all conviction, while the worst*
> *Are full of passionate intensity...*

When Yeats was 52 he married Georgie Hyde Lees, 25 years old, and entered into the most surprising period of his life. His wife understood him well and he fell deeply in love with her. She bore him a daughter and a son. Most surprising of all was the automatic writing that he depended upon from his wife for description of his system in *The Vision*, which he worked on from 1917 to 1931. It is difficult to understand why he felt so compelled by this occult endeavor.

The deep inner conflict continued to the end of his life. Yet he was steady in his political and literary commitment, and did not lose his capacity for love. He died in 1939 at age 73, having written his own epitaph. Last lines:

> *Cast a cold eye*
> *On life, on death.*
> *Horseman, pass by!*

But I would rather part from Yeats by citing this passage from his mystical meditation,

*Per Amica Silentia Lunae*

*We must not make a false faith by hiding from our thoughts the causes of doubt, for faith is the highest achievement of the human intellect, the only gift man can make to God, and therefore it must be offered in sincerity. Neither must he create, by hiding ugliness, a false beauty as our offering to the world. He only can create the greatest imaginable beauty who has endured all imaginable pangs, for only when we have seen and foreseen what we dread shall we be rewarded by that dazzling, unforeseen, wing footed wanderer. We could not find him if he were not in some sense of our being , and yet of our being but as water with fire, a noise with silence. He is of all things not impossible the most difficult, for that which comes easily can never be a portion of our being; soon got, soon gone, as the proverb says. I shall find the dark grown luminous, the void fruitful when I understand I have nothing, that the ringers in the tower have appointed for the hymen of the soul a passing bell.*

# VALUE NOTES TO YOUNG FRIENDS

Introductory Comment: I remember sitting alone in a Rome coffee shop trying to advance a paper on "productivity in higher education" which was overdue when I looked out the window and noticed a band of young people, probably high schoolers, lounging against a lamp post and parking meters. There were two girls and two boys in normal conversation. Then

another boy appeared across the street. Immediately, in a wave of exultation, all four called to him. He crossed over and it was like a lost friend had brought a gift of joy. Why they were all so delighted I do not know, but the scene had transformed from mundane to radiant. I sat mesmerized for a few minutes, then tried to get back to my paper---to hell with it---then began one of my Letters to Young Friends----I don't remember which.

I wrote these letters and notes usually on a Sunday evening, often in a coffee shop. This was work done obliquely, "do the deed shall breed the thought", which I secretly enjoyed, more than the required dictation I gave on Monday morning. Sometimes the need for more research would take part of the work week---a distraction but not unwelcome.

Reprinted here are 31 articles selected from over 150 published for college students during my years as college president.

1. The Girls of Tehran
2. Artificial Intelligence and the Singularity Part I
3. Artificial Intelligence and the Singularity Part II
4. Artificial Intelligence and the Singularity Part III
5. Alcohol and Co-dependence
6. Getting Real
7. Free Speech
8. Young and Reckless Behavior in a Declining Culture
9. Abortion
10. Marijuana
11. Reality Testing
12. The Bad Example of Professional Athletes
13. Facing Violence
14. Dinesen's Wisdom
15. Power of Love
16. Paradoxical Reality
17. Mimophantry
18. Mythical Reality
19. Soldierization
20. Professor Bloom's Critique of Relativism
21. Misbegotten Respect for Suicide Bombers
22. Lifting Lenin's Curse
23. Tiananmen Square
24. Solzhenitsyn
25. Celebrating Martin Luther King, Jr.
26. A Lesson From George Washington
27. A Personal Tribute to John Paul II

## The Girls of Tehran

I remember the Chinese students in Tiananmen Square twenty years ago. The Tiananmen revolt failed because the Chinese government was willing to use brutal methods of suppression combined with the timely economic expansion that began to create a rising middle class. Newspaper sources reported that over 3000 protesters were massacred. There was no possibility that the young revolutionaries could gain power despite the justice of their cause and their courage.

Is there a similar situation now unfolding in Iran? Whatever the outcomes we are witnessing a major historic event that demonstrates yet again the universal hold, especially on young people, of desire for liberty and justice. The young Iranians are the young Chinese are the young East Europeans are the young Africans, and further back the young Americans, expressing values of integrity and dignity that are instinctoid and are not washed away when their blood flows.

I think what makes the Iranian experience of 2009 different than our own revolution of the late 18th century is the central role of moral leadership taken by young Muslim women. Even when the male leaders retreat they hold their ground-- these are the girls of Tehran!

What is the reason and source of their defiance? Is it because they lost the most when the theocracy was created after the fall of the Shah and have the most to gain from its acquiescence to reasonable demands for reform and accountability? We have only glimpses of what these girls endure in their daily lives under a despotic theocratic regime.

In the streets it is best that they not be seen nor heard, keeping eyes focused on the ground, not daring to look at passersby. Azar Nafisi, author of "Reading Lolita in Tehran" (2003), explains that the streets are patrolled by militia called the Blood of God to make sure that women wear their veils properly, do not wear makeup, and do not walk in public with men who are not their fathers, brothers or husbands. At any moment they may be hurled into a patrol car, taken to jail, flogged, forced to wash toilets and humiliated in other perverse ways -- for their own education and protection. The humiliation of women stems from new sharia law that lowered the age of marriage from 18 to 9, reinstated stoning as punishment for adultery and prostitution, as well as other offenses not clearly defined.

In a recent case, the Iranian painter Delara Darabi, 22 years old and in prison since she was 17, accused of murdering an elderly relative, was hanged even though she had been given a temporary stay of execution by the Chief Justice. The British journalist Yasmin Alibhai-Brown reported, "She phoned her mother on the day of her hanging to beg for help and the phone was snatched by a prison official who said, 'we will easily execute your daughter and there's nothing you can do about it.' ..." Mother, I can see from my window the scaffold where they are going to hang me." Darabi's paintings reveal the cruelty to which she was subjected.

Domestic violence is a serious problem in all countries, but in Iran and some other Muslim countries it is validated by laws. There have been enlightened times when Muslim civilizations respected and honored females. Apparently this is not such a time in Iran. The Ayatollahs have induced a culture of hatred of women.

Some of us in the West have wondered why Muslims conceal or condone the persecution and violence against women and other backward practices? Why do some Muslim women seek to justify honor killings, forced marriages, polygamy and childhood betrothals?

Except that now we have the brave girls of Tehran! Against the massive forces of paranoia, cruelty and legally validated persecution and violence against women, they are stepping up to the front lines and declaring their opposition. Can they win anything? The possibility may seem remote, but they are telling us that this is not a time for hopelessness and despair.

From the tragedy of Hungary in 1956, to the Praque uprising to the Czech "Velvet Revolution," to the collapse of the Soviet Union, fundamental change succeeded despite enormous odds against it -- much due to the words of peace-bound literary leaders such as Vaclav Havel, Solzhenitsyn, and John Paul II. In her account of the struggle of women in Iran, Azar Nafisi adds to this power of literature -- not propaganda, Truth.

Currently in America it seems that we are struggling to find national consensus on our values in a time of complex negotiations with dictators and of our inability to recognize evil in the world even when it is clear for all to see. The meretricious argument of moral equivalency too easily prevails.

What is required for America to stand in support of the Iranian revolution? It is not a question of interference but of whether or not we shall continue to express the principles, ideals and aspirations that were crucial in the founding of our own nation and that have made America the best hope for a devastated world that again needs our example. Shall we be brave enough to stand alongside these young Iranians?

JOH : 7/10/2009

## Artificial General Intelligence and the Singularity (Part I of III)

Even though I place major priority on the value discussions in my "Letters to Young Friends", my spirit tells me that this is the most important Letter that I can offer for young people today. It is intended as a warning, a challenge and a reassurance of your ability not only to survive but to prevail in the exciting time of exponential change now upon us. I will begin by explaining my own interest in the subject, then asking you to respond in your own way.

When I was Dean at Niagara Community College in the late 1960s I joined the World Future Society and became an active member. By the late 1970s I had grown disillusioned with the Society's agenda and dropped out. I thought then that preoccupation with artificial intelligence was a wrong footed approach to invention of the future.( I have since humbly changed my mind.) But it was through that association that I first became aware of the significant differences between linear growth and exponential growth.

The lesson of exponential growth is well captured in the description of a lily pond which may grow plants at a seemingly innocent rate, doubling each day until half the pond is covered. The next doubling suddenly covers the entire pond. That is exponential growth. The effect has proven time and again in various activities, such as a bank savings account in which a 21-year-old puts aside $2,000 per year, never touches it and finds a yield of a million dollars when he retires at age 65.

The significance of technological change that is now occurring exponentially is outlined by the brilliant computer scientist and forecaster, Raymond Kurzweil, in "the law of accelerating returns". For an immediate penetrating description of Kurzweil's work go to the web and click on, *The Singularity Is Near*. A film based on Kurzweil's book of this title is now in production with a pledge of release in late 2009.

In a very creative example of why and how we now stand on the verge of the most transformative period in human history, the film uses a computer avatar named Ramona who gradually acquires self awareness. Ramona detects a secret attempt by microscopic robots (nano-bots) to destroy the world. Although her warnings are ignored because "she is not a person", she nevertheless stops the robot attack by virtue of her superior artificial intelligence.

While most people may be aware of sci-fi depictions of AI creations in movies such as Matrix, The Terminator, or I Robot ( from Isaac Asimov) few are aware of the broader significance of AI in all phases of human endeavor. A few examples:

*I am using Dragon software to dictate this article (a great help to me because I was never very good at typing); but even more sensational are INTERACT programs which allow us to converse fluently with someone in China even though we do not speak Chinese and our Chinese friend does not speak English.

*Carnegie Mellon University's school of computer science has a car, Ralph, that can drive itself.

*One of Kurzweil's inventions is a machine reader for the blind; another is the Kurzweil Synthesizer which accurately duplicates the sounds of real instruments.

*Cisco Collaboration Technologies is creating a set of computational tools for artificial intelligence that can be used to do things like predicting traffic jams, improving machine vision, and understanding the way cancer spreads.

*A computer mind chip that gives an individual immediate access to his own library."

These examples are certainly not mundane but they are at the low level of AI possibilities, pretty much already taken for granted--like our "Tom-Tom's-- because we are moving on so rapidly, from narrow AI to Artificial General Intelligence.

Ray Kurzweil and others now see the coming of self-aware machines of superintelligence within the next 30 to 40 years, perhaps sooner. This will happen because of the event of technological singularity. Kurzweil defines the Singularity as a coming epoch, almost upon us, in which the pace of technological change will be so rapid, its impact so deep, that human life will be irreversibly transformed. "Although neither utopian nor dystopian, this epoch will transform the concepts that we rely on to give meaning to our lives, from our business models to this cycle of human life, including death itself."(Kurzweil)

We are now beginning to reach the "knee of the exponential curve", which is the stage when the exponential trend becomes noticeable. Then the trend quickly becomes explosive. And the curve shoots straight up.

Kurzweil believes that the Singularity will represent " the culmination of the merger of our biological thinking and existence with our technology, resulting in a world that is still human but transcends our biological roots." He expects thinking machines to pass the "Turing test"--meaning its nonbiological intelligence will be indistinguishable from our biological intelligence by 2029. The nonbiological intelligence will be millions of times more powerful than our own unaided intelligence.

What are the implications of such astounding development if it occurs? How shall we learn to live with these machines? Is there much to fear from them, as Asimov's story suggests? Or in considering the "nanobots" of Ramona's story are we in danger of destroying our world by allowing nanotechnology to proceed with the development of these microscopic self-replicating mechanical structures? Will we lose control of the development of the New Creation? Is all of this fantastic discovery and invention playing God? What are the possibilities--and consequences—of a neo-Luddite attempt to halt the drive to the Singularity? Are Kurzweil and other singularitarians wrong in the first place as some critics argue?

These are premier questions and issues of your future. Will you be a singularitarian--or an informed critic-- or an "AI detective"? In part two of this series of "Letters" I shall attempt to provide a framework for discussion.

Letter to Young Friends ( April 10, 2009)

## Artificial Intelligence and the Singularity (Part II of III)

Throughout my career as an educator I kept my graduate association with the US Army Artillery School in Oklahoma. During my last visit there, I saw a tall, broad shouldered Sergeant walking down a stair -- with an artificial leg! I was stunned, and I believe you will see the significance. In conversation with him I learned that he was preparing to go back to Iraq as a functioning squad leader. The prosthetic device he is using is driven by microprocessors at each joint, just one of many new applications that permit amputees who previously would have been unable even to lead normal civilian lives now to return to the battlefield. In one sense the Sergeant is a special soldier, yet in a broader context of how our Army is developing he is not extraordinary.

U.S. Army Research, in conjunction with DARPA, is working on a "super warrior", 10 of which would be equivalent to today's brigade. They will have an exoskeleton that allows them to carry 180 pounds as though it were 5 pounds, run and leap like track stars, and will be plugged into a Pentagon grid. Add this new hardware capacity to predator drones that already exist. Combine this with new "smart" artillery which is deadly accurate and very fast. Yet even these recent developments pale in comparison with the robot army coming.

In this new era the military robots will have the intelligence to make battlefield decisions that presently belong to humans. They will have significant cognitive advantages over human soldiers. Herein lies the danger that the US office of Naval Research is now seriously considering. The perception that robots will only do what humans have programmed them to do falls apart in at least two ways: It fails to take account of artificial intelligence becoming Artificial General Intelligence; second, that programs are no longer written and understood by a single person. There are teams of programmers, none of whom know the entire program so no one can predict how large programs will interact without testing in the field -- an action unavailable to designers of military robots.

This does not mean that the robots cannot learn a warrior code, just as our human soldiers have done through superb training.(See my Letter on "Soldierization".) But it will be a dramatic undertaking and immensely important to develop the ethical dimension if we are to avoid the peril projected by Asimov in his story "I, Robot". Can this be done? Probably but not certainly. Could we simply stop the development entirely? Perhaps but not likely.

The dilemma posed here is but one of several in a future of continuing exponential growth -- ironically, dilemmas which may depend on non-biological super intelligence to solve. The compelling likelihood is that in your full maturity you shall either learn to coexist with subservient robots and conscious machines or face a battle for survival against these super intelligent machines turned psychotic. Do not be afraid! Face the existential fact that life is a challenge! The odds for positive outcomes are high.

The AI fantasies imagined by science-fiction writers have not materialized (not yet at least), but AI is already in more common usage than many of us realize. As Nick Bostrom (another AI scientist) has pointed out, AI inspired systems are already integral to many everyday technologies such as Internet search engines, bank software for processing transactions, software for large inventories, and in medical diagnosis. "A lot of cutting-edge AI has filtered into general applications, often without being called AI because once something becomes useful enough and common enough it's not labeled AI anymore." (Bostrom)

My generation has exemplified adaptation to rapid technological change, even those of us who are not technically savvy. Consider these developments of the past 30 years: the Personal Computer (as college president I first authorized expenditure for one TRS 80 in 1978); then ability to communicate greatly enhanced by fax machines in the late 1980s; and then the Internet, invented by US government but exploited tremendously by entrepreneurs in the private sector. At the same time on the bionic front, I know a man with two artificial knees and two artificial hips; the quality of his life is far beyond what it could have been 50 years ago.

As computers became more powerful they also became correspondingly less expensive to own and smaller in the bargain; in the near future they will look like pens that we carry in our pockets. Now it is almost standard that everyone has access to a computer. Of course there are issues (e.g. loss of privacy), but we learned to adapt and adjust in relatively easy fashion. Our world changed and we changed with it. But there is a dialectic at work here too: we ordinary people did not see much of this change coming; we are like passengers facing backwards on a train hurtling with ever greater speed into the future.

What my generation has experienced is mild on the growth curve compared with what your generation shall see. The issues will become much more profound, going to the very heart of what it means to be human. The first question is, can a machine with nonbiological intelligence become self-conscious? Kurzweil, Bostrom and other Singularitarians are convinced beyond doubt that such an event will occur during your lifetime. If so, how can humans ensure that these super intelligent machines are benevolent allies of humankind? What strategies and policies need to be considered now in order to ensure that the relationships between humans and machines will be positive? What are the prospects for -- and the potential consequences -- of trans-humanism, the merging of machines and humans in the same entity? Where is God in the equation for whatever shall evolve?

If we view the dangers as too great to allow continuing technological development along these lines presented, what are our options? Can we stop these trends? I would argue, citing Kurzweil, Bostrom and other AI scientists as well as their critics, that we may indeed modify our directions of development in the sense that we have always played a role in our evolution, but that the evidence is too overwhelming contrarily to think that we can, or should, place extreme barriers in the path of science and technology as it seeks to discover how Intelligence is flooding our world.

So far in human history, science and technology have steadily advanced, sometimes with quantum leaps. Yes, there are also wrong moves and stoppages. A recent example of the latter is a worsening of famine in Africa due to the movement opposing genetically modified food. In Africa and Central and South America people starving or on the edge of starvation are asked to give up the promise of expanding their food supply by elitist organizations for ideological reasons.

Science also has a natural overarching capability to go around irrational obstacles. The long-term trend of technological innovation is perpetual advancement. As Ray Kurzweil put it, "Only technology can provide the scale to overcome the challenges with which human society has struggled for generations. Emerging technologies will provide the means of providing and storing clean and renewable energy, removing toxins and pathogens from our bodies and the environment, and providing the knowledge and wealth to overcome hunger and poverty."

It is often said that education is preparation for the future. So what is your best preparation? This is just my opinion-- you must decide that on your own-- but in whatever field you find yourself I commend you to become an "AI detective" Look for the pros and cons, the dangers and potential benefits of emerging technology. You do not need to be a Singularitarian, but as an educated person you should have awareness of what this term means. Whatever your major, find a way to explore through electives in the liberal arts and sciences, such as biotechnology, nanotechnology, cognitive science, and philosophy of ethics (Kant) and aesthetics. In all of your coursework, strive to develop a positive but critical frame of mind. And if there are moments when the load becomes too much to bear, "choose something like a star... to stay the mind upon."(Frost)

Letter to Young Friends (April 15, 2009)

## Artificial Intelligence and the Singularity (Part III of III)

When the Singularity comes, as I believe it will when you are in your mid-40s, another great leap in the evolutionary process will change our world (and potentially the universe) in a manner similar to the human species becoming self-aware aeons ago. When that was exactly we cannot know, but it was then that God created us in his image, not physically but spiritually, with a capacity for moral choice and creative design.

Whether or not our new self-aware creations -- Thinking Machines -- will have a soul is a subject of debate in the community of Artificial Intelligence scientists. The level of intelligence that they will bring is also debatable but most projections place it much higher than our own. There is an important difference between our evolution and theirs: we did not create ourselves, but we are the agents creating these machines, at least until such time as they supersede us in their replication. In this sense we are a partner in the evolutionary process. I believe this is how God works.

But wait! Let's stop for a moment to reflect on what we mean in reference to God. First, God the Creator: The Primary Cause-- the architect of the universe -- did not need to be concerned about humankind, and in my view likely was not concerned, when He fashioned the laws by which the universe is governed. I believe in the power of prayer, but I do not believe that the Creator left a loophole for our whims of the moment to intervene in His creation without reference to the grand design about which we know very little. God is almighty, but insofar as the physical universe is concerned, not particularly benevolent.

But evolution is not just physical; it is also spiritual. With the emergence of the human soul there is a different sort of Deity which begins to express itself, not to spare humankind from "the problem of evil" but to provide guidance, compassion and the healing power of love. In our conscience and experience we can find the highest, noblest expression of this love. In the words of St. John, *"the Word was made flesh, and dwelt among us, and we beheld His glory, the glory of the only begotten of the Father, full of grace and truth."*

I would agree with those who contend that this belief can only be taken on faith. Yet there is a distinction between God as Creator, indifferent to our needs on this tiny planet, and God as Love, who will not leave us to face our trials alone. The mystery of the difference between physical evolution and spiritual evolution is magnified by its receding dialectical nature and the upending unity of all forces--the "all in all" of Christ --from material substance to spirit--from brute existence to self-awareness to the power of love.

Yet, again, hold on: on what basis can we believe these things? Is it science, or philosophy? I will contend for, and urge you to think seriously about, a new ground being formed which authentically combines science and faith in the invention of the brave new world through artificial intelligence. Faith in a loving God left out of the equation for guidance and wisdom is an omission potentially devastating.

If you are still with me you probably are wondering what all this has to do with artificial intelligence. Let us expand the term to " artificial general intelligence ,"and then the idea of unification has a lot to do with it. First, as I pointed out earlier in this series, artificial intelligence has been with us for more than four decades in ways we now take for granted; but no machine has yet passed the "Turing test" designed to determine if the machine could " think" like a human. When this point of technological singularity is reached--now well on the way--the exponential change curve goes straight up from specific/mundane to general. "When you have an AI system that can assist in the design of improved versions of itself you could go overnight to something radically superintelligent."(Bostrom) This shall be the next great flashpoint of evolution.

Unity is our watchword in dealing with artificial general intelligence -- unity of human beings and superintelligent machines. I am not thinking of trans-humanism here (although some AI experts like Kurzweil envision that kind of development), but obviously our challenge as creators will be to help ensure that intimate loyalty is structured into the "soul" of these machines, not simply as an "Asimov rule," but as part of a mutually held moral and ethical consciousness given to us by God.

Can a machine understand its human origins, its history ? Even more charismatic, can a machine become aware of God's presence? It remains to be seen. But there are ample reasons to believe that, aided by superintelligence, humankind may reach a higher ground, spiritually and materially, than we have ever known before. This is your ultimate challenge.

Letter to Young Friends (May1, 2009) Last in AI series.

## Alcohol and Co-dependence

Co-dependence is a disease of the soul. It can afflict anyone who lives with or loves someone who is addicted to alcohol or drugs. Just as an alcoholic is dependent on others to keep the addiction going until death, the co-dependent feels bound to meeting that person's needs. Eventually, it affects the co-dependent in all his/her relationships. The co-dependent may become addicted to a substance, too, but co- dependence is an addiction to destructive relationships.

A co-dependent person may have a fear of rejection, thus easily become victimized. Other traits of co-dependence include frozen feelings, anxiety, excessive delusion/denial, low self-esteem, even self-hatred. It is a fatal disease, but it can be diagnosed and treated as a mental health problem. The Twelve Steps of Healing process used by Alcoholics Anonymous for treatment of alcohol addiction has also proven effective for co-dependence.

In a dysfunctional family, particularly where alcohol or drugs are abused, the likelihood of young members becoming co-dependent is high. These are some of the rules in a dysfunctional family which can lead to co-dependence:

"It's not okay to talk about problems."

"It's not okay to express feelings openly."

"You must be strong, good, right and perfect."

"Do what you are told, not what you see."

The Twelve Steps program of Alcoholics Anonymous (Al-Anon) is easy to understand. I believe the twelve steps harbor three principles that are normative in human experience:

1. The truth of the Orestean Myth: We must accept responsibility for our actions.

2. Belief in a "power greater than ourselves." God is gracious to those who make the leap of faith. (The Al-Anon reference is to God as you understand him.)

3. Spirituality as a liberating force in our lives: Once discovered or re-discovered, spirituality fosters forgiveness, healing, health.

The Al-Anon approach and the emerging field of Co-Dependence theory and treatment are focused on the health of the whole person, including spiritual health. The Al-Anon reference to "A Power Greater Than Ourselves" is of a transcendent God, however we may define him/her. Such reference does not deny freedom of religion or compromise the standard of church-state separation, but it does frankly recognize spirituality, including belief in a transcendent God, as a dimension of human existence.

The Al-Anon program is all about power. Its vitality with the individual patient depends upon his/her recognition of how powerful alcohol is and what a threat it is to life itself. Since there is a power even greater, there is the hope for an intervention that would replace the destructive power of alcohol with the loving power of God. This is clearly a personal God while, at the same time, there is considerable room for personal religious or spiritual preferences and inclinations. Still, the method would not work if the God did not care about the person who is afflicted. Some step of faith is necessary.

This faith step consists of both personal belief - acceptance of a power greater than ourselves - and trust - commitment - or surrender to that power. This step of faith rekindles hope and leads on to further spiritual awakening as grace is received.

The field of co-dependence theory has shed light on the deepest and most pervasive problems of student life. Since co-dependence is rooted in dishonesty, the remedy is in truth. These are truths that every one of us may claim:

*I am a child of God. I have an equal share of personal integrity and dignity. My worth comes from my identity, not from what I do. It's okay for me to ask for help if I need it. I can accept responsibility for my own actions. I am free to express my feelings. I am capable of love.*

Note: This article is an edited version of one Dr. Hunter published in College Student Journal, "Exploring Co-Dependence and Spirituality in College Student Life", December 1992.

**Getting Real**

I've been thinking about this topic for a long time, ever since I sat in an intense conversation among students sorting out a problem. One guy was making the case - not lying exactly, but distorting the issue, making more of it than it deserved. Another student sat listening for a while then turned to him and said, "Get real, man!"

I liked that - a whole lot! For me, it lifted the problem to a fresh level and really got my attention.

The thing was, everybody understood, immediately. The second guy was saying, "Let's get to the heart of this matter which deserves serious consideration, but we can only make progress if we keep it in perspective and balance the pro's and con's; then maybe we can see clearly enough to make a whole where now things are fractured." It was all there in that simple admonition: "Get real!"

I don't think that advice can be much improved upon, but since it's my nature and role to philosophize about what I learn from students, I would like to offer a follow-up.

What this was all about is called "integrity," which is a universal (or normative) value. By "universal" I mean that all people everywhere share the desire for integrity in their lives. Even hardened criminals in prison will seek to measure behavior according to a code of integrity.

Integrity is the striving for authenticity and wholeness within our inner being.

It is matched in human values of the highest order by "dignity," i.e., believing in our own dignity, we are made able to believe in the dignity of others.

Dignity is the reliance upon the uniqueness of our personality and its entitlement to respect.

The value of integrity may be applied not only to the individual person but to the elements of an organization and the organization as a whole. In your activities, you represent the integrity of your school, for example. Dignity, on the other hand, is purely personal.

Now, of course, universality does not mean that these values are sacrosanct and always upheld. You may say, "this sounds fine, but I know some people who are dishonest to the core, they would steal from their mother blind. Where is their sense of integrity?"

Yes, anyone of us can violate our own integrity or fail to respect the integrity and dignity of others. (When we do, it's usually with regret, right?) Then, too, rationalization comes into play. We have a great capacity for self-delusion.

Because of these and sociological differences among people in different parts of the world, there are social scientists who dispute the notion of any absolutes beneath the relative. "Everything is relative" is their tired watchword.

But for those who are open to see, the evidence is clear that, despite our tendency to be sinners and scoundrels at times, there is a reverberating call, both immanent and transcendent, for the observance of the integrity and dignity of all human kind.

Within each one of us and bigger than all of us together, there is a God saying, "Get real!"

JOH: 1992

**Love of Truth**

*"Truth is so obscure in these times, and falsehood so established, that unless we love the truth we cannot know it."* (Pascal)

How do we know the truth of anything? Some philosophers tell us that truth is totally subjective. Another way of putting this argument is that we do not live in the world: we live in a picture or vision of it that we have formed. Others say that truth is external and objective, to be discovered by all who seek it. On the extreme end is the "true believer" who not only knows that he has the whole truth but is responsible to see that others accept it also.

But the lover of truth, I believe, is somewhere in between. Somehow he or she comes to recognize that the truth of anything is measured slowly, yet the desire for it is universal. Its revelation is the light of faith and hope.

The lover of truth does not confuse sincerity or passion with truth. He or she understands that truth demands great care, not because of any fragility, but because of the damage done through carelessness. Lies and bad faith do not always appear as such; they may wear the mask of truth.

The lover of truth is aware that it is easy to be deceived, especially by ourselves. He or she knows that the search is not easy. Those paths trodden many times by others may contain errors. New paths are often a thicket of difficulty. That is why to love truth may not be possible without charity.

Nor is it possession alone that is loved; it is not a question of making truth an idol. Truth is alive; it grows and deepens as a person develops. What was true at ten may have new meaning at twenty. It is not just an accumulation of "facts" though these are essential in the discovery process.

I write in this way to you because I believe we have come through a long midnight in education during which political ideology was more important on the college campus than truth, and we are still enduring it. But we have been shocked out of the predominance of ideologies, some as dull as ditch water but favored all the same, first by the collapse of communism and its intellectual underpinning of Marxism, and now by the relentless force of terrorism brought real to us.

Your generation has a great opportunity to restore basic principles. *Carpe diem!*

The search for truth isn't everything. There are other things just as important. (For example, beauty, friendship, joy, romance, motherhood, masculinity, femininity, solitude, peace, patience, compassion, the love of God, just plain work, the laughter of children.) But in the core of a school or college's "reason to be," truth sits in the highest chair. My hope and prayer for your generation is that as it grapples with the new world disorder you shall keep her there and resist those forces which would bring her down.

JOH: 1993, 2001

## Young and Reckless Behavior in a Declining Culture

I spent time on Prince Edward Island in Canada recently. While there I heard and read about a 19 year old athlete and underage girls (younger than 14) who became sexually involved. It is a sad story. Of course, all stories about wasted young lives are sad, but this one has a troubling, even frightening aspect.

The boy was an all star baseball player, a catcher highly regarded by baseball scouts and just given a contract to play for the Los Angeles Dodgers. (His name is well known in Canada but I will not reveal it here.) His fame now centers around his conviction for procuring illicit sex from the underage girls.

These girls are children. Like many seventh graders, they were silly, but the tragedy lies in their complete lack of direction and lack of moral sense. Apparently, they engaged in oral sex on older popular athletes to gain status of some description (?) despite having no other contact with them. They didn't talk, kiss, date or in any way engage in a social exchange. The boy is now facing a prison sentence of ten years, and his life is changed forever.

The girls too are paying a high price. An article in the Halifax Chronicle Herald states that they are being harassed at school and bullied on the school bus because they dared to testify against the "pride of the school." According to the news article, the girl's aunt is furious because the media has focused on what the conviction will mean for the athlete's career, but the impact on the girls has been largely ignored. But I wonder, where was the aunt, where were the parents, before this happened?

The girls testified in court that they and other friends routinely perform oral sex on boys. "It's everywhere," said one of the girls. "It's not really a big deal. It's just casual." The girls' naiveté (innocence?) takes me back to a statement by the President of the United States a few years ago that oral sex is not really sex. Well then, what is it? (Is the question narrow-minded? Is it "politically incorrect?") The superficiality of this moral relativism is radiant.

One person with a reasonable moral perspective on the case was Judge Nancy Orr. She said, "If half of the community thinks the girls were the perpetrators here, there is something seriously wrong with the message we are getting out to young people about appropriate sexual behavior and about what is criminal and what isn't in the eyes of the law."

Back to America, there is another equally sad story. (How many are happening in our communities that we know nothing of?) A pretty vivacious 17 year old girl's life is suddenly, horrendously altered by a sexual encounter with a boyfriend "who loved her." For that brief moment of ecstasy she will probably pay for the rest of her life because of a sexually transmitted disease that is hard to get rid of. How can we measure the cost — to her personal health? to her loss of esteem that she may not be good enough for anyone else? to her fear that she may not be able to bear children? and what of the boyfriend who transmitted the disease? Does he not suffer as well?

Along with AIDS, STD is devastating the lives of many bright, talented, otherwise wholesome young people across the country.

If our response to the AIDS/STD crisis is no more profound than to sell more condoms and constantly remind people to buy them, a lot of young people may become caught in a whirlpool of disease and addiction and meaningless relationships spinning away to desolation. A cure for these diseases would be wonderful, but what is the cure for a society which can no longer distinguish the values of permanence and love in the drive for sexual freedom and pleasure above all else? Why should a hedonist community care about victims? Its future is vanishing.

None of us are androgynous (male and female combined). There are and always will be differences between male and female in the human species. Male-female attraction and union is a primary force in God's creation. This green fuse is not just physical; it is spiritual--the longing for completeness--the "yin and yang" of reality --and the tension is moral.

The desire for intimacy is as strong as the denial of death. It has founded and destroyed empires, and created our most enduring myths and legends as well as the most beautiful works of art and literature. For all of history, up to now at least, such desire has been at the core of human drama.

There is mystery and beauty - and magic - in the life process that brings male and female together.

Can desire be corrupted? Passion trivialized? Yes, of course. Obviously, we are no longer in a Victorian age which sublimated the corrupt and the trivial. Desire and passion are exploited every day with TV images and consumer oriented messages. The connections of desire and sex and love may be a fair corrivalry for adults, but when the exploitation reaches to teenagers and to children who end up dismissing sexual relations as "no big deal, it's just casual," is this not symptomatic of a declining culture?

With an increasing number of kids, spiritual and moral values are not being internalized. Where are they going? They're in danger of ruining their lives before they reach adulthood, and if we're going to be of any help to them, we've got to get beyond the superficial doctrines of moral relativism whatever their source.

JOH : 2002

## Abortion

Is it any wonder that Supreme Court nominee Clarence Thomas refused to discuss "Roe v. Wade" in his confirmation hearings? This 1973 landmark decision that legalized abortion is one of the most controversial cases in the history of our Constitution.

It has divided the American people more deeply than anything else in the past twenty-five years. The division over the morality of abortion is likely to continue no matter what new decisions may be issued by the Court. It may be that the rights of women and the contending rights of an unborn child cannot be resolved legally in a way to end the controversy.

Indeed, it seems fair to say that this is an issue your generation will have to face even more seriously than mine has done, and you should therefore engage in an analysis of it.

Why is this so? The answer has a lot to do with technology.

When I was an undergraduate student in the mid 1950's, I heard about one case of abortion involving a student and how worried her boyfriend was. It was an isolated piece of information, probably more prescient than we realized, but there was no context of public debate and furor in which to place it.

This is not to say that the abortion issue has no history at all, but it is really quite recent that this issue has become so intense.

In the 19th Century and earlier, abortion was outlawed, but more significantly, it wasn't accepted by women as a safe or desirable practice. Because medical techniques were much more primitive in those days, abortion was highly dangerous for the woman. Combined with the strong moral and legal codes against it, this made abortions far less frequent than today.

There were unwanted babies then too, but infanticide and abandonment were more common solutions. These practices of course, were criminal; there was no contention that they were a matter of rights.

In an almost paradoxical way, the abortion issue demonstrates how pervasive and deep is the influence of technology on all of modern life. New reproductive technologies have had immense impact on cultural patterns and values and lifestyles in this century, and have shifted dramatically the regard for abortion in considering the welfare of women.

Surgical advances have greatly improved the safety of abortion for the woman. Other advances too have reduced the risk of complications. As the technology advanced, many women began to see the prohibition of abortion as the real danger to their welfare. From there, the idea of abortion as a right developed quickly. On the other side, of course, the rise in the number of abortions quickened the moral and legal arguments on behalf of the unborn child.

The technologies continue to advance. For example, apparently a fetus can be treated independently of treating the mother, including its removal from the womb and re-implantment. What implications does this have? How will the abortion issue be recast as we learn more through technology? More is coming.

But, whatever happens, it is unlikely that technology will decide the issue.

I think there will always be, at the least, a moral need to distinguish between freedom to terminate an unwanted pregnancy and freedom to kill an unborn child— terribly perplexing though this need may be.

JOH: 2000

## Marijuana

Some interesting new stuff about the use and abuse of Marijuana has recently come to my attention. Credits belong to research done at Duke University, Johns Hopkins University, National Drug Abuse Center, and summaries by Dr. Mitch Earlywine, University of Southern California (see especially, "A New Look at Marijuana", 2002.)

First, it's true that using marijuana is not physically addictive; it's not a "gateway" to other drugs; it does not destroy motivation; and it does not lead to violence. The main attraction to it is the relaxation and "good feelings" of a high and the loss of inhibitions. It is understandable why it is a drug of choice among young people. They see the hypocrisy in adults who express alarm about it and are themselves abusers of alcohol, which in many ways is worse. In this age when young people have more information available to them than previous generations had, it is also understandable why superficial conclusions are drawn that marijuana use has no dangers.

Earlywine dispels that notion in a compelling way. There are indeed dangers! Especially for chronic users! "Chronic users" are those who smoke five or more joints a week or more than 100 in a year. While these folks may not be physically addicted they experience "cravings" from the habitual use that are difficult to overcome.

The biggest danger is the potential effect on the balance of brain matter, gray and white. Duke University research shows that chronic use is altering the frontal lobe---scary implications! Johns Hopkins and the National Institute on Drug Abuse found similar results.

For their own knowledge and safeguard all students should check out these studies. There are other negatives as well. Learning is not possible when someone is on a high, and the legal problems of possession and selling can be devastating.

This review is not meant to scare you. I have great faith in young people's competence and good judgment but the college environment is now far more dangerous than when I was an undergraduate. And that means you must rely even moreso on your intelligence and courage to prevail as a whole person Protect yourself and others. Be a leader!

JOH : 2003

## Reality Testing

"Education is preparation for the future." How often have we heard this said? There is a philosophy reflected in our educational programs which offers hope and expectation for a future life. This philosophy is not wrong, but it may be misunderstood.

What does it mean to be a student, now? Here is a question about reality. Whatever else education should be, it has a lot to do with reality-testing. Students may be trained to do a job for a salary in the future, but education is more than training. Education reaches for the person, as being, not just becoming a skilled member of the work force.

Tomorrow, the lights may blink off, or shine differently, but reality-testing is what we are seeing and learning now, according to the lights of the present. Reality is always in the present. Regrets about the past, hopes for the future may drive us, but if we are coping with reality, we live in the present.

Of course, when we look at the misery of a large part of the world, we may feel that this reality is harsh or more simply, that it isn't fun. And so, people turn to drugs and alcohol to escape---only to wake up and find that misery and fear and degradation have increased. To the trapped, desensitized addict, reality is an increasing horror. The dream of heightened awareness is revealed as a terrible lie.

The truth is that every person has an interior capacity for awareness and intense perception, a natural ability to see beauty in things, to marvel at the unity and diversity of nature, to seek and give love, to be suddenly overwhelmed by the joy of life.

JOH: 1990

**Free Speech**

While in the United Kingdom recently, I was struck by references to a "no platform" policy which denies alleged racists and fascists the right to address student gatherings. This goes far enough to destroy the right to dissent, but it doesn't even stop there. On some campuses, it also means to ban or censure individual students for membership in unacceptable organizations. If this isn't fascism, what is it?

In America we have our own examples. There is evidence of growing racial and religious intolerance and disturbing practices aimed at preventing speakers from being heard, or even causing their cancellation. While some of this stuff may be explained as a puerile over-enthusiasm or emotional outpouring, the strong attack on civil liberties – – unconscious or deliberate – – cannot be explained away. If it is part of a wider malaise, or symptomatic of an undefined higher conscience at work, I think we had better get our basic principles in order.

The need for free speech is not when we agree: it is when we are divided and searching and perhaps frightened. While it is not absolute (you do not have the right to yell "Fire" in a theater), free speech is one of the most enduring but hardest won principles of democratic civilization.

JOH: 1990 (2010?)

## The Bad Example of Professional Athletes

Athletes today who insist on using performance-enhancing drugs are not just harming themselves, they are harming young people who look up to them. These so-called champion athletes, such as baseball's Barry Bonds, are demonstrating that to achieve great things in sports it is necessary, even desirable, to take serious health risks. Bonds hit 73 home runs in 2001. Now suspicion is high that it was done by cheating.

Of course, it is no longer certain that cheating in professional sports really matters. Recent comments from some sportscasters and writers clearly indicate that everyone knows or should know that the use of anabolic steroids is an increasingly common practice. But if this is true, of what real value are these athletic achievements by people who are betraying their sport as well as better men and women who still play by the rules?

I remember as a young athlete, even if I did not succeed, I had to play the game straight. My heroes were distinguished players like Stan Musial, Johnny Unitas, Bob Cousy, Bill Russell. They were known by all of us to be standup guys who always played the game clean and straight. What happened?

I remember a few years ago when Cal Ripken retired from baseball and was feted for his marvelous record of consistency and his work ethic, a columnist commented that we would not see his like again given the way athletes are pampered today. What a sad comment!

I know that these days it is considered naive to think that athletes should be good role models for young people. They are given many excuses for bad behavior, along with their millions of dollars in salaries. The recent trend of criminal violence on the basketball court and the ice rink confirms a situation out of control.

I think it is time to stop coddling these characters because of the dangerous example they set for young people and because they are destroying the sports tradition in America. Estimates of anabolic steroid use among high school boys now are as high as 11 per cent. These kids are at risk of muscle injuries, liver and cardiovascular problems and unknown emotional problems.

Yes, it is true that we should not be surprised by the breakdown. Just look around in the corporate world. We have just come through a period of stunning revelation of corruption and greed that is still not completely over. The sleaze in the last election was also an abysmal portrait of American politics. In public service, there are many artful dodgers of responsibility. In education, the teaching of moral philosophy is bankrupt. In religion there are exemplars of the ultimate hypocrisy in those televangelists who mock God by preying on the faith and emotions of believers. When lies and unethical practices and hypocrisy are so rife in society at large, how can we be surprised when it happens in sports as well?

But is not this all the more reason why we should take a stand in this arena where the influence is so great upon our young people? Is it not the responsibility of every mature athlete and all of us who want to champion some cause in life to express clearly to the young that cynicism and skepticism do not yet reign-that we and they can still hold to a creed of moral responsibility and intellectual honesty, even accounting for our disagreements and errors? Can we not still say that a victory that comes through cheating is not winning? A victory that is marred by corruption is not winning. That our aim always is to win with honor.

Young people who learn what winning is all about are prepared to win in life. Winning is about courage and valor, honor and integrity, responding to challenge, constancy and fatigue in hardship, grace under pressure, discipline, self-confidence, self-improvement, sacrifice, loyalty, team building and team work, comradeship and celebration and understanding that victory and defeat both are of value. In other words, winning is about ideals and values all young people need to embrace to have a healthy perspective on life and to be leaders.

If there are athletes who no longer stand for these ideals and values, why bother with them? To be seen on a field of glory they need to prove themselves by the lives they lead.

JOH : 1991

## Facing Violence

What does the horrific terrorist attack on our country September 11, 2001 mean for your generation? Think about that question.

Reported in USA TODAY, Kirk Cassells, a Skidmore College student said, "It changes everybody's life in the sense of our safety and hope. Stuff like this happens every day all over the world. You wonder when people will let go of the hate and the misunderstanding that drives them to do the wrong thing."

Kirk's reaction is understandable, but I suggest that there is more to learn that can be applied to our lives every day.

If Sept. 11, 2001, is a defining moment in our history — much like Dec. 7,1941, Pearl Harbor was — then we need to examine it on more than one level.

President Bush is leading us in a national response to terrorism, as he must. He calls it the first war of the 21st century, and he is determined to win this war. It's hard to know exactly what that means, but we do know it will take courage and wisdom.

One thing is absolutely clear: we are confronted by cold, calculating, uncompromising evil that will bring violence upon us in every way it can. Fuzzy-headed tolerance of this evil will only beget more of it. We are not a people motivated by hatred, but we will fight back, and we will prevail in defending our freedom.

But there's another level of violence too right here in our own society. We see images of it every night on television and in Hollywood films. We have also seen how violence affects our schools and colleges and the lives of individual students. It is sad to recognize how that violence in our midst has increased in recent years. Any student who has experienced it is also a victim of terrorism and it isn't just physical. Any person who has been violated suffers not just physical wounds but within his or her soul.

That is why we all have an obligation to give support to the victim, close friends especially, and to cooperate fully in the investigation of any assault.

Fractures and abrasions heal, but if the inner wounds are not treated, the effects will be felt in other ways because what is at stake is that person's integrity. What he or she has experienced is a little act of terror and it is very important to come out of it whole.

Often, the violator will count upon that terror. That is the clear implication of statements like, "Your ass is mine." Sometimes it works. The victim may fear the consequences of pressing charges, or he/she may hope that the crisis will disappear if it is ignored. But it won't. The inner soul knows that it has been violated, and until there is a re-affirmation of its integrity, the person will suffer - through bitterness or perpetual fear or some illness that seems to have no cause. I am not addressing here those spontaneous fights that sometimes happen between guys who quickly decide to forgive and forget. (The forgiveness is essential.) Maybe that's part of growing up. I mean those intentional acts of violence and threats of violence against a person in order to abuse and intimidate — the little acts of terror. This has become a problem on many college campuses, particularly involving male/female relations. None of us want it to happen, but that means we must be willing to act positively, with courage, when its shadow appears.

We live in a violence-prone society. There is no absolute guarantee against any one of us becoming involved in an act of violence. But there is one thing we can do to prepare ourselves for such a crisis:

Make a decision. In a very quiet state of mind, go deep into your inner being, and claim this knowledge of yourself:

1. I will not commit violence against another person.

2. I will not allow acts of violence to influence my life.

3. If I am confronted with a situation of violence, I will follow a path of courage and integrity.

Then, if you believe in God, follow with a prayer or meditative appeal that God shall uphold you in these affirmations for your life.

JOH : 2001

## Dinesen's Wisdom

"Who is Karen Dinesen?" She died in 1962. From old Danish aristocracy, she was born Dinesen, married Blixen, took pen name of Isak Dinesen, intellectually gifted, a woman of courage, a story teller, artist. She was, perhaps, one of those rare people who through experience and grace manage to get beyond illusions. She left much that is wise and good for us to ponder.

Dinesen discovered that life cannot be lived like a story; it is a story. The difference between the two conceptions is profound.

Karen Blixen went to Africa at the age of twenty-seven under the spell of an idea of herself that she was determined to follow. She suffered and learned from it. Nothing of her life in Africa met her pre-conceptions, yet her experience there was immensely important to her.

There she met Denys Finch-Hatton who was probably her equal intellectually though not artistically. He helped her to see and feel the rhythms of a beautiful and terrible nature which clearly separate the wild and the domesticated. To hold him, she told stories that fascinated him, and because she loved him, the stories grew powerfully. Finally she decided to write them down. Her stories unified her experience with her intellect and faith. Thus was born the art and wisdom of Isak Dinesen.

In this world, anything is possible, but the sin which corrupts and distorts is to play at being God. A story - a life - cannot be forced or made to come true. To be real, life must not be a fiction which we are trying to live up to. The story must be allowed to emerge, and for its emergence joy and suffering are essential materials. Imagination, as opposed to fantasy, allows us to see connections and possibilities as the story unfolds: what is happening to me? to others through me? how does this fit into the creative purpose of my life? what actions are required on my part? Such a view almost enjoins the active and the contemplative life.

The craving to impress your will and your being upon the world and to make the world your own is turned into a longing to be able to accept, to give yourself over to the universe - Thy will be done. (Dinesen)

*"He relinquished himself to it."* (Faulkner)

The most truly bold life is one which recognizes creative power, greater than self, and through that recognition forgets self and obtains grace.

In one of her essays, Dinesen tells the story of an old Chinese Mandarin who gave a ring to the Emperor when he came of age to reign:

"In this ring I have set an inscription which your Majesty may find useful. It is to be read in times of danger, doubt and defeat. It is also to be read in times of conquest, triumph and glory."

The inscription in the ring read: "This, too, shall pass."

The inscription does not mean that life should be lived passively. Dinesen explains: "It should not be taken to mean that in their passing, tears and laughter, hopes and disappointments disappear into a void. It tells you that it will be absorbed into a whole Story that *shall see them as integral parts of the full picture of the man or woman.*"

Dinesen's relationship with Finch-Hatton is depicted in the film, Out of Africa, created from a composite of five books by or about Dinesen. It is a good film.

Even better is a Danish film based on one of her stories, Babette's Feast. Babette proclaims the longing in the heart of Dinesen and perhaps every artist: *Give me the chance to do my very best.*

Karen Dinesen's life was not easy and more than once she thought of committing suicide but remained tough and always chose life at the end. She said of herself, "Nobody came into literature more bloody than I."

JOH : 1990

## Power of Love

> *"Scientific knowledge is power."* Francis Bacon

> *"Some day, after we have mastered the winds, the waves, the tides, and gravity, we shall harness for God the energies of love: and then, for the second time in the history of the world...man will have discovered fire."*
>
> Teilhard de Chardin

These quotations reflect two different ways of thinking and knowing.

Science is indeed a powerful way of knowing. But it is not the only way of knowing. There is an intuitive way and a mystical way. These ways may not describe the physical reality which is the domain of science, but there is ample evidence that the scientific paradigm (world view) does not contain all reality.

There is a question about reality constantly before us, so pervasive and so simple it's on the lips of every child: "Do you love me?" Where does this come from?

Science doesn't know much about love, which is the biggest reason you seldom find it in your textbooks. But rest easy, science/technology student, there are other ways to think about it, aren't there? – and not just physical.

Don't allow yourself to go into a paradigmatic freeze just because everyone and everything around you is screaming, "this is a material world." JOH: 1990

## Paradoxical Reality

> *"We live in a fantasy world, a world of illusion.*
> *The great task in life is to find reality."* Iris Murdoch

Obviously, the world is different for us in America than it was before the 9/11 terrorist attack on the World Trade Center. It isn't so different for most people in other countries, however. In some ways we have joined the rest of the world in the knowledge of imminent danger and the need to be constantly alert. We can't ever go back to that care-free, anesthetized view of life in which violence (more and more of it) was just something we saw on the screen.

At the same time, we still value most highly our freedom. As a nation, we still have the responsibility of leadership -- moral, political and economic -- as the world's only super-power.

So what are the things we should be thinking about? And not just what but how? Here I want to raise a topic that might get us started.

If you are not right, you must be wrong. Right? Wrong! Stay with me for a moment to see if we can make sense of how you can be right and wrong at the same time.

It's called *paradox*. In our culture we have not been taught to think much about paradox. For the most part we are linear, "either-or" thinkers. In other words we believe that things must follow in sequence, that there is usually one answer or explanation, a thing is either true or it is false. We like binary propositions.

A paradox occurs when two opposite things are held in a kind of tension. Nature has a way of holding opposites together. That is part of the mystery of creation.

There can be good and bad qualities in any situation which are difficult to unravel. Sometimes, in our eagerness to correct something clearly wrong, we lose something of value that we did not see in our first appraisal. Or, to put it another way, sometimes the solution to a problem creates another problem.

What is the practical value of this discussion? I am asking you to think about paradoxical reality because it is so obvious that we are not in control of our world, and we are going to have to learn to live with conflict which is increasingly multidimensional.

With the collapse of communism a decade ago, we thought about a "new world order" (words of President George H.W. Bush) . This world is neither new nor orderly, and we are going to have to adjust. I'm not saying here that "everything is relative," a tired and hollow doctrine that I'll come back to in a future article.

Nor do I mean that we should learn to live with violence and injustice. Far from it. In order to stop violence and bring justice we must be willing to act, but we must also be sure that our means are just and we have carefully considered results.

So it has a lot to do with truth. Sometimes truth is simple, but often it is paradoxical and therefore hard to come by.

In the Taoist world view, there is perhaps a greater understanding of paradoxical reality than we have understood in Western culture. The "yin-yang circle" teaches us that night becomes day, weakness is strength, goodness presupposes evil. All of life is a paradox.

If this is reality (we could debate it), how do we keep our balance? An awful lot depends upon our respect for truth and our concomitant desire for goodness, beauty and justice in the world. Each seeks the other while admitting to the pervasion of enemies, like weeds among the flowers in a garden not easily cultivated. It helps if we can hold opposites in mind at the same time, without losing faith in the transcendent light that ultimately shines through everything.

JOH: 2001

## Mimophantry

"... here is also the virgin plant, which they term the sensible tree, which after the least touch of one's hand I see fall down withered, and then revived after a little space." -Fr. Andrew White, West Indies, 1634

Fr. Andrew was describing the mimosa plant, which is remarkable for the sensitivity of its leaves, hence the name, sensitive plant.

Everybody knows what an elephant is.

A "mimophant" is a hybrid species: This term may be used (I think) to describe that remarkable person who, like a mimosa, is very sensitive to his/her own feelings but quite capable of trampling like an elephant over the feelings of others. You would think that someone ultra-concerned about his/her own feelings and needs would be equally concerned about other people's, yet this is not always the case, is it?

You may have noticed that "mimophants" also aren't used to taking responsibility for their own welfare (or morale). They may have talent and skills, but when problems come up, it's somebody else's fault. They're energy sappers, not radiators.

A sub-species, "mimophant-jokester," are those people who delight in playing practical jokes on others but become angry when the joke is on them; they can dish it out but can't take it.

Then there are "mimophant-mommas and papas," nice folks suffering from their overindulgence.

Okay, enough of this malarkey. Let's get serious about it for a minute. I'm not suggesting that the fun term, "mimophantry" be taken seriously in social research, but many of my colleagues in education will agree that there is a growing affliction of excessive self-absorption in schools and colleges today.

As America became more affluent over the last century, we began to value happiness for our children more than their character education. The result has been too many kids--even from families with modest means--who have too much money, too many things, too much protection, and too little challenge. Too much of a good thing can be toxic.

When parents seek a perfect life for their children, without pain or disappointment, those kids are stripped of the opportunity to develop their maturity, to learn from pain and failure, to be honest with themselves, and to be empathetic.

Often these kids are hollow inside -- deprived because they have been too advantaged and getting away with too much all their lives. And they know it.

I'm primarily concerned with those of you in this fairly large group who are now trying to succeed in college. Your success is my job, but it's getting more difficult for me and your professors because many of you are not strong enough. You've been spoiled, and you expect an unearned entitlement to continue.

But I am not writing from despair. Far from it.

First, I know your potential and your resiliency. A basic question for you is, what kind of person do I want to be?

JOH : 1993

## Mythical Reality

When I was growing up, my teachers sought to put me on the right track by de-mythologizing (or "de-bunking") everything. I learned that anything mythical was false, unreal, unhistorical or unscientific and therefore either insignificant or bad. I liked my teachers. They were well intentioned, not cynical in their desire to separate myth from truth, but I realize now what a terrible disservice it was to me personally when I bought into this crimped way of looking at the world.

It was many years, in fact fairly recent, before I began to understand how powerful the myth is, and more importantly, how essentially true and fundamental to a coherent, sane explanation of reality it may be.

I realize now that to impart culture as though history is what happened and myth is fiction distorts immeasurably our understanding of who we are and where we come from.

Myth is a reflection on reality, a way of explaining through generations what actually happened. Let's take an example.

At the center of nearly every civilization is a remarkably similar Creation myth. Basically, it is an account of how the world came to be as a gift from God.

In primitive times, when it was feared that the gift would be taken back, human sacrifice was offered. To ensure that spring would come again, a king or a deity would be taken into the hills to be torn apart and scattered. The world was saved in a dionysian frenzy.

There are two essential parts to the Creation myth: the world is a gift, and the world's survival is threatened.

Many would say that we are now above this bunk. We know that spring will come again. Science and technology will take care of us. Anyway, we don't sacrifice people that way anymore.

Ah! Are we really so superior?

Creation also means Creator. If this world is God's gift, we have more than selfish reasons to protect and keep it clean, don't we? It's becoming pretty clear that selfish reasons won't suffice, and that's also part of the Creator-Creation myth.

The myth explains a relationship of God, man and nature in which man cannot stand alone nor dominate.

JOH: 1993

**Soldierization**

The first real job I ever had was Executive Officer of a battery of 155 self-propelled howitzers. Just twenty-one years old I was assigned after being commissioned at the Artillery Officer Candidate School, Fort Sill, Oklahoma, renowned as the home of the "King of Battle," U. S. Army Artillery. This was many years ago.

I returned to Ft. Sill recently, arriving the same day as the 13th Field Artillery Battalion was returning home from Iraq. For four days I had the opportunity to meet and converse with young soldiers and a few older officers, each of whom has a personal story. Not all of them were combat veterans; some were going through "soldierization"-- civilians being turned into soldiers. It is a wondrous process of training and indoctrination of

Army values that I must admit is better--more effective-- than what I experienced in my time.

Ft. Sill is the oldest of five Army training posts. Its origins are with the famed Buffalo Soldiers, and it is now the artillery training base for both Army and Marine Corps. Volunteer soldiers who are destined for artillery take their training here. The first goal is to transform civilians into soldiers.

Young people enlist in the Army for various reasons. Bonus money is probably the biggest recruitment tool. They come from various backgrounds and probably have not experienced a regimen of motivation, discipline, physical fitness and training similar to Army or Marine basic training.

Their initial training consists of three phases. The "Patriot Phase" teaches personal health, courtesy, self-respect and respect for others, drill and ceremonies, inspections and first aid --- a personal orientation and introduction to Army values. Second is the "Gun Fighter Phase" focusing on weapons training, obstacle course, and hand-to-hand combat. Third is the "Warrior Spirit Phase." Here there is a strong emphasis placed on team work, individual tactical training, hand grenade, gas mask, live fire exercise --a rounding out of the basic combat training intended to put each soldier onto a warrior path of development. Upon graduation, each soldier goes on to Advanced Individual Training.

In all three phases there is an environment of total control intended to inculcate the Army values:

Loyalty-Duty-Respect-Selfless     Service-Integrity-Honor-Personal Courage.

These values are what make a soldier. Each time that a soldier slips in the standards of performance expected of him/her, the question is, "What value did you violate?" There is rigor and realism in this combat training, but for most of the young men and women who experience it, there is also a new sense of freedom and self worth.

I have met and talked with many of these young men and women and have an enormous respect for their growth and development through the Army. Without exception, those whom I met showed uncommon courtesy. On an Army base "Sir" is voiced all over the place, yet I saw no lack of individual pride. Some had served in the Gulf War, some had just returned from Iraq, and some were waiting for their first assignment. (It is the Army's intention that every soldier will serve productively in the first unit to which he/she is assigned.) The steady look in their eyes was the same that we have seen in the combat pictures of young NCO's on television and in the newspapers-- looking barely out of their teens-- who knew exactly what to do on their mission. The training and doctrine so much in evidence at Ft. Sill, doubtless on other posts as well, has given us the best Army in the world. A lesson from Viet Nam has been learned well by this army: "Never send a soldier into combat untrained." This is the new Army's contract with America.

I was at Ft. Sill for an OCS reunion but more specifically for orientation to the new leadership training and the values it espouses. One night as I was returning to my BOQ I was stopped for a gate check (surprised that the security was not even more intense). The MP on duty noticed my OCS cap and began asking me about my time at Ft. Sill. In the Army, there is great respect accorded to the "greatest generation"-- the Veterans of World War II. Now I don't go quite that far back, but I think that is where this soldier placed me. I'm not sure these young guys have a good sense of chronological history: Viet Nam and everything before it seem to coalesce in their minds. He asked me what I had done in the service. Later, I realized that he was primarily interested in my training. When I told him that I kept going to schools, some of which he was familiar with such as Ranger school, he became even more attentive. Then he did something that totally surprised me. With his eyes fixed on mine, he snapped to attention and gave me a sharp salute, "Thank you, sir!"

Having met these young military people, I am even more astonished by the observations of so many television commentators, journalists, academicians, and some of our political leaders and representatives who prior to the war in Iraq, and all during the war, could not overcome their doubts.

Chris Matthews of NBC said that if we go to war in Iraq, it will be a "military catastrophe." Maureen Dowd echoed in the NY Times: "While these leaders were not part of the Viet Nam war, couldn't they at least, like read about it?"

Even after it became clear that a blitz krieg victory by our forces was in the making, with less than 200 casualties, it continued-- the din of criticism of military tactics, the over-hyped and just plain false reportage of civilian casualties, the cynicism expressed about the military failure to protect museums and immediately stop the looting (the breadth of which no one predicted).

These critics did not get it just a little bit wrong, they were totally wrong!

Their arrogance is dumbfounding to military officers. In truth, it was the Army itself, not our political leaders, that learned the hard lessons of Viet Nam and resolved to build a new and better Army. We may or may not have a long-term strategic victory in Iraq. It's too early to tell. But the success of our forces in the field ought not to be sullied.

One of the deplorable attempts to do so is the case of Jessica Lynch, from our state of West Virginia. Several sources have said that we did not need the force to rescue Jessica Lynch that we applied. One of the principles of protecting both our troops and civilians is to apply as rapidly as possible an overwhelming force to get the job done. Whether or not it was needed, this was the right approach to rescue Pfc. Lynch. To have to apologize for it now is absurd.

These commentators are unable to see what is really happening in Afghanistan and Iraq. A completely new military force with capacity to conduct several simultaneous operations at great speed, prepared to deal with uncertain, unpredictable circumstances which require tactical decisions at the unit control level, simply made it impossible for the Iraqi forces to respond to their multiple dilemmas created by the overwhelming combinations of force and speed. They could not communicate effectively and simply collapsed. Before the war it was predicted that the oil fields would be set ablaze, but the Iraqi forces couldn't even get to the oil fields.

Another error is that all of this was done simply because of American technological superiority. While it is true that we have technological superiority, the technology enables the soldier in the field; in the end the victory is won and the sacrifices are made by this new generation of warriors and their families.

There is indeed a need for a sharp analysis of the errors in our efforts to free the peoples of Afghanistan and Iraq. It should focus first on civilian authority. There are problems beneath the surface which threaten the stability of this Army in ways that enemies in the field could not. The honesty of media coverage is also a serious issue.

There is a weird way of turning the world upside down in the thinking of some of our journalists and "talking heads" who readily ruminate about America's perceived failures. Many are remarkably sensitive to the grievances of terrorists yet cannot see that despite our mistakes we are a democracy which is trying to lead the way to peace and freedom in places like Somalia, Kosovo, Afghanistan, Iraq and the Middle East.

Whether or not our troops should go to these places is a question for civilian judgment. Our troops do not question civilian command. They are ready to serve and rightly proud of their role. And there is no moral equivalence. Unlike their adversaries, they do not murder civilians. They do not torture children.

The major force for order in the world is America's influence, nurtured by our military power. But we don't have an imperial army. Those who do not understand the difference and preach self-abnegation and withdrawal are still afflicted by the spirit of Munich which partly caused World War II.

American military officers have been involved in many conflicts in many different parts of the world. Another of which I have some personal awareness occurred in El Salvador. One of the common and false criticisms is that we trained the Salvadoran death squads and were partly responsible for massacres. The truth is that after a long and terrible civil war that ravaged the country, the Salvadoran military hierarchy agreed that they must come under civilian control. Thus peace finally came through treaty signed in January 1992 establishing a democratic government. Why did they so agree? Because of the influence of their American military colleagues.

The battalion return at Ft. Sill was poignant. Not all of our troops shall be returning alive of course. Shown on public television was a scroll of the names of those who died in Iraq with their ages-19, 20, 21, 27-a few in their 30's, but the majority under 30. And of course there were many more like who have been seriously wounded and traumatized. Those who died were like so many other young people who were struck down before they reached the prime of life and did not get the full opportunity to achieve their hopes and dreams. What other victories and achievements they might have gained we cannot know.

JOH: 2005

Professor Bloom's Critique of Relativism

Several years ago, I wrote a review of a book by Allan Bloom, a University of Chicago philosophy professor, titled, "The Closing of the American Mind. "

The book became a phenomenal best seller, apparently chosen by many people who do not ordinarily go for heavy doses of philosophy.

As predicted, it made no friends for Professor Bloom in Academe, where the book was subjected mostly to scorn and derision. For awhile, it was almost a standard at higher education conferences to cite Bloom's error and arrogance in attacking higher education. Some critics cite Bloom's hatred of students; some cite his lack of a curriculum reform; others (closer to the mark) question Bloom's emphasis on German philosophical influence, particularly Nietzsche. The State University of New York's former Chancellor, Clifford Wharton, called it "racist." The controversy was very interesting.

Poor Professor Bloom has had a very rough time. His academic critics include many whom I suspect have not read the book but think they have caught its general spirit.

I agree with Bloom's colleague at the University of Chicago, Mortimer Adler, who said that there has been no worthwhile criticism of it yet published. He detests the criticisms as much as he dislikes Bloom's philosophical analysis.

Why, then, was Bloom's book a "best seller?" Obviously, it struck a chord with the general reading public which it did not with the intellectual elite (which may be another reason for the latter's resentment.)

I would like to suggest that it is Bloom's main thesis -- obscured by the criticisms -- which seems compelling to a lot of ordinary people who are smarter than we in higher education are sometimes willing to grant. That thesis concerns the false-profoundness of prevailing views in higher education that everything is relative in a materialistic universe. Relativism and materialism teach that to postulate any absolute values is like believing in fairies and witches.

These dominant philosophies of our age rightly project liberal openness and tolerance as enduring universal values but wrongly conclude that there are no others. Just as Bloom's critics question his inept conclusions about higher education, many other readers question the "conventional wisdom" of materialistic relativism -- a tired and hollow doctrine no longer sufficient to sustain a free society or a safe world.

Or maybe Bloom's readers do not make a philosophical interpretation. Perhaps they simply identify with his thoughts because they see the critical need for a moral center: There must be some value anchors, something to hold onto, in a world which all too clearly is out of balance. In this sense, Bloom's book is a reminder of a remarkably prophetic poem by W. B. Yeats:

### *The Second Coming*

> *Turning and turning in the widening gyre*
> *The falcon cannot hear the falconer;*
> *Things fall apart; the center cannot hold;*
> *Mere anarchy is loosed upon the world.*
> *The blood dimmed tide is loosed, and everywhere*
> *The ceremony of innocence is drowned;*
> *The best lack all conviction, while the worst*
> *Are full of passionate intensity."*

For many people, spiritual values and the "old verities and truths of the human heart"(Faulkner) are still important. For many, God is still alive in a cynical world.

Bloom's store of knowledge is impressive, but he is not original. He is simply opening an old door that enters into a room which is well-lighted. For the higher education community, it is a room full of classical artifacts; it is also a room where religious values may be comfortably discussed. Not everyone may choose to enter, because there is free will and free choice, but it is an option that the gray dogma of relativism shall not close from the mind.

JOH: 1991, 1999

## Misbegotten Respect for Suicide Bombers

In my last letter on the collapse of the Soviet Union, I referenced the work of Robert Conquest, who documented the price paid by the peoples of the Soviet Union for the cause of the state religion of communism framed by Lenin and Stalin. It likely shall be a long time before Russia, the Ukraine and other countries of the former USSR recover from this failed experiment with totalitarian doctrine which tried to bend all human values and interests to its service.

Question: Is that what is happening again in the Islamic world today? I am stimulated to raise this question by an AP news report I have just read about a world conference of Islamic leaders who tried to focus on defining terrorism. The results of the conference were to my mind stunning, hard to believe.

The major conclusion was that terrorism should be defined by the United Nations; in other words the conference couldn't do it and therefore failed. In itself this would be understandable. But these Islamic spokesmen went on to proclaim - and this is the stunning part - that they were opposed to all forms of terrorism except the Palestinian suicide bombers - they were not terrorists - they were religious martyrs. Here we have it all again: the deconstruction of logical thought combined with the complete lack of any standard of humanity.

How any religious leader can argue that intentional and indiscriminate killing not of soldiers but innocent people, including children, is justifiable by a higher cause is indeed difficult to understand. The astonishing thing is we are beginning to hear from some American commentators willing to rationalize the argument.

It is not reconcilable, I believe, with belief in a loving God.

It's certainly true that the complexity of the problems in the Middle East seem irresolvable. The suffering and sorrow endured by both the Palestinians and Israelis is heart sickening. Forty years ago when the looney tunes philosophy, "God is dead," was in vogue, the journalist I.F. Stone said, "If God is dead it must be that he died trying to solve the Palestinian-Jewish problem." Well, at least we have that mindless pejorative behind us.

God is not dead. He's alive and still works through men and women of good will. Both the Palestinians and the Israelis are in need of prayer and more of it.

What's your perspective? Politically speaking, I believe that President Bush is trying to do the right thing and he is joined by some other world leaders, such as Tony Blair of Great Britain, who are balanced and responsible in their view of the dispute over Israeli peace and Palestinian land.

Their efforts will be made even more difficult, however, if respect for suicide bombers should grow and define terrorism in such a way as to exclude these horrible acts. If that should occur it is hard to see anything but an apocalyptic end. Such a reigning religious doctrine -- already being taught to eight and nine year olds in Palestine - - would bring the most brutish human condition the world has yet known. For if such a monstrous evil did dominate the human heart, how could there be any room for forgiveness and atonement?

If Karen Dinesen is correct it will not come to pass. She wrote that "the thought of forgiving ones enemies will always everywhere be deeply admired; I know that this is so among Muslims who are otherwise pretty fierce in that direction and among Orthodox Jews...for a noble minded Muslim the overall view of how to live a good life coincides, where the best of them are concerned, with good Christians.'"

Let us hope and pray that this is indeed the case and we can hold to the distinction between Islamic faith, rightly understood, and an unfit moral corruption traveling under the veil of Islam.

JOH: 2004

## Lifting Lenin's Curse

Sometimes it seems that life goes along in an unchanging pattern. Then a cataclysmic event occurs, and we know that life will not be the same. This happened to America on September 11, 2001. Back in 1991, just ten years before, in the Soviet Union events were telescoped and presented to a world immediately changed.

Historians will write mega volumes about the summer of 1991-- the collapse of the Soviet Union, coming quickly after the removal of the Iron Curtain across Eastern Europe. Lenin's curse had finally been lifted.

It came so fast that a lot of scholars who called themselves "sovietologists" had to re-think their methods, and a lot of other folks who were charmed by Marxist-Leninist vision -- in Europe, Central America, Africa -- were completely discredited. The ash-heap of history was redefined.

It's not clear what will take its place, but totalitarian communism is dead or dying. This crime against humanity had its roots in a birds-eye view of history by Karl Marx who thought that "class struggle" would bring the demise of bourgeois capitalism, emergence of a classless society without private property, and a gradual withering away of the state.

Marxist prophecy never happened where it was supposed to, but in Russia in 1917, a revolution was captured by Lenin who brought about a new communist state in the name of Marx though not in the Marxist way. Lenin founded a new religion of great power -- without God.

What Lenin had in mind was not just a new state but a "new man." There were to be no Russians or Ukrainians or any other nationality, only Soviet citizens. There was no need for churches or synagogues because the "new man" would face squarely the fact that life was totally material and would live in peace, without spiritual crutches, because of his loyalty to the state.

What a price was paid for this doctrine! Robert Conquest, a very competent sovietologist, estimates that under Stalin 25 million Soviet citizens were killed by it. In the 1970's the great Russian writer, Solzhenitszyn, began to outline the truth of the new system in books like Gulag Archipelago. A lot of the plain horror is now coming out. every day, sometimes by those who perpetrated it, like KGB agents. For example, a report on Olympic athletes of East Germany (formerly a communist state) reveals the complete contempt for the souls of these athletes by those who wanted them to be "winners." A process of body engineering involved feeding massive quantities of steroids to children who were potential athletes. Those who could not metabolize steroids were released from the program. It was all done in full knowledge of the side effects. One document is of a famous sprinter who suffered liver damage, yet officials kept her on steroids because she was a key member of a relay team. The athletes were forbidden to talk to their parents about the steroid use or to consult physicians outside the program.

In the end, more powerful than the state are the ethnic and spiritual forces in the lives of Russian and Slavic peoples. Who can tell their future? The legacy of communism will not be easily overcome. Religious and ethnic conflict can be demonic too, as we know from the Middle East. Nor does the western brand of materialism have much to offer people starved for freedom, spiritual as well as political. But out of the Russian people's experience, there may be another, greater hope.

Perhaps Anthony Ugolnik, a Russian Orthodox priest and English professor, expresses that hope when he says, "The Russians are ahead of us in realizing how life is a unit, how the soul and body, faith and culture are inter-related."

But I think even more hopeful are the lyrics of a young Rock band in Moscow called Black Coffee. Here they are, as reported by Ugolnik, a fresh reflection on life and enduring values in Russia:

*"See the wooden churches of Russia, feel their warped*
*and ancient walls, come close and ask them about life.*
*In these timbers, beats a heart, lives a faith.*

*In the midst of our chaos, suddenly, underneath it all, emerged your*
*eternal peace. In the scene I am painting for you, notice small detail, old*
*church perched on a hillside. Clearly, there is no limit on the horizon.*

*The ancient churches stand still. Their life is without limit,*
*in time and in space. In these timbers still beats a heart, still*
*lives a faith. Hush, hear the heartbeat. Seize the faith."*

JOH: 1991, 2001

## Tiananmen Square

China is perhaps the last place in the world where re- commitment to the principles of the American Declaration of Independence would be expected. Yet there it was, for a short while last May for all the world to see, in Tiananmen Square of the city of Beijing. The calm yet passionate demonstration by Chinese student was perhaps the most significant reflection of the universal power of the ideals of freedom and justice and democracy that we have seen in this generation. The shift of action to realize these ideals in a historically closed, tradition- bound society is both ironic and inspiring.

The brutal end to the students' dream on June 3-4 and the subsequent repression and lies by the Chinese government may have been predictable, but it is also testimony that violence requires the lie for its justification, and the lie can ultimately only be sustained by violence.

Newspaper sources have reported that over 3000 students were massacred in Tiananmen Square. Our first difficulty perhaps is to internalize what that means. It is like all the students of this college being killed at once. In place of tanks running over people, imagine soldiers storming the dorms and spraying machine gun fire in every room, as university students were killed in Bangladesh in 1971. The first thing is to see that these students are just like us.

244

The second challenge is to understand what these events mean. The killing has happened before for similar reasons. It is aimed not just at life, of course, but at the ideals, principles, values which are in conflict with the prevailing ideology -- stated simply, that to hold the nation together, people must think the same way.

By the conventional wisdom of "cultural relativism", the events are indeed tragic, but the Chinese students were naïve, and the response was not only predictable but understandable in a cultural context: these values don't fit China; they could not be expected to endure there. This level of tolerance is itself ideological, lacking critical reflection.

What happened is perhaps better understood in the context of the evolution of thought. Freedom and justice and democracy may be sociologically relative, but there are also categories of thought which are universally born and working their way to expression in all societies. Fundamentally, these ideals which the Chinese students expressed and gave their lives for are related to the immanence of dignity and desire for integrity in all people everywhere.

How men and women think, what commitments they make, and what and why they sacrifice are supremely important. Derivatively, that is why the cause of the Chinese students and what happened to them in Tiananmen Square, June 3-4, 1989 deserves our intensive scrutiny and reflection.

JOH: July, 1989

## A Lesson From George Washington

There have been a stream of books out in recent years on our founding fathers. One is on the life of George Washington by Richard Brookhiser.* It's excellent -- solid research, well written. Brookhiser is not one of those deconstructionists who like to debunk everything and show the kids that there really aren't any heroes in American history, just a bunch of scalawags. In his view, Washington was definitely in the heroic mold, human though he was, and he is rightly called the father of our country.

It struck me in the reading how similar the events and the problems of his time were to those of our time. Great differences too of course. We were not a super power during Washington's presidency.

I had forgotten that 9-11 was not the first time New York City had been attacked by enemy forces. In 1776, the city was invaded by the British - now ironically our foremost ally. Brookhiser estimates the British forces had at their command ten ships of the line, dozens of other ships, and 32,000 professional soldiers. The American Army under Washington had no Navy, no ships and 19,000 soldiers - most of them untrained. In New York City, they were completely routed. There were eight battles fought between 1776 and 1778. Washington lost six of them.

On 9-11 we lost the two TradeTowers. Washington lost the entire city. Ultimately of course we won the war, but it was not because Washington was a superior military strategist or our troops were so much better in combat. The turning point may have come in 1778 when the French came in on the American side. (Yes, ironic now, isn't it, that but for the French we may have entered the 19th century still British subjects.)

There is evidence, however, that even without the French intervention the revolution would ultimately have succeeded. Brookhiser thinks the rebels won for two reasons -- two qualities that Washington insisted upon -- perseverance and flexibility.

I began by saying there are both similarities and differences between our time and Washington's time. No matter what problems confront us, we are not called upon to sacrifice the way that Washington and the patriots of 1776 were. But we are called upon not to be selfish, to thrust beyond our own personal interests; and when we do so, we render our interests more enlightened, and we feel good about ourselves. Isn't that true?

The difference is between self-sacrifice for a great cause and simply refusal to withhold on our commitment to other people.

There are also similarities. What can hold the family, the school, the community and the nation together in trying times are those same qualities we can see so clearly now in those revolutionaries: persistence and flexibility. There is a paradox here, a paradox of leadership in a democratic institution or society.

The paradox is this: If you are a leader there are times when you must simply take charge and move decisively regardless of what people think; if you don't things will fall apart. Washington understood this. He was very decisive but he also understood that success in the end depended on the people he was leading. "My brave fellows," he would frequently say. Compare that to Frederick the Great, a contemporary regarded as a "brilliant military strategist," who would say to his troops, "Do you dogs expect to live forever?"

Another great general, Napoleon, said that "the first quality of a soldier is constancy in fatigue and hardship." Washington abundantly displayed this quality: during eight years of command he never allowed himself to take furlough.

But it was his other leadership qualities that steered away from Napoleonic totalitarian vision and kindled the fire of democracy. During the war, there were many disputes with the Continental Congress, whose members grumbled about costs. Washington pressed hard and often, sometimes with a sense of despair, for the needs of his army, but he refused to accept arguments that he should override Congress, thus implanting from the beginning the principle of civilian authority over the military.

Washington was a democrat by instinct. He saw himself as a temporary leader of equals. He knew that this time would pass. One of his greatest contributions to democracy, now so inured that we hardly think about it, came when he refused to be king and accepted the office of president of the new nation only as its temporary steward. It was this paradox of his leadership that allowed flexible responses yet within the framework of commitment to the goals of the revolution.

Washington died in 1799 and was buried without any funeral oration. But John Marshall of West Virginia wrote of him as "the hero who lives now only in his own great actions." Henry Lee, father of General Robert E. Lee, eulogized him as "first in war, first in peace, and first in the hearts of his countrymen."

The influence of George Washington has been pervasive and deep throughout American history. One of the most important lessons he exemplified is that we must strive for flexibility of response to our needs and problems while maintaining a strong focus on our basic values, and persevere. *Cursom Perficio.*

\* Richard Brookhiser, <u>Founding Father: Rediscovering George Washington</u>, Free Press, 1996. (Available through Amazon.com:books)

JOH :2005

## Solzhenitsyn

In a recent Letter on the demise of communism, I mentioned Aleksander Solzhenitsyn.

Solzhenitsyn is a Russian writer, exiled from the former Soviet Union in 1974. He lived for a few years in Vermont, then returned to his native land when the Soviet Union collapsed. In 1970, he was given the Nobel Prize for Literature.

His Nobel Prize Address, *One Word of Truth,* is a stunning portrayal of the power of art and literature to defeat the lie. He has some personal traits I don't like, but there is no denying that Solzhenitsyn is both a great writer and a prophet.

What makes Solzhenitsyn so remarkable is that not only is he a writer with a total world view, he has made a direct connection between literature and morality -- not as a propagandist, as so many writers do, but as a true artist. His works express universal values and will live on.

What is it that a writer should write about? Not political issues of the day, for these are likely to be short-lived. Rather, the writer as artist goes to universal themes, essential questions about humanity, which take us inevitably to definitions of good and evil.

Solzhenitsyn shows us that the evil man is not set apart. He begins, believing that he is doing good or at the least, is acting in accord with approved ways. Solzhenitsyn explains the relationship between good and evil and the crossing over to an irretrievable condition of evil. With powerful insight, he revealed the root of evil in the twentieth century to be unconstrained ideology and saw its collapse in his homeland.

Solzhenitsyn is well known in western circles, but he is not very popular. Why?

Basically, he does not fit into current western theories about freedom and art. Solzhenitsyn sees freedom as spiritual, not political in nature. His theory of art rests on two fundamental concepts: (1) truth is absolute, (2) reality is objective. Both ideas grow from belief in a personal God who created and sustains the world. Art is a gift from God.

In contrast with this view, other artists of this century see themselves as creators of independent spiritual worlds. They are doomed to failure, by Solzhenitsyn's view, because lacking orientation to God, they have no moral order to rely upon and drift into confusion and despair. But Solzhenitsyn's disaffection from the west is more than disagreement about art.

In *Gulag Archipelago*, Solzhenitsyn wrote about an entire country which was brutalized and annihilated by a cruel and inhumane system. Enduring humanity is one of Solzhenitsyn's themes. Human freedom and goodness can live in the human soul, despite degradation and suffering, and can triumph. His own life proves it.

So, when he was exiled and came to the west, he was astonished to see a different kind of enslavement. He was not "grateful" for his new freedom. He saw that western materialistic values have led to greed, corruption, and alienation from God-all destroying the human spirit as much as concentration camps do.

Solzhenitsyn probes the truth of the human condition and experience in the twentieth century with great power and moral vision. No writer is more worthy of your attention.

JOH: 1991,2000

August 3, 2008

Alexander Solzhenitsyn died in Moscow today at age 89. In his last years, he somehow reconciled with the current government of Russia led by Vladimir Putin, former KGB official.

Although some of his final statements are perplexing, it is not too difficult to understand the historical context in which he set his argument.

The Harvard historian, Crane Brinton, framed a theory of the stages of revolution that shows the last stage as a dialectical return to the state that had existed historically. The notion that Russia could break permanently from its totalitarian tradition is specious. To recognize the hold of history does not refute or contradict the idea of spiritual freedom existing bilaterally with stability and security. Whether or not this will be the case in Russia remains to be seen.

JOH

## Celebrating Martin Luther King, Jr.

Let me confess: my words are not sufficient to honor Dr. King, but I'll tell you what I think: In my view of American leadership I rank Abraham Lincoln and Martin Luther King side by side. Though 100 years apart, they are the paramount champions and martyrs of the quest for a united nation founded on liberty and justice for all. One white leader and one black leader -- we cannot recognize one and not the other, for they were equal in the task God ordained for them.

Dr. King is a continuing inspiration for all of us, and a national hero at a time when America needs heroes. But then, when was ever a time that we did not need heroes?

I think what also sets him apart from many political leaders is that he was a very graceful man.

He had the grace of boldness in standing for what is right -- that we know certainly. But he also had the grace of kindness -- wherever he went he took something of the love of God -- the grace of a thankful, uncomplaining heart -- and my, was he not wonderfully graceful in his use of language?

We who follow him should be grateful to God -- for his example and his legacy to guide us in the continuation of the cause of brotherhood, which he so ennobled.

It is the case that we never know where the influence stops of men and women who excel as Dr. King did. A very recent example of that is work of Investigative Reporter Jerry Mitchell in Mississippi which is finally bringing to justice the Ku Klux Klan leader Edgar Ray Killen for the 1964 murders of civil rights workers. Without his courage and dogged pursuit of the truth these events may have remained unvindicated, locked away forever. It's no accident in my view that Mitchell was inspired by Dr. King. Mitchell said, "It's been a matter of faith for me throughout this whole thing. God's hand is in it. It just doesn't make sense otherwise."

I believe that's what Martin Luther King would have said too.

So the quest goes on; the struggle goes on. But now at least we can sing together:

*"Sing a song full of the hope that the present has brought us, Facing the rising sun of our new day begun."*

JOH

## A Personal Tribute to John Paul II

*"I have looked for you. Finally you have come to me. And I thank you."*

These dying words from Pope John Paul II, God's great servant, uncompromising apostle of life, may be interpreted in many ways in years to come. I believe they were uttered as he met God face to face.

I attended the funeral of John Paul II and experienced first-hand the deep love of this man by thousands present from all over the world. History will remember him as spiritual guardian of the sanctity of life and great moral leader and teacher of the salvific power of faith. He came in an era when western civilization has fallen into moral chaos. He will be remembered for having sparked the flames of freedom, ascending as Vicar of Christ when bloody communism seemed dominant in the world. Less than twenty years later the Soviet empire collapsed due in a large way to his influence.

"Be not afraid!" "Be not afraid" he said over and over again even in the darkest of days. Along with Roosevelt, Churchill and Reagan, he was one of the great liberators of the 20th Century, yet he had no armies, no guns, no bombs, only religious and spiritual authority.

Born in Poland, it was there his leadership first emerged. Without him, it is unlikely that the spirit of freedom defined in the Solidarity movement of the 1980's would have caught hold. When triumph came the stage was set for the idea of freedom to begin to roll in other parts of the world.

I remember the Sandinistas in Nicaragua, the FMLN in El Salvador, and the accompanying new power of "liberation theology" which converted many Catholic priests to Marxism. I saw the giant cross in downtown Manaqua with the face of Karl Marx superimposed on the figure of Jesus Christ. John Paul II would have none of it. He fought his own battle for Christ against poverty, always with human freedom in mind.

Some criticize him for not being more assertive about pedophiles in the priesthood, not allowing women to be ordained, and other matters of reform. I make no judgments on those Church matters—not my business. I am not a Catholic. Yet I see his splendor, anchored in conservatism. He reminds me of Disraeli's comment: "All great minds are conservative."

Throughout the Pope's many travels, his message was catholic- - the true definition, universal. He was the first Pope to visit synagogues and mosques.

Given the hedonistic culture and addictive society in which young people are growing up today (is it any wonder they cannot distinguish freedom from license?) it is indeed heartening to observe how this Pope inspired many of you and stirred so much outpouring of grief:

Last week a 20-year old boy flew to the Vatican and slept in the street. Asked why he was there, he replied, "to pay my respects to the Pope. If I don't see him today, I'll be back tomorrow."

A young woman at the Holy Name Cathedral in Chicago said, "I felt propelled to come here today because my heart felt so heavy." "It just hurts", she added. "He needs all the prayers of his people."

Hearing of the Pope's final moments, another 20-year old who lives in a home for at risk youth prostrated himself in prayer on the ground in front of a church in New Orleans.

A beautiful young girl in Krakow, Poland said, "I don't know how we can go on without him. He was my father."

Outside of my family, no other person's death has brought tears of sorrow to my eyes as did this man. Perhaps others join me. For whom does the bell toll?

John Donne tells us: *"Do not send to know for whom the bell tolls. It tolls for thee!"*

JOH : April 11, 2005

## Facts, Lies, And Rumors

The Neil Simon comedy, Rumors, is delightful. Beneath the comic situations, Rumors reminds us how tangled up our lives become when facts are confused with inferences and how easily rumors take on life of their own.

In the use of logic, the first thing, of course, is to learn the difference between fact, inference and opinion.

Facts can be empirically verified through observation or measurement.

"The sun rose this morning." If it did, that's a fact. (If it didn't , you're not reading this.)

"The sun will rise tomorrow." Most likely, it will, but that's not a fact---it's an inference.

"There is a global warning trend." If there is, you would never know it by the temperature of one day or even one year. The accumulation of facts over a long time is the only way to discern this trend. These big inferences ought not to be made or taken lightly.

There are different kinds of facts (or data contexts)---political facts, economic facts, academic facts, etc.

Then there are opinions. You've heard it said, "everyone is entitled to an opinion." True. But not all opinions have the same worth. In general, an informed opinion is much better than one based on ignorance. Analysis usually makes a difference.

Which gets us to values. In the academic world, if you can imagine it, there used to be an idea that facts could speak for themselves. Now we know better. There is always a fusion of facts and values in human situations because the human person makes the facts dynamic through perceptions and interpretations.

Now we're talking about truth and lies---and rumors (which are usually, but not always, lies).

Some people are just careless about facts. Others like to spread rumors because they think it makes life more exciting. To get a reaction : float the rumor and see what happens. When you hear a rumor, it's a good idea to check it out before passing it on.

The problem with rumors is that they can do a lot of damage. A rumor may b e partially based on fact, but more often than not, it exaggerates the fact or leaves something out. That's when it becomes a lie.

Lies are not always malicious, but when they are (i.e., deliberately used to hurt someone), it is the worst form of human corruption.

JOH

## Rational Process And The Mountain Of Irrationality

As a college student many years ago I was blessed by what was called the "liberal arts tradition" in the hands of admirable professors who recruited me for it. One introduced me to literary criticism, and another to the "Socratic method"----both aimed at search for truth. At that time we had not yet fallen into the trap of "no such thing as truth---all is relative."

While I was not an all-star student in those days, almost inadvertently I discovered something magnificent that set me on a course eventually to become my professional life. It is a process of rational inquiry and dialectical arrival at conclusions. I was not alone. We were inspired by the idea that even if our skills were inadequate or our notions too strong, the process or method would retain its integrity and lead us back to it. It goes something like this.

Keep three skills in balance: inquiry, acknowledgment' and advocacy. There is truth to be found but none of us will ever have sole possession of it. You never know what you don't know.

We see the world from our own perspectives. Each of us has our own story. Learning someone else's story or side of the issue may let us see something we didn't see before. In this learning conversation, we ask questions about the information. Examine the empirical data. Trace our interpretations of it.

The process goal is always the same: What is the truth? Not what is most popular---or what is easiest to accept.

Socrates stressed humility in the face of truth, but there is also room for enthusiasm! In fact, without it you can't get very far.

The method does not rob you of your advocacy but it will test your assumptions and interpretations, strengthening or refining or amending them, helping you to clarify your position. The conversation ends with acknowledgment that there may still be something missing, something more to learn. At the same time if we are responsible for making a decision, we do not shrink from the responsibility. Rather we trust in our informed judgment.

Tough, honest criticism is essential, but throughout the process there is respect for the other guy. It's demonstrated by acknowledging each other's position. To acknowledge, of course, is not the same thing as to agree. We may achieve a synthesis, or it may be that we simply agree to disagree, at least for the present. Even with the same information we may come to different conclusions. Why? Because of different assumptions, different interpretations. Without mutual understanding of the process it will simply stop. Embarrassed, friendly adversaries withdraw to the protection of banality.

In my youthful naiveté it never occurred to me that such a beautiful approach could be undermined by our culture. Or that there was another world view oriented to fantasy.

Now there is something happening in our culture as it interacts with fantastic ideology which is threatening the process of rational inquiry and coarsening the dialog.

Within our democratic society, the decline of rational method and the resulting incivility is traceable to both political excess and cultural fascination with image-making and entertainment in which image is more important than truth. We are bombarded mercilessly by images of all kinds, but the significant force is the image-spinning, the manipulation, distortion, even lies by professional media handlers who are very skilled and clever. They can turn the world upside down, building a mountain of irrationality.

JOH

### The Role Of Women In War

During World War II (the 1940's) "Rosie the Riveter" was a popular stereotype because she filled in for the men away at war. Along the way, she proved that women could handle the industrial jobs which until then had been reserved for men. Other women served in the army and navy but not in a combat role. After the war, many women did not like going back to the little shop or home. Perhaps feminism as a movement began then.

Or perhaps the roots go as far back as the seventh century to Celtic Christianity. There lies an interesting and ironic tale of history.

The Celtic Church was active in prohibiting the use of women in war. There are pitiful accounts of women forced onto the battlefield before this enactment. The following is from W. J. Watson, "The Celtic Church and Paganism," Celtic Review, 1918 (out of copyright):

*"The work which the best of women had to do was to go to battle and battlefield, encounter and camping, fighting and hosting, wounding and slaying. On one side of her she would carry her bag of provisions, on the other her babe. Her wooden pole upon her back, and it had at one end an iron hook, which she would thrust into the tress of some woman in the opposite battalion., Her husband behind her, carrying a fence stake in his hand and flogging her on to battle. Adamnan's mother chanced on a day to come on a battlefield. Such was the thickness of the slaughter into which they came that the soles of the women would touch the neck of another. Though they beheld the battlefield, they saw nothing more touching or pitiful than the head of a woman in one place and the body in another, and her little babe upon the breasts of the corpse, a stream of milk upon one of its cheeks and a stream of blood upon the other."*

Adamnan was the ninth Abbot of Holy Iona, an island in what is now Scotland. Inspired by his mother, he did not rest until he had secured the emancipation of women from war.

The Church's effort gradually evolved into a charter for women, not only in regard to warfare, but in promoting the role of women in upholding standards of morality and sanctity of the family as well. They were to be protected from the barbarity and ferocity of men. A code of chivalry was evolving.

For the Celtic Church, the women's charter was a way "to please God by doing things that are agreeable to Him, and so to grow like unto Him."

In today's world, of course, it is important to recognize the equal right of women in all endeavors including the making of war. A circle has been joined.

Maybe it's just me, a product of an older culture, but I have difficulty warming to this idea that young men and women should be equal on the front lines of combat and die in equal numbers. Is this progress?

JOH

## Coping With Change

Sometimes, as we see and hear of the ravage of drugs and alcohol, the question naturally occurs: are we still dealing with healthy people in our educational institutions? My answer is, with the great majority of students, yes! If this answer were wrong, we would need an entirely different theme than "coping with change."

Only healthy people can cope with the pace of contemporary change. But this does not mean that they shall cope. To cope means to have skills, imagination and perspective. These are also the traits of the educated person. In this sense, education is distinguished from training.

People can be trained to do a specific job, but what happens when that job is no longer there? Coincidental with growing unemployment are expressions of need for an upgraded work force coming from business, industry and the military. They consistently point out the value of these kinds of attributes: ability to communicate---computational ability---creative and adaptive capacity---inter-personal skills---critical thinking skills---alertness.

Employers know that such employees are also more motivated, more reliable, and more trainable. In the future, it is likely that these skilled people (as distinguished from "skilled workers") shall be in even greater demand. The question is, how shall this workforce be created?

We cannot avoid the proposition that we are all students and leaders or should be. How well schools and colleges develop qualitatively depends to a large degree on how seriously this proposition is taken throughout the organization. We must all be students and we must all be leaders!

I leave you with two things to think about:

- The desire to learn is infectious. Instructional technologies have been shown to quicken the rate of learning and should be employed, but it is still the enthusiasm and example we bring to our relationships with others in a learning environment that best motivates us and them.
- In a technology-intensive society, we are faced with a learning imperative. This means first that students must have mastery of basic skills---reading, writing, speaking, listening, and computation---which are then honed as critical and creative thinking skills. It also means that learning cannot be confined to a place and time in our lives. Formal learning is a life-long process. We are never too old to start, but we are always too young to finish.

Some people say, I cannot learn, it's too difficult. Not so! It's a matter of getting started right.

The more we learn, the easier it is to learn. It is only when we decide to take a break from learning that we begin to falter and stagnate.

Well educated people understand this imperative and naturally live by it. Continuing education becomes part of their life-style. It is ironic, perhaps, that educated people take advantage of educational opportunities while the poorly educated are not interested and fall further behind.

JOH

**Today's Teacher**

How should we then live?

Today's teacher, school or college, is caught between two forces of cultural decline. The challenge is first, to understand that both are detrimental to the teaching profession and students, and second, to pronounce them for what they really are.

The first is political correctness, writ large. One of our most savvy education writers, Diane Ravitch, in her book, *The Language Police,* renders a searing indictment of the way school textbooks are processed by today's publishers in order to maintain market share.

Under the threat of political power groups, both left and right, they have surrendered to censorship and bowdlerization. Most of the unsuspecting public are unaware of the ridiculous and damaging "dumbing down" caused by anti-bias and sensitivity guidelines used by textbook publishers, as well as state and federal authorities. I was astonished to read Ravitch's meticulous and extensive documentation of how literary quality and historical accuracy are compromised in order to escape controversy.

But the censors go even further: Apparently, some of our most famous classics have been dropped from select reading lists, including, outrageously, Mark Twain's *Adventures of Huckleberry Finn*. Ravitch is spot on with her comment that this is a novel "teachers and students alike must learn to grapple with… which they cannot do unless they read it!"

How shall an independently-minded, professionally trained teacher cope with this Orwellian undertow? If this question were the sum of the challenge, it wouldn't be so bad; educators know how to right wrongs in the profession. But this is only one part of the challenge calling us to an educational renaissance.

Students today--children from a young age—are being assaulted with language and images that violate and de-sensitize their souls. They hear words everyday that I cannot use here because they would not be printed (nor should they be) – at least at present. The vileness passes vapidly amongst us, not just taken for granted, but more than occasionally with approval of its "artistic merit."

"Sensation" was a much glorified exhibit held a few years ago in London dedicated to "grunge" and "punk" and other crudity that probably was original. One huge painting was of a woman who had tortured and murdered several small children and thus became a celebrity. It hung along with other pornographic paintings of nude women. The mother of one of the slaughtered children protested the exhibit, and indeed there was a lot of outrage about it. (The Brits have not given up yet.) Still it was declared to be a great artistic success because it broke through taboos and set a new standard for art.

Let us not be suborned by this argument for trash that merely titillates and exploits salacious appetites. There is a difference between art and popular entertainment culture that seeks to shock and degrade its participants.

The current issue of *International Art Journal* carries photographs of paintings judged to be the best of 2010. Several are beautiful; some are interestingly strange; none are pornographic.

Are teachers and parents and others who are responsible for the welfare of children just supposed to buy the argument that protestations of our declining culture come only from the yahoos among us-- the unsophisticated prudes and religious bigots who simply don't understand the purpose of art?

There is a circle of ironic challenge to be grappled with in the teaching profession. On the first front , we should not accept censorship. The spirit of free inquiry does not allow it.

But there is significant difference between *"censor"* and *"censure,"* and we owe it to our children to be tireless in applying the latter in those cases of violence-exalting, frivolously vile and satanic exploitations that endanger and darken our culture rather than enlighten it.

JOH: April, 2010

## Notes on Bewilderment and Hope

John Dewey said, "Life is compartmentalized." That was true of my life. Sometimes to my disadvantage, I had several compartments that kept me occupied, or preoccupied, in ways that sometimes conflicted. One such compartment was my interest in American foreign policy, garnered mostly from my days of teaching history and government. I often preferred this reading pastime to catching up on the administration documents that should have taken priority.

Following is a bit of "jam writing" – – disconnected pieces on issues that need to be connected, but I doubt my ability to find the connecting theme for the bewilderment and the hope that I have always felt on our American foreign-policy. The topics are as follows:

*High stakes in the Iraq//Afghanistan war; selling out our veiled sisters

*Anti-Americanism in Europe and the ongoing Islamist threat to the survival of Western civilization

*Continuing decline of civility in public discourse and the challenge of climbing the mountain of irrationality

*Pax Americana and the liberating message of John Paul II

"Despair, is only for those who see the end beyond all doubt." (J.R. Tolkien)

Unfortunately, for our grandchildren, world problems are becoming more complex, and the more likely it is for folks to give up on the complexity. Surely, it is one of the great tasks of education to teach students to face complexity with courage. It's no good trying to simplify issues with sound bites of 25 words or less, but it's even worse to assume that there are no answers or solutions anymore. Yes, we are living in a time of bewilderment, yet there are also signs of hope, and for those of pioneering spirit, there is still positive response to challenge. Events move so rapidly and antithetically now that it is foolish to claim complete knowledge or definitive judgment. No one can pretend to stand outside of the events being observed. Yet we must reason and act. In doing so, if we find a more promising way of looking at things, we need to summon our will to admit our limitations and embrace the new opportunities without allowing displacement of strategic values.

The Bush administration made many mistakes, but the "forward strategy for freedom" was not one of them. If we value our freedom, the cause of democracy and liberalism must remain our central foreign policy imperative. Tactics are something else to dispute, but in an age of world wide terrorism, this strategy is the best answer any nation or international organization has put forward.

We better get used to it: whatever is done in our foreign policy may test our democratic institutions. The risks are exacerbated because we do not know if those institutions can work as effectively in the world of the 21st century.

A dialectic is at work. The strength of democracy is still being determined even if it is the world's best hope.

The Bush and Clinton administrations and now the Obama administration have fumbled badly in the tactical pursuit of common strategic objectives. Perhaps because of the complexity, we do not have the statesmen of our history. Resources are being squandered; and we are facing a crisis of systems failure, which, if not resolved will put our nation on a slope of decline. Our enemies and some of our anti-American zealots may relish that thought, but the consequences for the rest of the world will be just as devastating for them as for us. The abnegation of American leadership would usher the world into a new dark age. The fault with the isolationist critics who castigate America's leadership role is not lack of patriotism but lack of vision.

It should not be surprising that it is the Afghan and Iraqi women who have been most supportive of American intervention and are so strongly committed to free elections. In Iraq under Saddam, not only was voting a joke, but women were habitually imprisoned, raped, tortured and killed.

According to Affra al-Barrack, who spent seven years in an Iraqi prison, some women were hanged by their feet during menstruation, so that they became "poisoned by the infection generated by their own blood." This is a demonic hatred of women characteristic of Islamist extremist groups noted for their " honor killings" and penalties applied to rape victims. Women were most active in traveling around Iraq to register female voters.

Do these women deserve our support? Is their freedom and justice worth the lives of American soldiers? How about British, French, German, Canadian, Dutch, Belgian, Spanish soldiers? If we should just "get out," as feminist groups totally disconnected from their veiled sisters demand, what are the consequences in the lives of Middle Eastern women? In all of the emotional rhetoric about America as "rogue nation," is there any real consideration given to that question, or is the answer simply, "well, whatever happens, it was Bush's fault."

An extraordinary memoir by Azar Nafisi, "Reading Lolita in Tehran," is an account of what happened when Islamists took over Iran. Nafisi was a left wing conspirator who worked to overthrow the Shah with dreams of ending tyranny in her country. In 1979, she went home to celebrate the fruits of the revolution – – and for the next 20 years watched as colleagues, relatives, friends, were arrested, tortured and assassinated. The defining moment for her came when a highly respected woman judge and scholar was put in a sack and stoned to death. Nafisi left her beloved country with her husband, and lives with the guilt.

Fouad Ajami, with in-depth knowledge of Arab culture, consistently offers penetrating analysis of the high-stakes in the Middle East:

*"The remarkable thing about the terror in Iraq is the silence with which it is greeted in other Arab lands... Those who, in Arab lands beyond Iraq have taken to describing the Iraqi Constitution as an American – Iranian Constitution give voice to a debilitating incoherence. At the heart of this incoherence lies an adamant determination to deny the Shiites of Iraq a claim to their rightful place in their country's political order... The American project in Iraq overturns an edifice of material and moral power that dates back centuries. The Arabs reeling against US imperialism and arrogance will never let us in on the real sources of their resentments..."* (Fouad Ajami, "Heart of Darkness," Wall Street Journal, 9/28/2005)

A decade earlier than our intervention in Iraq was our delayed intervention in the Balkans. In 1990, Europe and the United States split over how to deal with the collapse of Yugoslavia. A UN peacekeeping force maneuvered by the European Union was deployed in former Yugoslav states of Bosnia and Kosovo. In 1995 these "peacekeepers" stood aside as the Serbs murdered 7000 Muslim men in Srebenica. Then began the "ethnic cleansing"– – the systematic rape of Muslim women and girls, numbers estimated as high as 60,000. By the end of the decade over 200,000 people had died in the Balkans on Europe's watch. The genocide stopped when America finally decided to intervene. We, of course, were criticized for taking so long to do it, and then for the bombing campaign.

It seems clearly evident that the Bush administration made some mistakes in Iraq. Foremost was the disbanding of the Iraqi army after its defeat, the failure of intelligence, and the Abu Ghraib prison incident. The latter seriously undermined America's prestige in the Middle East, for was not this the same pattern as Iraq under Saddam? President Bush should have demanded immediate investigation and accountability at the highest level. Action to dismiss Sec. Donald Rumsfeld might have protected the administration against an onslaught of reasonable criticisms from that point.

In 1961, Sen. William Fulbright spoke of these essential American values:

*"It is not our affluence, or our plumbing, or our clogged highways that grip the imagination of others. Rather it is the values on which our system is built. These values imply our adherence not only to liberty and individual freedom, but also to international peace law and order, and constructive social purposes."*

During the Bush administration, this credo was undermined.

This aftermath, however, is a different matter than the decision to remove Saddam. Furthermore, if we could have depended on earlier European assistance in dealing with Saddam, that decision may not have proved inevitable. Throughout the 1990s, France and Russia tried to weaken the UN weapons inspection program in Iraq. We now know why, of course, by the scandal of corruption in the UN sanctioned oil sales program, the stolen profits from which Saddam used to build palaces while Iraqi children starved.

The cynicism everywhere is most intense when the observer refuses to recognize the enormity of the scale of murder of innocents and the most horrific tortures imaginable – – descriptions too pornographic for the printed page. Western human rights groups calculated that at least 300,000 Muslims had been murdered by Saddam's regime since the end of the Gulf War in 1991. Thousands more, including children, were imprisoned and tortured. This vile regime, one of the worst in modern history, was ended by the invasion of American troops.

In order to stay the course in the Middle East, we need European countries as allies, and they need us because of the enduring hatred – – a culture of death ("I die, therefore I am) – – that confronts all of civilization.

It will require the energy and example of a united America with better leadership than we have had in recent years.

## Distinguishing "Islamist and Islamic"

We need, of course, to distinguish the <u>Islamist</u> terrorists from <u>Islamic</u> communities of devout Muslims who yearn for peace and freedom as much as we do. Hopefully, at the same time, we shall avoid the mistake Europe made when it failed to recognize the domination and carrying power of the Islamists whenever there is a vacuum in law and order.

This is what Europe now struggles with "big time." Grimness of the problem was portrayed by Ajami in the 2004 Wall Street Journal article (cited above):

*"The geography of Islam – – and the Islamic imagination – – has shifted in recent years. The faith has become portable. Muslims who fled their countries brought Islam with them... A new breed of Islamists radicalized the faith there, in the midst of the kafir (unbelievers).*

*The new lands were owed scant loyalty, if any, and political religious radicals savored the space afforded them by Western civil society... You would have thought that the pluralism and tumult of this open European world would spawn a version of the faith to match it. But precisely the opposite happened: the faith became sharpened for battle..."*

In "The Cube and the Cathedral" George Weigel explains Europe's simultaneous collapse of morale and moral authority as the outcome of a Christophobic secularism. The most spectacular evidence of the suicide of an entire civilization is Europe's declining birthrate unable to sustain its population, except for Muslim immigrants. Demographic estimates by the UN are that Europe's native population will decline by 100 million or more in the next 50 years. The Muslim minority will double in size by 2015.

Atheistic humanism has dominated Western Europe for a century. Only in East Europe, most notably Poland, has faith been vibrantly alive. The message of hope was brought by Pope John Paul II.

In balance of power diplomacy, there is a doctrine of "raison d'etat," first put forth by Machiavelli, that states should not be subject to the same moral constraints as individuals. Charles de Gaulle said that "the state is a monster," by which he meant that only state interests were relevant.

This approach will not work in confronting the challenge of terrorism, however, because the moral stakes are so high. We must know clearly what we are for and what we are against, and then formulate intelligent strategies of alliance, without apologies. This is not the same thing as trying to effect a balance of power. There is no power balance to be achieved with terrorism.

European aspirations are to move away from hegemonic military power as the guarantor of peace and security to an open system, and to rely upon multi lateral pressure for resolving crises and brokering treaties. Notwithstanding the need for closer attention to and better diplomacy with our allies, America cannot adopt policy based on European aspirations that would neutralize our power – – the power that has given Europe protection and strength as it proceeds with new doctrines. This is very unrealistic.

It's obvious to everyone now that the Bush administration had bad intelligence on Saddam's weapons of mass distraction (WMD), and for this there needed to be accountability and corrective action. But how did we get launched into the hyperbole and burlesque of **Bush Lied**! and **Illegal War!--?**

Allegations about lying are just about the most serious charges that can be levied against a president. They should be investigated thoroughly – – and they were! The Senate Intelligence Committee, after intensive study, issued a unanimous report in July 2004, signed by the co-chair, Sen. Jay Rockefeller, and seven other Democrats, that charges about Bush lying were without merit. One of the conclusions in the committee's report reads:

*"The committee did not find any evidence that administration officials attempted to coerce, influence or pressure analysts to change their judgments related to Iraq's weapons of mass distraction capabilities." (Wall Street Journal,* July 12, 2004)

If President Bush had been lying about WMD, then so was Sen. Rockefeller when he relied on CIA evidence to claim in October 2002 that "Saddam's weapons pose a very real threat to America." Also lying about the WMD threat were President Clinton, while he was in office, and Senators Hillary Clinton and John Kerry.

The exaggeration and invective for partisan purposes detracts from healthy criticism, criticism that is needed. It is a disservice to the cause of open, honest debate essential in the democratic decision-making process. Both of our major political parties have developed "spinning the facts" into an art and science, but there must be some minimum standards of honesty and civility on both sides of the aisle. Is this not obvious? Should we not measure maturity and sense of responsibility in all who hold positions of authority accordingly?

## Pax Americana?

On the side of creative diplomacy, Robert Cooper, a distinguished British diplomat, makes the case for a hopeful Pax Americana, different than George W. Bush and the neoconservatives imagined, nevertheless an enhanced strategy for freedom and democracy led by the United States. (See Robert Cooper, *The Breaking of Nations,* McClelland and Stewart, Ltd. 2004.)

It could be argued that the main difference between Europe and America is that following World War II Europe lost its "will to power" whereas after the trauma of 9/11, America rediscovered it. Cooper recommends that both Europe and America need to re-examine their positions. He argues that it is not necessary or desirable that the European Union abandon its desire to solve problems by negotiation and legal means. But it is dishonest and self defeating that the use of military power should be left to the United States. Cooper argues cogently that both military power and multi lateral legitimacy are essential. If we had this kind of understanding and determination during the period of confronting Saddam over alleged weapons of mass destruction this may have been sufficient pressure to persuade him, thus obviating the need for military intervention to enforce full inspections.

The important goal, in the best interest of both America and Europe is to restore the road of reconciliation. This may require new flexibility on America's part, but effective strategy will also depend upon greater cooperation and participation on the military dimension by European nations, especially France and Germany, which in the past have offered the excuse that there is honest disagreement with the US on what constitutes "common interests ."

The security of Europe has always been a common interest. It is not plausible that Europe has a lesser stake in dealing with terrorist regimes than does the US. This introduces a host of other considerations, including economic and trade policies which are complex in their own right.. Yet, joining in a genuine effort of multilateralism realistically conceived may offer hope of reconstituting one of the most reliable alliances of the modern world. As Cooper concludes:

*"When it comes to security issues, it is still a world of every country for itself. And security is the foundation of all things. It is a mistake therefore to exaggerate the degree of order and legitimacy in the world. But it is also a mistake to believe that such a community could never exist and that we should not set it for ourselves as an ultimate and a very distant goal. Such an objective may well be unattainable.. But if this is so then the alternative is the law of the jungle and that, with the development of technology, looks increasingly nasty. The attempt to do better is not merely a moral imperative; it may be necessary for our survival."*

## "The Gospel of Hope Does Not Disappoint"—Pope John Paul II

Hope is always present as a measure of faith in a loving God. We cannot know for certain how God may intervene and through what instruments revealed as opportunities. Even when things are most bewildering, there are spiritual, moral and intellectual forces which can be marshaled.

The evidence of things hoped for and made manifest is revealed in the faith and work of John Paul II. This holy father understood that, despite Europe's Christophobia, it was Christianity that taught the values of human dignity and laid the foundation for the ideas of democracy and liberty. In *"Ecclesia Europa,"* John Paul called his fellow Europeans to courage and hope:

*"Do not be afraid! The gospel is not against you but for you... Throughout the vicissitudes of your history, yesterday and today, it is the light which illuminates and directs your way. It is the strength which sustains you in trials. It is the prophecy of a new world, the sign of a new beginning. It is the invitation to*

*everyone, believer and nonbelievers alike, to blaze new trails leading to a Europe of the spirit in order to make the continent a true, common home filled with the joy of life."* (Quoted in Weigel)

This message is universal. Those who are ready to give up on the complexity of our situation, those who cannot see beyond the next day or even the next hour, can find renewal in a serious reflection of it.

It was John Paul II, more than any other leader including Ronald Reagan, who was responsible for the collapse of communism in Eastern Europe and ultimately the demise of the Soviet Union. When Europe had forgotten God and started on its path of hopelessness, the Communist empire was in its ascendancy. The new religion of communism counted all power in material terms. When Stalin was asked if he should be concerned about what the Pope had to say, his response was classic: "How many divisions does the Pope have?"

Europe is now struggling in the wake of 20th century exclusive reliance on relativism, secularism and materialism. The enemy at the gate is homegrown, in-bred Islamist terrorists, justified by an ardent corruption of true Islam to give up their lives for the cause of crushing an alien civilization. This barbarism can be defeated, but Europe does not yet know how. It's possible that America does not know how either, having already breathed in "Europe's problem."

It has always been when things look their darkest that new leadership emerges, as for example, when Patrick finally again reached the shores of Ireland, destined to become the savior of classical antiquity in a dark age. Behind him was the break of day.

My heart goes out to these young people yearning for freedom in places like Iran and Russia. Do they feel loss of hope in their dark days?

Let's not discount the possibility of this spiritual intervention. We face a dark complexity in a split world. Yet, despite our bewilderment, I believe the balance will swing again and the visible will regain its hold. Our part, dear friends, is to summon the courage to continue facing up to the challenge.

November 2010

# Acknowledgements

## and

# Select Bibliography

In an autobiographical work of this sort, it is difficult to categorize and cite all of the sources, primary and secondary, of my obligation over the almost 50 years of my career. The following selections appear to me at this time as the most prominent. When thousands of books, letters, documents, reports and pieces compose the canon which the mind and heart have stayed upon, it is possible that indelible jewels among them were lost along the way. My last ambition will be to recover them and refine and annotate these lists.

Would that I could say, as Google does, "The selection and placement of stories on this page were determined automatically by a computer program." Alas, my computer literacy is not that high.

My first obligation is to acknowledge my literary sources, especially those for Burns and Yeats. My travels to Scotland helped me to find a marvelous old tome written by P. Hateley Waddell in 1967 (and weighing about 12 pounds) which is an irreplaceable treasure on Burns, now out of print/copyright. I am primarily indebted to M.L. Rosenthal and Richard Ellman for Yeats' poetic lines and life analysis. The excerpts from *The Fiddler of Dooney* and *Politics* are quoted with permission of Simon & Schuster, Scribner Poetry. An excerpt from Yeats' *Per Amica Silentia Lunae* is in the Gutenberg Project e-book released in August 2010. Bartleby.com is an excellent on-line source for Yeats' poems. The valedictory poem by Rudolph Schirmer is from Michael H. Macdonald and Andrew A. Tatie, *The Riddle of Joy,* William B. Eerdsmans Publishing Co. 1986.

Also, I am especially grateful to the editors and translators of Solzhenitsyn's works. How could we do without them?

Some quoted material is ubiquitous, contained in many sources. For Murphy's Laws, see Paul Dickson in Wikipedia. I first found Tennyson's poem, Ulysses, in a book seemingly uncopyrighted given to me by my mother, English Idylls and other Poems, first published in 1842 by Thomas Y. Crowell and Co.

Higher Education and Organization Development*(partial list of books influential during my formative years of administration)*

Warren G. Bennis, *Changing Organizations*, McGraw-Hill, 1966

Daniel Bell, *The Reforming of General Education*, Columbia University Press, 1966

Robert R. Blake *and* Jane S. Mouton, *The Managerial Grid* , Gulf Publishing Company, 1968

Peter F. Drucker, *The Practice Of Management*, Harper, 1954

Amitai W. Etzioni , *Modern Organizations, Prentice-Hall, 1964*

Abraham H. Maslow, *Eupsychian Management*, Irwin- Dorsey, 1965

George S. Odiorne, *Management by Objectives*, Pitman, 1965

Douglas McGregor, *The Human Side Of Enterprise* , McGraw-Hill, 1960

Harold G. Shane, *"The Educational Significance Of the Future"*, *World Future Society, October, 1972*

Alfred North Whitehead, *The Aims Of Education*, McMillan Co., 1929, 1957

José y Gasset Ortega, *Mission of the University*, translated by Howard Lee Nostrand, W.W. *Norton, 1944*

Immanuel Kant, *Education*, translated by Annette Churton, University of Michigan, 1960

John Dewey, *Art As Experience*, Capricorn, 1958

Eric Hoffer, *The Ordeal of Change*, Harper and Row, Publishers, 1963

Allan Bloom, *The Closing of the American Mind: How Higher Education Has Failed Democracy and Impoverished the Souls of Today's Students*, Simon and Schuster, 1987

Diane Ravitz, *The Language Police*, Alfred a. Knopf, Borzoi Book, 2003

Jerry L. Martin and Anne D. Neal, *Defending Civilization:How Our Universities Are Failing America and What Can Be Done About It*, American Council of Trustees and Alumni, 2002

John O. Hunter, *Values and the Future: Models of Community College Development*, Banner Books International, 1977

## Science, Systems and Artificial Intelligence

Ray Kurzweil, The *Singularity Is Near*, Penguin Books, 2005.

J. Storrs Hall, *Beyond A I* , Prometheus Books, 2007

James D. Watson, *The Double Helix*, Signet Books, 1968

Thomas S. Kuhn, *The Structure Of Scientific Revolutions*, 2nd Ed. University of Chicago Press, 1970

Claude Lévi-Strauss, *The Elementary Structures Of Kinship*, translated by Bell, von Sturmer and Needham, Eds., Beacon Press, 1969

Stephen W. Hawking, *A Brief History Of Time: From the Big Bang to Black Holes,* Bantam Books, 1988

Ervin Laszlo, *The Systems View Of The World*, George Braziller, 1970

Sylvia Nasar, *A Beautiful Mind,* Simon and Schuster, 1988

Historical and Cultural Analysis

George F. Kennan, *Around the Cragged Hill,* W.W. Norton, 1993

----------------------, *Memoirs 1925- 1950*, Atlantic Monthly Press Book, 1967

Nicolas Berdyaev, *The Origin of Russian Communism*, translated by R. M. French, Ann Arbor Paperback, 1960 (First published 1937)

Aleksander Solzhenitsyn, *The Gulag Archipelago*, Abridged Edition, translated by Thomas P. Whitney and Harry Willetts, Harper Collins, 1985

--------------------------------,*"One Word of Truth"*, Nobel Lecture, translated by Nicholas Bethel, Stenvalley Press,London, !970

--------------------------------,*Lenin in Zurich,* translated by H.T. Willetts, Farrar, Straus and Giroux, Inc. 1976

Edward E. Ericson Jr. *Solzhenitsyn: The Moral Vision*, William B. Eerdsman Publishing Co., 1980

Victor Sparre, *The Flame in the Darkness,* translated by Alwyn and Dermot McKay, Grosvenor, 1979

Kenneth Boulding, *Conflict And Defense: A General Theory*, Harper, 1962

Azar Nafisi, *Reading Lolita in Tehran*, Random House,2003

John W. Kiser, *The Monks of Tibhirine: Faith, Love, and Terror in Algeria*, St. Martin's Griffin, 2002

Isak Dinesen, *Letters from Africa*, University of Chicago Press, 1981

Jean LaCouture, *DeGaulle*, The New American Library Translation, *1965*

Robert Cooper, *The Breaking of Nations*, McClleland and Stewart Ltd. 2004

David Herbert Donald, *Lincoln*, Simon and Schuster, 1995

John Preble, *The Highland Clearances*, Penquin Books, 1963

Thomas Cahill, *How the Irish Saved Civilization*, Anchor Books, 1995

Theodore Dalrymple, *Our Culture, What's Left Of It*, Ivan R. Dee, *2005*

--------------------------, *The New Vichy Syndrome: Why European Intellectuals Surrender to Barbarism*, Encounter Books, 2010

--------------------------, *Not With A Bang But A Whimper: The Politics And Culture Of Decline*, Ivan R. Dee, 2008

Roger Kimball, *Tenured Radicals*, Ivan R. Dee, 1990, 1998

## Philosophy and Religion

Immanuel Kant, *Religion Within Limits Of Reason, in The Philosophy of Kant by* Carl J. Friedrich, Ed., Random House, 1949

John Paul II, *Rise and Let Us Be on Our Way, Warner Books, 2004*

John Paul II, *Crossing the Threshold of Hope,* Alfred A. Knopf, 1994

George Weigel, *The Cube and the Cathedral,* Basic Books, 2005

Garry Wills, *What Jesus Meant,* Viking, 2006

Marcus J. Borg, *Jesus :A New Vision,* Harper and Row, 1987

Robert Louis Wilken, *The Spirit of Early Christian Thought,* Yale University Press, 2003

Michael H. Murray, *The Thought of Teilhard De Chardin,* The Seabury Press, 1966

Augustine, *The Confessions,* translated by Edward B. Pusey, Washington Square Press,1960

Ernest Becker, *The Structure of Evil,* Free Press, 1968

--------------------, *The Birth and Death of Meaning, 2ⁿᵈ Ed.* The free Press, 1971

Victor Frankl, *The Search for Meaning,* Beacon Press,2006 (First published, 1946)

Michael H. MacDonald and Andrew A. Tadie, Eds. *The Riddle of Joy: G. K. Chesterton and C. S. Lewis,* William B. Eerdmans Publishing, 1989

C.S. Lewis, *Surprised By Joy,* Harcourt, Brace and World, 1955

David Adam, *Border Lands: Celtic Vision,* Sheed and Ward, 1991

Erik H. Erikson, *Gandhi's Truth: Origins of Non-Violence,* W.W. Norton, 1969

Thomas Merton, *The Seven Storey Mountain,* Harcourt, Brace and World, 1948

Robert Daggy, Ed. *The Alaskan Journal of Thomas Merton,* New Directions Publishing,1988

Martin Luther King, Jr. *Letter from Birmingham Jail, April 16, 1963,* African Studies Center, University of Pennsylvania

Lau Tzu, *Tao Te Ching,* translated by John H. MacDonald, Arcturus, 2009

Dag Hammarskjold, *Markings,* translated by W.H. Auden and Leif Sjoberg, Alfred A Knopf, 1972

<u>Fiction</u>

Alexander Solzhenitsyn, *One Day in the Life of Ivan Denisovich,* Bantam,1976

Robert Littell, *The Stalin Epigram,* Simon and Schuster, 2009

Richard A. Clarke, *Breakpoint,* GP Putnam's Sons, *2007*

Michael Frayn, *Copenhagen,* Anchor Books,1998

<u>Yeats</u>

John Kelly, Ed. *W.B. Yeats Selected Poems* JM Dent Everyman's Poetry, 1997

Richard Eberhart, Intro. *A Poet to His Beloved: The Early Love Poems of WB Yeats ,* St. Martin's Press, 1985

Richard J. Finneran, Ed. *The Yeats Reader, Revised Edition,* Scribner, 1997

M.L. Rosenthal, *William Butler Yeats Selected Poems and Plays, Fourth Edition*, Scribner, 1996

Richard Ellmann, *Yeats: The Man and the Masks*, Dutton Paperback, 1948

Marjorie Howes and John Kelly, Ed. *The Cambridge Companion to W.B. Yeats*, Cambridge University Press,2006

William Butler Yeats, *Mythologies*, Simon and Schuster, 1959

Burns

P. Hately Waddell, *The Life and Poems of Robert Burns*, David Wilson, Glasgow, 1867

Andrew Noble and Patrick Scott Hogg, Eds., *The Canongate Burns, Volumes I and II*, Canongate Classics, 2001

John Cairney, *The Luath Burns Companion*, Luath Press Limited, 2001

*A Critique Of The Poems Of Robert Burns*, Printed by John Brown, 1812

Other Poetry Anthologies

Louis Untermeyer, Ed. *Modern American and Modern British Poetry*, Harcourt, Brace and Company,1955

Neal Frank Doubleday, *Studies in Poetry*, Harper & Brothers,1949

Harold Bloom, Ed. *The Best Poems of the English Language*, Harper Collins Publishers, 2003

John O. Hunter, Ed. *For the Love of Poetry*, unpublished manuscript, 2009